Solving Problems with Dowsing

A book for new dowsers

Over 15 ways to improve your dowsing, even if you are working by yourself, don't have a lot of resources, never had training, and have no idea where to start

by Henry Dowser

Excerpted and expanded from the books *Dowsing and Manifesting*, and *Dowsing and Self-Healing*.

Available from www.amazon.com, and other fine bookstores and merchants
ManifestingHeart Group home page: http://groups.yahoo.com/group/ManifestingHeart

Any course offerings, webinars, conference calls, or related products, would be announced there, or on feelmuchbetternow.com. We do expect to offer CD's with specific exercises from this book, in time, also. We will be offering trainings, as well, in time. You can reach us at imaginalhealing@gmx.com. We will not respond to any questions about specific ailments, for reasons cited in this book. This book was adapted and expanded from the larger books, *Dowsing and Manifesting*, and *Dowsing and Self-Healing*.

ISBN-13: 978-1482688573
ISBN-10: 1482688573

What are your fondest dreams?

How would you feel, if they were real, right now?

Table of Contents

The best and most beautiful things in the world cannot be seen or even touched.
They must be felt with the heart[1]

What if you could get any information you wanted, just by asking the right question?

What if you could have more fun in your life than you ever dreamed possible?

What if, in doing so, you made it easier for others to realize their dreams, also?

---

1   -Helen Keller.

Why not commit random kindnesses[2], and senseless acts of beauty?

Have you noticed that we are only truly alive when we are connected?[3]

2   *Random Acts of Kindness*, ed. Conari Press, fwd Daphne Rose Kingma.
3   Kahlil Gibran. *Turning to one another*, by Margaret Wheatley, says "*truly connecting with another human being gives us joy.*" *If you realized how powerful your thoughts are, you would never think a negative thought* -Peace Pilgrim

Solving Problems with Dowsing **7** A book for new dowsers ISBN-10: 1482688573

I. Dedication and Introduction

This book is dedicated to my ancestors, my family, the unborn generations to come, and to seekers everywhere. This book is dedicated to those who realize that a large part of their mission and purpose in life is helping others, and it is designed to help them do that.

This book is written in appreciation of my own teachers, who helped me greatly. This book "pays forward", or passes on their lessons. I have followed my fascinations, in my life, as much as I could. This has made my life considerably more interesting. This book is also dedicated to helping others learn the special magic and fun of following their fascinations.

You may wish to make that a rule in your life- to pay attention to, and <u>follow, your fascinations</u>. I studied what fascinated me, in college, including dowsing. College was fun. My life has been much more fun, as a result. I have met people who studied subjects they hated, in college, and then worked in jobs they hated. They don't seem very happy. Joy is the core of what most people seek. Life is about finding joy, and sharing it. This book is my offering and sharing of joy, to those interested.

This book is intended to teach in a spiral path, the way indigenous cultures teach. Points may be repeated, in different ways. The objective of this book is to take you to the next level, so you can address problems and issues effortlessly[1].

Dowsing is fun. Dowsing is play. Do you remember that feeling you had, when you graduated high school, and you knew you were going to enter into the big world? Learning how to dowse introduces you to a whole new world, in the same way. For many, it is even more exciting. *You cannot force dowsing. You can only <u>allow</u> it.*

---

1 I also express my appreciation to Enya, Loreena McKennit, Celtic Women, J.S. Bach, Mozart, Henry Purcell, Beethoven, Jean Phillipe Rameau, Claudio Monteverdi, Josquin Desprez, Adriano Banchieri, Guglielmo Ebreo da Pesaro, Francesco Spinacino, Antonio Caprioli, Gasparo Alberti, Andrea Antico, Francesco Patavino, Bernardo Pisano, Pietro Paolo Borrono, Francesco de Layolle, Costanzo Festa, Pierre Attaignant, Simon Boyleau, Francesco Canova da Milano, Balthazar de Beaujoyeulx, Mattio Rampollini, Tomás Luis de Victoria, Thomas Tallis, William Byrd, Palestrina, Thomas Morley, Guillaume Dufay, Johann Jakob Froberger, Diego Ortiz, Antonio de Cabezón, Orlando di Lasso, Gregorio Allegri, Francesca Caccini, Alessandro Piccinini, Vittoria Aleotti, Gamelan orchestras, water harmonica players, and several others who supported us in writing and editing this book.

There is a major shift required for successful dowsing. Most books on dowsing assume readers know this. A dowser needs to shift out of the world that consists only of what we can see, hear, and feel, with our gross senses, and into the unseen world from which the seen world emerges[2]. Expressed another way, the dowser realizes that matter, the particle, is not all there is, that there is also the quantum probability wave, of potential, of energy, of spirit. A dowser realizes that consensual reality, as taught in schools, is really only the reality of the conscious mind, and the physical world. It is not a complete model.

A dowser is something like a Robinson Crusoe, on an island, who never saw the sea. One day the dowser sees the sea- which is an old symbol for the deeper mind- and realizes the material world behind him/her is a small island in a vast sea. Robinson Crusoe might make a fishhook, and line, to fish. The dowser uses the fishhook of the well-formed question, and casts it into the deep mind, the Void of all possibility. In time, intent pulls forth the answer.

Dowsing makes no sense from the viewpoint of those who think the island is all there is. You can point out the sea, you can bring them salty water, but they will be in denial until they finally open their eyes, to see the sea. Let them wonder where you got the fish. Don't try to explain anything. Just smile, and say something like, "Oh, I guess I was just lucky."

You can lead a kid to college, but you can't make him think. So it is with other people. You will be happier if you only feed interest, and then only enough to get them on their own path. Yes, you can see how they can greatly open up their possibilities, but if they don't want to see that, respect their position, and move on.

Tamarack Song's book *Entering the Mind of the Tracker: Native Practices for Developing Intuitive Consciousness and Discovering Hidden Nature* very nicely shows the interplay between an individual animal, and the "spirit", the energy, the potential of the invisible pattern of the animal.

---

2 The cover photo is intended to show that matter is on a matrix, which is mostly invisible.

Indigenous trackers[3] also have to get out of the purely material, to be any good. Trackers enter a dowsing state of mind, to track. Dowsers are trackers.

Dowsers understand that life is a continual balancing of the flow of energies. Sun Tzu's *The Art of War* gives one an idea of how this works. <u>The keys to balancing and healing are removing the obstacles to the flow of compassion and love.</u> All life is based on love. Any life form not acting out of love has been severely traumatized in some way. It's not important how or why.

The key is to <u>remove the root causes</u>, the obstacles. Then the flow will remove the stagnant energy. Healing, solution, or growth will follow, in their own unique time and way. They may come from a simple realization that is not necessary to act out life's traumas in one's body[4], and life. Individual human consciousness is part of the hologram of the universal mind. We are all fractally connected, in the Universal mind.

If you extend your individual consciousness, you can know about the entire Universe[5]. As you reach wholeness yourself, you will find opportunities to help others reach their wholeness. Nature's way is to bring parts together to form a whole. So one who can invoke healing and wholeness, including through dowsing, will generally attract those who need it[6].

The Japanese word *Sensei* literally means "born before". It has the suggestion of someone who is a little bit further down the path, only[7]. I don't claim to be any smarter than you are. I'm delighted to share my experience of the path with you, knowing it will speed your progress on it, so that you will not have to flounder as much as I did. You may also follow your fascinations. All you need, to have a life of great interest, is to stay in the present moment. Do this, and you live in eternity[8].

---

3   *Journey to the Ancestral Self*, by Tamarack Song, is an outstanding discussion of what it is like to live in a dowsing culture, where dowsing is part of everyday life. The book in your hands is an introductory book. I cannot improve on Tamarack Song's book. For someone who wants to understand dowsing, at a deeper level than any book I've read, on dowsing, I recommend getting that book, though be warned: it is very advanced. I get nothing for saying this.
4   P. 76, *Dr. Judith Orloff's Guide to Intuitive Healing*, Dr. Judith Orloff..
5   P. 6, *A Cosmic Book: on the Mechanics of Creation*, Itzhak Bentov.
6   P. 144, *The Divining Heart: Dowsing and Spiritual Unfoldment*, Patricia and Richard Wright.
7   It is commonly used in the U.S. for a teacher of Japanese martial arts.
8   P. 124, *Heading Toward Omega: in Search of the Meaning of the Near-Death Experience*, Kenneth Ring.

Solving Problems with Dowsing **10** A book for new dowsers ISBN-10: 1482688573

Albert Einstein was a dowser. He learned to ask precise questions[9], and said himself formulating the right question was the most important thing one could do. Your life is the crystallization of the questions you ask. If you want to improve your life, or your dowsing- improve your questions.

Some parts of this book may not seem rational. They aren't rational. Dowsing works with the deeper parts of the mind, which run by a very different set of rules. One could even call them meta-rules, rules that aren't the rules we are used to.

Dowsing has been part of humanity for a long time. You can learn it, and you can use it to improve your life, and the lives of others. It is fun! You will find yourself growing into wholeness, as you use dowsing. Dowsing is something like going through a pitch dark warehouse, with a flashlight. After a few visits, you realize something of how big the warehouse is, and that you have many more possibilities than you ever dreamed possible.

What if life was perfect, just as it is, and all we had to do to realize that, was to put our attention on that?

---

9 The Theory of Relativity grew out of a question Einstein asked- *what would it be like to ride on a beam of light?*

II. Getting started in Dowsing

What is dowsing? _Dowsing is the focused use of intuition, perhaps with a readout device, a scale_, in Raymon Grace and Walt Wood's simple terminology. Intuition is awareness that someone tunes into, with intent. Awareness is always on, but not always listened to. Dowsing scales could be using a very simple yes/no/wrong question scale, a protractor or chart to get percentages, or a very complex heads up display, in imagination, as in the movie _Ironman_. Dowsing is also expression of intent. Asking the focused dowsing question turns dowsing on.

Does dowsing work? In a word, <u>yes</u>. It cannot not work, unless you shut it down with your conscious mind's choice, to ignore it. Dowsing is like breathing, or blood circulation, it is always working in the background, because your awareness, and intent, is always on. It is processes your questions 24/7. You don't have to choose to pay attention to it. Indigenous peoples lived in a dowsing state of mind, and could often foresee danger before it came. The Western Culture we live in had mind and heart cut in two, because the Church was threatened by Science, and they agreed to split the unseen world and the seen world. Politics causes problems.

In the physical world of Newton, and Descartes, there is no action at a distance, other than gravity. The whole is merely the sum of the parts, and we live only in a physical world. But that is only a paradigm, a belief system[1]. Only those who can see the invisible can do the impossible. This book will do something I don't see in many books. It will offer more useful belief systems, and meta-beliefs, so that you can see the invisible, or at least, what is invisible from Newton's perspective. Most dowsing books seem to assume this. It is useful to have a foundation, a supportive belief system, that supports dowsing.

---

1 Let's test that belief system. In a crowd, stare at the back of someone's neck, intently, let's say 30 yards or meters away. If they aren't drunk, or stoned, or asleep, in time they will turn around. If you keep staring at them, they will meet your eyes. This is not possible in the Newtonian Universe, because this is action at a distance, which is not gravity. Yet it happens. The Newtonian world works in the "island" of the physical world, at human scale. It does not work everywhere. I may say this again, just to drive this point home. When you realize you are more than just your body, you have entered the world where dowsing is possible.

Solving Problems with Dowsing **12** A book for new dowsers ISBN-10: 1482688573

Here is a metaphor for dowsing. Let's imagine you are in a confined place, and need to see around a corner, but can't put your head there. You can reach out with your right arm. You put a mirror in your right hand, and now you can see around the corner. The mirror is your dowsing tool, it lets you see what is otherwise blocked. This is *reflective* dowsing.

There is another kind: *projective* dowsing, which is the projection of intent. Let us imagine you have a flashlight, or torch, in your left hand, and you shine it on the mirror. Now you are putting light on what you perceive, and shifting it[2]. Both dowsing phases are discussed in this book.

Dowsing has been used for 98% of human history[3]. It is as natural as breathing, or seeing. In the so-called civilized world we live in, there is a lot of noise, and static, which blocks the conscious sensation of dowsing. Language, as symbol, and abstract thinking, may actually suppress dowsing[4]. Enter the deeper mind, and dowsing is almost effortless.

Let's use another metaphor. When I was a kid, we would buy shoes at a Department store, usually Sears, Roebuck & Co. The grocery store did not sell shoes. As I recall, we had to first locate the Department store. Then, we had to locate the shoe department. We would get to the style we wanted. Then a shoe salesman would come out, size my feet, and get 2-3 selections of shoes. I would try them on, pick what felt best, and we'd buy them[5].

---

2 This distinction is somewhat artificial, because all dowsing, as with observation, is *projective*, it shifts what is observed. That is a Quantum Mechanics idea, which, as you progress, you will find very real.

3 For the materialist who wants "proof" of this, go live a year in the woods, with nothing of civilization with you, other than maybe clothing, and an ax, and a knife. You'll have your proof, and it will be absolutely unmistakable. You won't be able to satisfy materialists, but you will know this beyond the shadow of a doubt. A month would be enough for some. Some Mexican healers live in the wilderness, just like this, as one example of what's possible. A word of advice: never argue with idiots, no matter how educated they are. They will taint you. Just smile, and change the subject.

4 How many word and analysis-addicted scientists, otherwise rational, are in total denial, or perhaps also anger, about dowsing, and anything that cannot be physically sensed? Don't bother them. They have their own process, they will move through bargaining, depression, and acceptance, in their own time.

5 Anything physical can be used as a metaphor. This is extremely important, in dowsing, because your deeper mind will give you feedback in images and symbols that you know. Many phenomena and pieces of information are simply beyond our current ability to model in language. Remember the movie *Red October*? When the sonarman picked up the submarine as seismic activity, because that was the only way the computer could perceive it? Your mind has to do this in dowsing, sometimes, so be very aware of this. You need a graphical user interface for your dowsing- which could be Yes/No/Wrong question signals, scales of possibilities, or even sets of archetypes as measurements. We'll talk about all this.

Solving Problems with Dowsing **13** A book for new dowsers ISBN-10: 1482688573

For dowsing, first we get to the store- the correct state of mind, the EEG state. This must- must- be at least the Alpha EEG, of about 7-14 Hz, and maybe deeper[6]. Then we have to go to the correct department- just as a dowser must narrow down the scope of what s/he seeks, with finely crafted questions. Then we get preliminary feedback, and work with the subconscious mind- the sales staff- to refine what we seek. The subconscious mind goes to the superconscious, which has access to the infinite inventory room of the zero point field, the Void of all possibilities. It comes back, and presents the answer, perhaps as feeling.

I am so very amused at critiques of dowsing. They say it doesn't work, that it has been debunked, because it can't work. The French Academy of Sciences determined, in the 1840's, that meteorites couldn't exist, because there were no stones in the sky. About 1908, the New York Times had an article stating that heavier-than-air flying machines were impossible. In the late 1890's, the head of the U.S. Patent Office proposed closing this office down, because everything that could be invented had been. If people want to be disempowered, to never plug into power, that's their choice, who are you to interfere in their lives? Would you rather be right, or effective? Effectiveness comes from staying in the question, not staying in the answer or conclusion.

When I was a lad, I was surrounded by people who said that Jesus[7] was the only truth. They forgot to add the all-important tagline, "for me". In college, I was surrounded by people who said Science was the only truth. They also somehow forgot that tagline. The Universe is far, far bigger than our religious and scientific models of it. The Subconscious mind takes in more than 60 million bits of information per second. It filters the information, based on your belief systems, and gives you what the filters allow through, as 6-8 bits of information.

---

6 Please don't let this technical stuff make you nervous. Remember going sailing, or maybe biking, or walking, on vacation, and you entered a really relaxed state of mind, that felt great? That is Alpha. Watch pre-teen kids playing, they are naturally in Alpha. Some of them are fantastic dowsers, till the adults tell them it doesn't work, or get scared of it, also.
7 In an extremely limited understanding, which didn't include understanding the Semitic culture he grew up in, historic precedent, and a number of other data that even biographers would consider. Aramaic is radically different from English; Douglas-Klotz had to use 10 translations, in English, to approximate the meaning of the Aramaic Lord's Prayer, as one example. But that is off-subject. The lessons for dowsers is to always be learning, always be humble, as there is always room to grow.

Solving Problems with Dowsing **14** A book for new dowsers ISBN-10: 1482688573

There are scientists who believe we are only a body, and the conscious mind. Have you ever been driving, and suddenly came back to awareness, and wondered where the last 10 miles went? Or studying, or writing a paper, and suddenly you realized you were 5 pages ahead, and weren't aware of it? Who was "driving the bus", metaphorically[8]?

Science measures at most 10% of existence- the replicable, easily measured part, that can be modeled in language, and conclusions. It is only a department in one store in the shopping district, metaphorically. I like it. But it is only one channel, on a "cable provider" that has billions of channels that I've been able to count. Dr. Richard Feynman noted that the observer principle, in Quantum Mechanics, is very important. What you observe is what is real, to you. What you do not observe is not real, to you.

Some years ago I had training in Hawaiian healing methods, related to what some would call Huna. The first thing the instructor said was to open your mind to infinity, to infinite possibilities. If you work with someone, and you have a belief system that something is impossible, that is a very powerful hypnotic suggestion. Perhaps in some absolute sense, something might be impossible, but what does it cost you to believe it is possible, to open up to new outcomes[9]?

The human organism is more sensitive than any measuring device currently in existence. Lyall Watson details 35 known senses, in his book *Lifetide*. Oh, wait, you say, you learned of five, in school? Perhaps they didn't know everything, in school?

Then there is the Amazing*[ly Disempowering]* Randi, with his million dollar prize for anyone who can demonstrate paranormal phenomena to his satisfaction. In the first place, he has a million reasons to ensure that no-one will ever meet his standards. He is firmly planted in the Denial/Anger phase of acceptance.

---

8   Elsewhere, I talk about staring at the back of someone's neck, until they turn around. You can stare at any person, or situation, with total awareness, in a state of no thought, for a while. This will transform it, and you, but you won't understand unless you do it. This is actually a way to dowse, if you enflame your mind with a question, or leave it totally blank. This makes no sense in a Newtonian universe, however.
9   *Would an infinite being choose to limit itself? These limiting beliefs- are they really yours? Who do they really belong to? Maybe you could return to sender?*

He is also solidly in the Beta EEG, which in Lipan Apache, was called the "land of the living dead", because it is the place of the purely physical, where no paranormal activity can occur. Dowsing does most absolutely <u>not</u> work, in the Beta EEG that scientists work in. Randi entrains his test site, and anyone who enters it, in the Beta EEG state, which ensures that nothing paranormal will work. Breathing doesn't work in a dead body. That doesn't mean breathing is impossible, though.

Never deal with skeptics. Their disbelief taints the morphic field around them[10]. I find skeptics[11] toxic. They don't feel good. I stay away from them. Results are the only report card, and I get enough results to be satisfied. *Have fun playing*, instead[12].

If you limit yourself to the world of the flesh, all you get is the physical. This is something like the people cited in the movie *Supersize Me*, who limit themselves to only eating food from McDonald's. Apparently this is possible, but I couldn't do it. You can choose to do that, just keep in mind that choices have consequences. Dowsing also demands respect, for the larger picture, in a form most "civilized" people have forgotten.

Dowsers I know tend to be very respectful. Those who demand to "test" dowsers are, generally, grossly disrespectful. The testers are doing the metaphorical equivalent of trying to manufacture electronic circuit boards in a very dusty plant, or the doctors who, prior to Semmelweiss, would do surgery on live people, right after doing autopsies on corpses with diseases, without washing their hands[13]. History is full of examples of people who refused to change with changing circumstances.

---

10   Their morphic resonance is not useful for you. There are many people who simply ignore phenomena that do not fit their limited theories of how the world works. That's their choice. Respect their choice, and live your dreams. I mentioned to a professor, in 1979, that *Science* magazine had noted that genetic manipulation was being done, in the laboratory. He assured me it was pseudoscience, and wanted to know nothing more. I wonder if he eats corn, now? People whose perception is always tuned to the same view of reality are like a television set stuck on one channel. P. 109, *The Elves of Lilly Hill Farm*, Penny Kelly.
11   *It is difficult to free fools from the chains they revere.* -Voltaire
12   There is a story of a wise rabbi. A student went to him and said he was so confused, because he had been taught he could disprove anything. The rabbi said, "Can you prove you have no nose?" The student said, "Why certainly, to begin with..." The rabbi punched the student in the nose. The student stopped, shocked. The rabbi said, "So, tell me, what hurts?" Awareness can be like that.
13   Doctors of that time thought Semmelweiss was crazy for washing his hands, before surgery, and hounded him the way dowsers are hounded by some scientists today. Note that pattern. Mahatma Ghandi said, "First, they ignore you, then they laugh at you, then they fight you, and then, you win." Could it apply to dowsing?

On the old *Kung Fu* TV series, Caine was once asked why he was in a library. He responded, "The search for light and truth is never-ending". It must be true, it was on TV, right?

The Universe is so big that there is no "The Truth". There are only viewpoints We are always growing, we each have our personal truths. We can learn from each other, but we don't even know   0.000000000000000000000000000000000001% of what is actually going on. We have a puzzle with that many pieces, in total. We have a tiny fraction of pieces, and most people don't even have the same pieces.

Some years ago, some students from Yale came to an American Society of Dowsers conference. to debunk dowsing[14]. Most dowsers smiled and walked away. Ray Willey decided to play with them, so he passed their tests. They couldn't believe it, since, in their world, dowsing doesn't work. So they decided he had cheated, but they couldn't figure out how.

Why, why would you argue with someone in denial? Can you convince an alcoholic, in denial, to stop drinking? No, you cannot, not even with medical reports proving severe liver damage.

You cannot convince materialists drunk on the material senses, either. If they tell you dowsing doesn't work, smile, and say, "Yeah, I guess you're right", and just walk away. Dowsing responds best to situations where data obtained through it would help someone improve their condition, in usually very unmeasurable and non-repeatable ways. This normally does not include dealing with people who have advanced degrees in shutting out their subtle senses, and awareness. Scientists usually filter this kind of experience out of their perception.

There are people who will assure you they don't know how to draw pictures. They don't. They can debunk art, saying it doesn't work- and it doesn't, FOR THEM. You can, however, see the results other people got, with art, and say that the debunker is talking about the personal, not the universal.

---

14   There is no fool worse than an educated fool, except perhaps a politician.

When I wanted to learn art, I went to someone with results, who could draw well. I did so, in a class using the book *Drawing from the Right Side of the Brain.* I learned to draw, well. Listening to people say that drawing was hard, the "debunkers", wasn't helpful, I found. That is also what I did with dowsing.

A. Dowsing is always on; we just tune into the flow of awareness already present

Dowsing[15] is best proven in direct experience. Some years ago, I did a formal VisionQuest. I sat in a spot in the woods, with four gallons of water. I had no food. I had a sleeping bag. I asked for a Vision of my mission and purpose in life. I got it, though it was so subtle I didn't know it, for a year afterwards. I also realized what a loud, noisy cacophony civilization is- with cars, radios, machinery noises, and so on. Dowsing works better in silence.

If you are in the woods for a while, and get to the point where a whisper sounds like a shout, where you clearly hear the symphony of nature as the wind strums the plants, and birds sing solos, dowsing is easier than watching television. The Universe is always broadcasting, and you won't know that unless you tune in. The Apache used dowsing. They didn't call it that, however Geronimo knew where the cavalry was, at a distance. Lozen used her arms like a radar antenna, to scan for the Cavalry.

Indigenous peoples lived dowsing. The Lipan Apache had names for states of consciousness very similar to the Beta, Alpha, Theta, and Delta EEG's. They were, respectively:

1. Land of the Living Dead
2. Land of the spirit that moves behind all things
3. Land of the Spirit
4. Land of the Master

---

15   Dowsing is like electricity, always on, but you have to plug into it, by getting into the dowsing state, and turning the switch of your appliance, with a carefully formed question, to put it to use.

If you plan to work with dowsing, you must- you must- enter the Alpha EEG state, at least. Jose Silva's outfit has been training people in this since the 1960's.

There are some who claim his methods have been debunked. You can debunk anything, if you want to. That doesn't mean it doesn't work for others. As you move through the levels of dowsing, you will work with deeper and deeper levels of consciousness. Those at the advanced end of the scale move into the Gamma EEG state.

Dowsing, and really all intuition, depend on fractal resonance. The mental image you form with your question allows the resonance to occur[16]. People using intuition get endless lessons in the complexity, simplicity, and beauty of the web of life. Progress in intuitive work, and any other spiritual activity, follows the path of the clockwise golden section spiral.

1. In the first circle of the spiral, one learns to locate the target, and ask further questions, to get information about it, something like a metal detector. Spiritual awareness is required for the next stages, which means materialistic people cannot enter them[17].
2. In the second winding of the spiral, one learns to find targets out to the horizon, something like a direction finder.
3. In the third winding, one finds targets through metaphors, such as maps, archetypes, and dowsing charts.
4. In the fourth winding, one moves beyond dowsing devices, including physical senses, to device-less dowsing, and in time, knowing the response before the device could indicate. At this level, one enters the heart.
5. At the fifth winding, cooperation with nature occurs, along with an opening of the heart, if that hasn't already happened. Intent becomes critical at this stage. At this level, one has access to the subtle strands of everything. One affects them, whether intentionally or not.

---

16   Pp. 48, 52, *The Divining Heart: Dowsing and Spiritual Unfoldment,* Patricia and Richard Wright.
17   This is roughly the Purgatorio, if you like that metaphor.

6. At the sixth winding, one enters co-creation with nature. Heart creativity expands at the sixth winding. One can intend or request, perhaps using an open-ended question to allow for infinite possibilities, that something new come into this reality, a new pattern, and it does. We fully realize that the surrounding world mirrors what is within, and what is within mirrors what is without. This could include even instant repair of a broken bone, or new healthy tissue to replace diseased tissue[18]. This is the gateway into the Gamma EEG state. Oh wait, that is outside of your belief systems, pretend I didn't say that.

7. At the seventh winding, one works directly with the Creator. At this level, one touches the harmony of all created matter, and how thought and action affect everything[19].

This book you are reading was excerpted and expanded from the larger books, *Dowsing and Manifesting*, and *Dowsing and Self-Healing*. The purpose of these books is to take you from the first to at least the sixth level, above, and to open the door into the seventh. They are long, because it takes some time to shift the disempowering belief systems we have in Western culture. In a truly indigenous culture, you could learn this stuff as a child, from elders, as part of daily life, and not need books. In Western culture, books are often our elders.

If you need medical help, please seek appropriate advice from medical professionals. If you have a problem with the brakes on your car, seek out a mechanic, in the same way. We accept no responsibility for misuse of ideas in this book, though we don't see how anyone could misuse them. The sole purpose of this book is to help readers find and share joy, as they improve their lives, and help others, using deeper parts of their consciousness, in dowsing, and shaping their world, with intent.

Let's talk about the dowsing process.

---

18 P. 131, *The Divining Heart: Dowsing and Spiritual Unfoldment*, Patricia and Richard Wright. This has has been reported repeatedly in Hawaii, for example.
19 We cease interacting with surroundings, we are the surroundings. This is very difficult to describe with words. How does one describe communion in abstract bits of separated meaning?

1. Intuition offers extremely useful feedback. **Feedback lets you clear out the obstacles to using the Law of Resonant Attraction, which is a conscious shaping of the flow of life.** I've found I need the feedback.
Start with kinesiology. I use kinesiology for yes/no answers. When you look at anything, the soul has already said yes, or no. Then the mind kicks in, and starts analyzing[20]. I might run my fingers back and forth on a surface, and notice that if my finger sticks, the answer is no. If my finger runs quickly, the answer is yes. I feel _yes_ and _no_ in my body[21]. Stand up. Say, "*I am a clear channel to my higher self.*" Then say, "*My name is* [whatever your name is]". You will likely find yourself leaning forward, or some other change will occur. Then say "*My name is* [a name that is not your name]". You will find yourself leaning backwards, or in another direction. This is simple dowsing. When you dowse for a while, and pay attention to your feelings, you will just feel the response in your body. You could move to dowsing, with a device. Dowsing, and what is said here, are from the realm of the heart[22]. For this kind of work, it can be helpful to have a dowsing device[23], that will at least generate "yes", "no", and "wrong question" responses.[24] This is for feedback.

---

20   P. 62, *The Reality Creation Technique*, Frederick E. Dodson.
21   Yes, and truth, are probably a light feeling. No, and lies, feel heavy.
22   Kinesiology, and dowsing, are the connection between the body and spirit, the mind and the physical world. P. 18, *Power vs. Force*, David Hawkins, M.D., Ph.D. The October 13, 1967, *New York Times*, had an article by Hanson Baldwin on dowsing, in Vietnam. The December 11, 1967 *London Times* wrote about Major Harold Spary, who helped find water through dowsing, during the North African campaign, in WW II. Pp. 111-2, *Psychic Energy: How to Change Desires into Realities*, Joseph Weed. *The Divining Hand*, by Chris Bird, cites an American who helped General Patton's forces find water, at the same time, and also Luis Matacia's work with the U.S. Marines, using dowsing, during the Vietnam war.
23   Dowsing devices are basically readout devices, they are ideomotor response amplification devices that help you communicate with the deeper levels of mind. Pendulums, bobbers, L-rods, and Y-rods are a few examples of these. Some scientists hate dowsing. That's fine. They can hate it all it they want. It's not my fault Newton and Descartes cleaved their thinking. When you enter the dowsing morphic field, and follow its rules, you find it works. That's all I need. I don't care what other people hate. In the USA, the American Society of Dowsers has conventions where training in this is offered. If you aren't aware of how to dowse, and you want a concise description, you could look at www.lettertorobin.com for their free download. It's not new. When the Apache leader Victorio needed to know the location of his enemy, his sister Lozen would stand with outstretched arms and pray. As she turned to follow the Sun's path, her hands would begin to tingle and change color when she faced the enemy. The intensity of the sensation indicated the distance to the enemy. -James Kaywaykla, quoted by Eve Ball, *In the days of Victorio: Recollections of a Warm Springs Apache, II.*
24   I'm amused by religious people who are afraid of dowsing. The *Urim* and the *Thummim*, cited in the Bible, are unquestionably dowsing devices, clearly used as such. Even Wikipedia notes this. The prohibition on divination cited elsewhere was poorly translated from the Hebrew.

Solving Problems with Dowsing **21** A book for new dowsers ISBN-10: 1482688573

2. Dowsing systems are basically focused awareness with a readout device. If you want a pendulum, put any weight on a string. If it doesn't move itself, move it, tell the pendulum what the *yes, no,* and *wrong question/can't answer* directions are.

3. Your first dowsing test is always *is my energy system in balance?* If not, use intent sequences to put it in balance. Drink a lot of water, to be sure you have good receptivity. Dehydration interferes with intuitive/dowsing accuracy, and the energy system.[25]

4. Yes, as with all intuition, when you start out, it feels like you're making it up[26]. Then again, you're making everything up. On dowsing charts[27], see where the forward swing is going. If your bobber or pendulum isn't acting right, or is going crazy, you may have asked the wrong question. Ask a different question.

   You can tell your pendulum to put to work like Walt Woods' pendulum, or any other master dowser[28]. You can tell it to produce winners. With practice, you can use a virtual pendulum, that is, an imaginary pendulum[29]. Sometimes the intuitive answer comes through before I get my dowsing device working.

5. Dowsing not only <u>gives answers</u>, reflectively, it can project <u>energy</u>, and carry <u>intent</u>. For feedback, check the energy level before and after shifting, on a scale of 1-10 to start.

---

25 The above is more than sufficient. But for those who need piles of information, *The Emotion Code*, by Dr. Bradley Nelson, describes many other methods of body dowsing, with more detail than I have room for.
26 Because your brain interprets reality, and does not portray it. This is the difference between a living animal, and sausage.
27 Robert Detzler, as one example, is a prolific producer of dowsing charts. Google "dowsing chart", also.
28 That recipe can be applied to many other things; you could tell your energy work to work like that of Jesus, say, or your meditation to be like that of the Buddha, or your visualization to be like Einstein's, your compassion to be like Mother Theresa's. These archetypes are available for your use on call. I was raised Protestant. I find Catholic bookstores have some very useful portrayals of useful archetypes, notably angels, at good prices. A Shia Muslim might want to have the courage of Ali, for example. A good Apache teacher might be a Coyote teacher.
29 I use a protractor, to pick up percentages, with the pendulum. These are easy to find.

Before you start a procedure, Dowse with your device, or intuition[30]: *Do I have permission?* [Yes or No] or *Can I? May I? Should I? Is there any reason not to?* [Y/N] You can use a bobber or pendulum to spin energy in and out of a person, situation, or condition. You could also use your hands, and even do it just with your mind. One can see it more easily with a device. A percent scale dowsing readout is also very useful[31].

6. Here is some simple Torsion Physics, to use with projective dowsing: *Clockwise [CW] spin* installs or invokes *energy, Counter-Clockwise [CCW] spin* pulls it out. When you pull bad, or out-of-place energy out of a situation, using the CCW spin, let it pile up, in your imagination, let its negative intent cease, feel it turn into prosperity, which is frequency 8 on your dowsing scale[32], and/or fifth dimensional energy to enhance spiritual evolution, and put it back in, with a CW spin. You increase intent with a CW spin, and decrease intent with a CCW spin[33]. If I ask a question of my dowsing system, CW may indicate peace, love, joy, and prosperity. CCW would indicate fear and greed. Yours might be different. Notice that this is applied torsion physics. Or, don't.

7. You can measure the energy of anything[34]. Dowsing is a point in time phenomenon. When you're dowsing energy levels, it may be useful to **dowse the average energy level for a period of time**, such as one month.

---

30 This is so easy! Pay attention to your feelings. There are two feelings: stuck, or perhaps heavy, and free flowing, or light. As answers to questions, they mean *think again*, and *good idea!* If you prefer, no, and yes, that's fine. Sit in heartspace, and ask the question, for all answers exist there. If you aren't sure how to do this, take several deep, relaxing breaths, relax deeply, go to your heart, and let the answer arise, without an expected outcome. All answers are already available there. Only your conscious mind separates you from the answers. This comes from Robert Winn, who does fascinating breathwork trainings. When starting out, this seems very subtle. Continue making distinctions, and it gets easier and easier.
31 Pp. 62, 130, and elsewhere, *Ten Thousand Whispers*, by Lynda Madden Dahl, notes that these percentages are flexible, and depend very much on your energy state. Your body temperature is also variable, too, isn't it.
32 Numerology and Doreen Virtue's book on angel numbers are one place to start, if these frequencies interest you. Most importantly, find what the frequencies mean TO YOU.
33 In Sufi whirling, motion is usually CCW, to raise the energy up from the earth, and to raise one's own energy. A CW spin is grounding, and invoking. Physicists define spin as being on its axis of rotation, CW or CCW. p. 100, *Quantum Reality*, Nick Herbert. You don't need a pendulum, you can do this with your awareness.
34 Data has meaning in comparison to, in relation to, comparable data. Compare today to yesterday, last month to the same month last year, or compare a before and after energy level. The level of the Dow-Jones Industrial Average, as one example, is meaningless without comparable levels before. Even body temperature is only useful in comparison to observed averages, and previous levels.

If you are working with manifestation and dowsing, you can test the percent manifested of a particular creation[35], and any blocks keeping it from manifestation. It is necessary to do this from a meditative heartstate, so that you don't disturb it by your observation.

Do not be attached to this, and also don't worry if it goes down, because progression is not necessarily a straight line graph. You can dowse the present time, or the past. You can dowse the future, but not from the present. You have to dowse the future as if it were the past, from a point on the other side of the date you are interested in[36].

8. **Ask very precise questions that elicit exactly what you want, not what you don't want[37].** If you ask, "Is it raining outside?" you will almost always get a *yes*, because somewhere, outside, it is indeed raining, somewhere on the surface of the earth. If you ask, "Is it raining in a 100 yard/meter radius from this house?" you get a much more useful answer. Your life is the crystallization of the questions you ask. Ask better questions, and your life changes for the better[38]. Focus helps intent, also.

9. If you search the Internet for dowsing devices, you will get a great many sites that tell you they don't work, it's all in your mind, and so on. Test these sites for percent true, with your dowsing device. For someone who lives totally in the flesh, they are true enough, but for people who are realizing their potential, they test at less than 5% true. If you prefer disempowering ideas, why are you reading this book? Disempowering ideas are available for free on almost every channel of your Television, all over the Internet, from authority figures, and from many people on the street.

---

35 99.9% of manifestation occurs out of your conscious awareness, before you ever get anything physical.
36 P. 242, *Intuition Technology*, John Living, Professional Engineer.
37 P. 70, *Psycho-Cybernetics*, Maxwell Maltz.
38 Precise wording is also critical to any statement of intent. In the form is the outcome. Pp. 140-141, *Lucid Dreaming*, Robert Waggoner.

If you want to empower yourself, start by <u>finding what works</u>, not with using disempowering ideas that other people want to sell to you. The Amazing[ly Disempowering] Randi has over 1 million reasons why he will <u>never</u> find anyone who can meet his impossible standards. He never will find the proof he claims he seeks, because he is not open to finding it. He is so powerful at, and invested in, creating disempowering states that he disempowers anybody foolish enough to enter his energy field. If you want a better life, use HeartSpace, not RandiSpace.[39]

Do not have anything to do with such people[40], if you can help it. You cannot prove anything to them. Dowsing devices, and intuition, were used extensively for over 98% of human history, despite their denial. The Tassili caves in Morocco show unmistakable Y-rods, for example. *De Re Metallica*, a mining text written by Georg Bauer in the 1500's to find silver in the place from which the dollar got its name, Joachimsthal, shows Y-rods in use to locate silver veins.[41]

10. The first place to start is to **fix yourself**. Emotion is fuel for intent. Ask yourself daily, for a while, "**How do I feel?**", and track down and adjust anything less than your default, normal state of peace, love, joy, happiness, freedom, contentment, and so on.

That is dowsing. We'll talk more as we got along. No book can describe every possibility. Books can, however, suggest general possibilities within classes of ideas. This book does that. The model of reality you create, based on what you read here, will probably be unique.

---

39 When you find disempowering ideas in hardsell mode, you want to ask, "Who benefits?" Who benefits from keeping you disempowered? Why would they be hard-selling doubt like timeshares that turn out to have negative value, if there weren't benefit for someone? How much is The Amazing[ly Disempowering] Randi paid to disempower people, I wonder?
40 Don't waste your time, energy, or attention with them, they entrain people in lack of power. When you lie down with dogs, you get up with fleas. Those who run with wolves must learn to howl. Those who argue with fools become fools. When you deal with people who militantly hard sell you on doubt, the best thing you can do is say "I guess you're right", and leave.
41 *The Divining Hand,* by Christopher Bird, has a story by a man who dowsed water wells for General Patton, in North Africa, during WW II. Could it be that the people who say dowsing doesn't work use it secretly, but don't want you empowered?

Solving Problems with Dowsing **25** A book for new dowsers ISBN-10: 1482688573

No sequence in this book is absolute, though some sections might be. In all cases, you may end up downloading additional information, and adding to or changing a sequence. That's ok, and desirable. You are an individual. There are very few one size fits all formulas.

Your beliefs can free you, or imprison you, because you create your beliefs, and your beliefs create your world by filtering it[42]. I see beliefs as tools. It is best to take the most appropriate tool for a job. A belief that something is impossible is not a useful tool. Great things achieved by humans started from the belief that they were possible, not that they were impossible.

Part of learning is learning to unlearn, to empty out what we think we know, to enter into unconditioned responses, **to live as, and in, the question.** We are given what we need to grow, when our cups are not already full. Service must be the intention[43].

We are all a part of one another, and ultimately part of pure consciousness, God, or whatever term you use for infinity and infinite consciousness. The simplest entities, a leaf, a fish, a Cedar, a mountain range, a quartz crystal, are all marvels of the Creator's art[44]. Healing into wholeness means realizing we are already whole, not merely an absence of unpleasant symptoms.

Pierre Teilhard de Chardin argued that human evolution is going towards a trans-human state, which involves the birth of the unified planetary mind, aware of its essential divinity. He called this the Omega point[45]. The end of the movie *2001: A Space Odyssey* portrayed this. It could be that the near-death experience is taking humans into the next stage of development (of wholeness) by unlocking previously dormant spiritual potential[46]. Intuition does the same thing.

---

42   Wouldn't it make sense to filter out what is not useful? You can change your filters- your beliefs- so that this happens.
43   Pp. 134-5, *The Divining Heart: Dowsing and Spiritual Unfoldment*, Patricia and Richard Wright.
44   P. 220, *Heading Toward Omega: in Search of the Meaning of the Near-Death Experience*, Kenneth Ring.
45   P. 252, *Heading Toward Omega: in Search of the Meaning of the Near-Death Experience*, Kenneth Ring.
46   P. 255, *Heading Toward Omega: in Search of the Meaning of the Near-Death Experience*, Kenneth Ring.

Totally aside from that, dowsing is just a lot of fun. It is an artistic activity. I enjoy it as much as I enjoy woodwork, calligraphy, art, making Chinese *Penjing* or Japanese *Bonkei*, storytelling, music, and the other forms of art I engage in.

Projective dowsing is an art form. It creates what the Navajo people call *hozho*, which I will weakly translate as sparkling, harmonious, joyful, healing beauty.

It's kind of like getting an abandoned lot, in the city, covered with trash, and through careful work turning it into a beautiful garden park, with a small waterfall, fish in a pond, birds singing, beautiful flowers, a seat to enjoy it all, wind chimes, wind harps, rose arbors, a statue of an elf made using Sacred Geometry, and so on. That is my metaphor for dowsing.

We used to live in paradise, till we threw ourselves out of it, with the separation of the conscious mind, in judgment and fixed opinions. The Angel with the flaming sword is our own higher self, which still holds the sword we used to cut it off from us. Enter into that, and we enter Paradise again. Please note this is a metaphor, not some religious interpretation.

What is the most beautiful place you have ever been? What would it be like to live in that kind of beauty, most or all of the time?

For water dowsers... isn't water often a part of beauty in landscape, even in the desert?

B. Understanding how perception, dowsing, & the world, work together

The purpose of this section is to offer empowering ideas based in the paradigm of energy, not of materialism. Some of what is said here is based on Quantum Mechanics ideas. If these words remind you of difficult times in school, train yourself so that every time words related to science show up, you immediately come up with another word, such as ice cream, chocolate, or maple syrup. Wholeness cannot be understood using only the intellectual mind. It is heart-based, and must be felt, recognized, and even welcomed[47], from one's entire being.

Every thought and observation is an information compression. Every thought and observation contributes to, and shifts, the cosmos we observe[48]. Belief systems create and shape what we think we see. Real growth and healing involves being guided and supported through changing perceptions[49].

Observation is a powerful gift[50]. You are connected with, and even shape, what you perceive. Observing a stone is actually observing the effects of the stone on the observer[51]. There is a subtle partnership between light, matter, and ourselves[52].

At our core, we are holographic beings, living within a holographic universe. The 3 and 4 dimensional world of ourselves, and everything else, is a virtual reality created and perceived by our senses[53], just as a bunch of binary signals create the image on your television screen. We are connected holographically and fractally to the great unifying field of consciousness. Health and happiness occur when we are in harmony with the Unified Field. Disharmony is communicated through the feelings in the body. Helping a situation, or someone, to heal, means listening and feeling first, and then thinking[54].

47 P. 12, *The Human Hologram: Living your Life in Harmony with the Unified Field*, Dr. Robin Kelly.
48 Do myths and stories re-arrange the past? They certainly do at a personal level- the story you tell about your past shapes you. Do they at a Universal level? Does our story of the Big Bang shape how the Universe came into existence? I'll let you dowse that mind-bender.
49 P. 29, *The Human Hologram: Living your Life in Harmony with the Unified Field*, Dr. Robin Kelly.
50 P. 37, *The Human Hologram: Living your Life in Harmony with the Unified Field*, Dr. Robin Kelly.
51 P. 39, *The Human Hologram: Living your Life in Harmony with the Unified Field*, Dr. Robin Kelly.
52 P. 43, *The Human Hologram: Living your Life in Harmony with the Unified Field*, Dr. Robin Kelly.
53 Pp. 10-11, *The Human Hologram: Living your Life in Harmony with the Unified Field*, Dr. Robin Kelly.
54 Native peoples in North America used cradleboards. This meant infants learned to observe and perceive carefully,

The person with the issue learns to live and love life in the now, in harmony, in a fractal blueprint of unity[55]. This is very similar to the Navajo concept of bringing a person back to the original healing beauty, of *hozho*, in the *Healingway*.

Once we understand ourselves as human holograms, we realize that we can focus our consciousness for the greater good. That is where dowsing becomes very helpful. Dowsing, whether water dowsing to get pure water, cleaning out a street level drug market, or high level work, is about contributing to the greater good. Dowsing is service. I'll go so far as to say dowsing is Love, or at least its expression.

Rational intellect combines with compassionate intent, and our heart consciousness can solve many more problems than the mind alone[56]. Our bodies are continuously formed around a holographic matrix in the universal field of consciousness[57]. Balancing the Yin and Yang polarity of life is extremely helpful.

The first law of thermodynamics notes that energy cannot be destroyed. It can only be changed[58]. This is very important. Since everything is energy, everything can be shifted. This is done with intent. This is *projective* dowsing.

The holographic world that transcends time and space is the *implicate order* of David Bohm. The world we see is the explicate order. Balancing the two, as polarities, the Yin and Yang, plugging Yang into Yin, lets us access the infinite energy of the implicate order, the zero point field; scalar, torsion or fractal free energy, or grace. Symmetrical geometric shapes occur as footprints of dimensions beyond the purely physical, symmetry outside the chaos[59]. Photons could be carrying, or at least transmitting, universal information. Some suggest that the photon has a toroidal, or doughnut shape[60].

before jumping into a situation. Usually Americans will jump into a situation first, without thinking, and cause problems, as that is how they grew up. The first approach is finesse; it costs less, and gets better results.
55   P. 14, *The Human Hologram: Living your Life in Harmony with the Unified Field*, Dr. Robin Kelly.
56   P. 15, *The Human Hologram: Living your Life in Harmony with the Unified Field*, Dr. Robin Kelly.
57   P. 25, *The Human Hologram: Living your Life in Harmony with the Unified Field*, Dr. Robin Kelly.
58   P. 26, *The Human Hologram: Living your Life in Harmony with the Unified Field*, Dr. Robin Kelly.
59   P. 28, *The Human Hologram: Living your Life in Harmony with the Unified Field*, Dr. Robin Kelly.
60   P. 34, *The Human Hologram: Living your Life in Harmony with the Unified Field*, Dr. Robin Kelly, and Dan Winter.

Colors are based on the angle we view the torus from. It is useful to pay attention to patterns of information, in dowsing. Contrast makes it possible to see. An image with no contrast has only a field of color to perceive. Dowsing means noticing ever finer contrasts, and patterns, and distinctions.

The quantum world is one of instant non-local connections, and our measurements are involved in the outcomes. Human attention, and even intention, affect results retroactively[61]. Our bodies are fractal, including DNA, which may be relevant for DNA's non-local connections to quantum realms. The network of connective tissue, known as our cytoskeleton, provides support for our tissues, and the semiconductor electrical circuitry known as the Chinese meridian system[62].

The physicist Bevan Reid notes that virtual energy and pure space become beams of bio photons, or bosons, which form the foundational matrix for all living matter. Our physical body is in constant communication with the virtual energy of space. Space is not empty. It has an infinite number of tiny spiral vortices, or wormholes, sometimes called quantum foam. Each one acts as a portal in the library of universal information.

The fabric of space-time consists of an infinite number of portals to other dimensions. Our body downloads information instantly from this. We could call this constant exchange of information resonance, or base-line dowsing. DNA molecules can receive, process, and project light[63].

Brainpower alone is not enough to heal chronic, complex illnesses[64] or problem situations. The heart is important, also. As an example, pleasurable emotions such as joy, happiness, excitement, enthusiasm, and contentment can significantly reduce the likelihood of developing heart disease, or community problems.

---

61   P. 48, *The Human Hologram: Living your Life in Harmony with the Unified Field*, Dr. Robin Kelly.
62   P. 75, *The Human Hologram: Living your Life in Harmony with the Unified Field*, Dr. Robin Kelly.
63   Pp. 79-82, 96, *The Human Hologram: Living your Life in Harmony with the Unified Field*, Dr. Robin Kelly.
64   P. 120, *The Human Hologram: Living your Life in Harmony with the Unified Field*, Dr. Robin Kelly.

Even watching funny movies can help the heart. A healthy heart holds joy, yet adapts swiftly to pressures and stresses of daily life. Yin and Yang are perfectly balanced in it, or perhaps the parasympathetic and sympathetic nervous systems are in balance. Perhaps the heart is the seat of the soul. The heart is the core of the human bio-field, which is linked holographically to other fields of consciousness, in the one great unified field.

The heart, connected to this field, communicates subtle variations in information and consciousness as feelings[65]. It is more sensitive than any measuring device[66].

Black holes at the center of galaxies may behave like much larger fractal hearts, gently pumping energy into outer space, as hot plasma[67]. Quantum entanglement occurs as a vital part of living processes[68]. Karl Pribram showed that information could be spread holographically within the brain[69].

Sensory information is spread through the visual cortex in the pattern of a Fourier transform. Sir Roger Penrose, the quantum physicist, said that the quantum and classical world of space-time meet in the microtubules in each cell. Here, the quantum world collapses down into the physical world of our consciousness and perception[70]. He also suggested that efficient fractal packaging and microtubules form a quantum computer[71].

Our perceptions of what we see, hear, feel, and so on, are to a great extent based on our expectations. In a certain sense, what we perceive is what we expect[72]. Beliefs govern our feelings, thoughts, and actions, and influence every aspect of our lives. They are electrochemical signals that broadcast throughout the body. Most beliefs are stored unconsciously[73], as a model of what feels real.

---

65   P. 117, The Human Hologram: Living your Life in Harmony with the Unified Field, Dr. Robin Kelly.
66   The heart is the only real dowsing device, then.
67   P. 118, The Human Hologram: Living your Life in Harmony with the Unified Field, Dr. Robin Kelly.
68   P. 97, The Human Hologram: Living your Life in Harmony with the Unified Field, Dr. Robin Kelly.
69   P. 122, The Human Hologram: Living your Life in Harmony with the Unified Field, Dr. Robin Kelly.
70   P. 127, The Human Hologram: Living your Life in Harmony with the Unified Field, Dr. Robin Kelly.
71   P. 128, The Human Hologram: Living your Life in Harmony with the Unified Field, Dr. Robin Kelly.
72   -Dr. Steven LaBerge, cited P. 17, Gamma Healing, Chris Walton.
73   P. 16, Gamma Healing, Chris Walton.

To a very large extent, men and women are a product of how they define themselves. They create beliefs about life and self, based on models derived from innate ideas, and experience of the culture and environment we grow up in. These beliefs crystallize at a deep level of our psychosomatic systems, in the mind, and brains. The nervous system is associated with endocrine systems, and even blood and sinews.

People act, speak and think according to these deeply held beliefs, and belief systems[74], on automatic, for much of their waking days.

The heart sends emotional and intuitive information signals to the brain and body, and it can remember, feel and sense[75]. Your heart senses a probable future intuitively, and then conveys this information to the brain, to prepare you for a response[76]. Everything is already whole, and healed, in the heart. All information is accessible in the heart, because there is no separation from it, as there is with the conscious mind. Without the separation, all information is available there.

The heart is where the original beauty, the *hozho* of the Navajo/Dineh people, the perfect plan, the ideal, exists. Healing is just remembering who you truly are. The being that you truly are is in your heart, not in your head.

Body cells can be understood with material or energy models. In every culture and medical tradition before ours, healing was accomplished by moving or shifting energy[77], and restoring the "flow". Your mood affects your immune system, directly, at the molecular level. Every thought and emotion has a biochemical level.

The mind is literally a whole body phenomenon. Mind and body are inextricably connected with our thoughts, affecting our biology[78], and dowsing. Over 95% of your daily thoughts,

---

74   -Dr. Jeremy Hayward, cited p. 25, *Gamma Healing*, Chris Walton.
75   P. 79, *Gamma Healing*, Chris Walton.
76   P. 80, *Gamma Healing*, Chris Walton.
77   -Prof. Albert Szent-Gyorgyi, Nobel Laureate in Medicine, cited P. 88, *Gamma Healing*, Chris Walton.
78   P. 29, *Gamma Healing*, Chris Walton.

feelings, and actions each day are governed by learned programs in your subconscious mind[79].

The subconscious mind talks to us through the body[80]- ideomotor response, for example- and even through events in our lives. Belief is strong enough to totally reverse the chemical action of a drug[81]. The placebo effect even works for surgery[82].

Being childish, playful, and silly, and laughing happily, invokes the subconscious mind[83]. The more we work with the subconscious mind, the easier it all gets[84], because it is like plugging into power. The Indian metaphor for the conscious mind working with the subconscious mind is the elephant boy getting on the elephant[85].

Empty space is full of energy and information. Their interaction with observers creates the physical world, and makes dowsing possible. Quantum energy and information fields interact with the body and mind, which influence life[86], directly. Connective tissue fascia are the largest organ of the body. The molecules in this have a crystalline structure.

Crystalline structures receive energy and information very well[87]. We are vibrational beings of energy and information, within larger fields of energy[88]. We are connected to all other energy fields, including those of other human beings.

We live in a quantum, interconnected universe, full of energy and information. Universal mind is a sea of fluctuating energy and information, from which everything in form arises, and to which everything returns. All information is accessible in it.

---

79   P. 37, *Gamma Healing*, Chris Walton.
80   P. 49, *Gamma Healing*, Chris Walton.
81   P. 60, *Gamma Healing*, Chris Walton.
82   P. 64, *Gamma Healing*, Chris Walton.
83   I read a book by I think Chuck Pfarrer. He had a friend who walked into a tough bar, with a feeling of imminent violence. He shouted, "OK, who's the toughest, meanest Mfer in this place?" A huge man got up, and said, "I am." His friend then said, "Good. Take over for me. I have to go to the bathroom." The entire place broke up in laughter, and the bad energy vanished. This is an example of projective dowsing, using language.
84   P. 125, *Cosmic Ordering for Beginners*, Barbel Mohr, Clemens Maria Mohr.
85   I grew up in Southeast Asia. At that time, elephants were the bulldozers, and log lifters. An Asian elephant can lift a log, on its tusks. However, it needed the guidance of the elephant rider, to do so. Both had to work together.
86   P. 93, *Gamma Healing*, Chris Walton.
87   P. 95, *Gamma Healing*, Chris Walton, and many other sources. Consider crystal radios, or silicon crystals in computers.
88   *Luminous beings we are, not this crude matter.* -Yoda

It is the zero point field[89]. We are quantum entangled with everything in the Universe, inside a holistic, interconnected reality of concentric rings, and geometric forms. Our thoughts, beliefs, and emotions can both influence the world of matter[90], and respond to changes in the world[91]. This is dowsing.

The closer scientists examine atoms and particles, the more they discover how everything is dependent on, and indivisible from, everything else. The elementary structures of physics may not be particles at all.

Elementary particles interact through temporary or virtual quantum particles. The back-and-forth flow of virtual particles is known collectively as the zero point field. In quantum field theory, particles cannot be separated from the empty space around them.

Matter is a relationship between two fuzzy things: particle energy traded with other particle energy, and with the background field. The relationship between these creates what we call matter, and our sense of mass, or density. Inertia is resistance to being accelerated in the zero point field. An object is a collection of electric charges, in interference patterns, interacting with other energy.

Non-locality, or quantum entanglement, unfolds such that once subatomic particles are in contact, they are forever influenced by each other, instantaneously, over any time and distance, without force or energy. Entangled particles can get into a state of coherence, where they behave like a giant wave.

Dr. Richard Feynman noted that the role of the observer is critical to quantum physics. The only thing that transforms the potential of a subatomic particle, which exists as a smeared out, uncongealed wave of possibility, into something solid and measurable, is the observer. A dowser is an observer.

---

89 Pp. 108-9, *Gamma Healing*, Chris Walton.
90 Consider greek sculpture, which was carefully carved, by the ratios of sacred geometry. It was an intentional embodiment of the invisible divine order, in matter. Roman copies don't always look good, because those who copied weren't always aware of this. Sculpture, originally, was intended to affect human minds, so they would tend towards divine order in sacred geometry.
91 Pp.113-4, *Gamma Healing*, Chris Walton.

C. The Universe is a joint venture

The Universe is a joint venture between the observer and the observed. Observation, even after the fact, determines the final outcome. One could see the entire Universe as one giant possibility wave, immanent, awaiting birth into existence, through observation. We are the Universe co-creating itself. When we look at an electron, or take a measurement, we influence its final state[92].

The model of the human hologram recognizes that information is very important in our Universe. We receive information, as awareness, in its purest form, through intuition, feelings and instincts[93]. This is dowsing.

The heart has its own magnetic field, with opposing poles, and a central zero point of balance. It seems to be the focused receiver of information from the unified field. Once received, the information is relayed by the heart to the rest of the body, holographically, and through biochemicals[94].

The model of the human as hologram recognizes that outside of the physical universe, and our understanding of energy, is the realm of pure information, which forms our bodies, and informs our minds and hearts[95]. When we are one with the unified field, we notice magical moments, bliss, spontaneous joy[96].

A useful sequence for self-healing, and healing situations, then, would involve noticing feelings, acknowledging them, expressing emotions, seeking useful information, and taking corrective action[97]. One then uses feedback to guide further action.

We are part of a global consciousness, and we can get in and out of the global field of consciousness to make connections with others nonphysical energy. This communication happens each and every moment, whether you know about it, or not[98].

---

92 Pp. 7-16, *The Bond: Connecting Through the Space between Us*, Lynne McTaggart.
93 Pp. 145-6, *The Human Hologram: Living your Life in Harmony with the Unified Field*, Dr. Robin Kelly.
94 Pp. 147-8, *The Human Hologram: Living your Life in Harmony with the Unified Field*, Dr. Robin Kelly.
95 P. 185, *The Human Hologram: Living your Life in Harmony with the Unified Field*, Dr. Robin Kelly.
96 P. 193, *The Human Hologram: Living your Life in Harmony with the Unified Field*, Dr. Robin Kelly.
97 P. 162, *The Human Hologram: Living your Life in Harmony with the Unified Field*, Dr. Robin Kelly.
98 P. 121, *Gamma Healing*, Chris Walton.

Your thoughts are not only connected to others. They also impact, influence, and change the world of matter. They have actual affect on the material world[99]. Your perceptions, thoughts, and beliefs are information compressions.

Some report it is even possible to indirectly change the structure of DNA, or the acid alkaline balance, simply with intent[100], shifting energy.

Altered states of consciousness tune the receiver wavelengths of our brains and bodies to different frequencies[101]. We can pick these up with our normal waking consciousness[102].

Intuitive awareness comes through as information without emotional charge, and information laced with compassion[103]. It is always downloading. We just pay attention to it, to realize it is there[104]. One can act on it, with finesse, and trust, to get results. Let's play a bit:

D. Introductory remote viewing dowsing

1. Be aware of something you want to know more about.
2. Close your eyes.
3. Lay on the grass, in the sunlight, arms out to your sides.
4. Relax, and breathe deeply.
5. Picture the whole earth, seeing its color, and the pale bluish glow that comes off it.
6. Then narrow the focus of your imagination, so it gets narrower and narrower.
7. Notice what attracts your attention, and focus on it[105].
8. Notice that this is dowsing.

---

99   P. 125, *Gamma Healing*, Chris Walton.
100   P. 129, *Gamma Healing*, Chris Walton, and Kishori Aird's and Claude Swanson's books.
101   You switch a radio from FM to Shortwave bands, and get a whole new kind of programming. Those who limit themselves only to FM restrict the kind of information they can receive. To use another analogy, once you find out how to use the Internet, a whole new kind of information becomes available to you.
102   P. 183, *Gamma Healing*, Chris Walton.
103   P. 195, *Dr. Judith Orloff's Guide to Intuitive Healing*, Dr. Judith Orloff.
104   If you had the TV, Radio, blasting at high volume in your house, you might not hear the telephone ring, as an analogy. However, when you turn these down, you can hear the telephone. This is one of the advantages of meditation. Tom Brown, Jr., notes that if you are in the woods, and are to the point where a whisper sounds like a shout, a whole new world of information opens up to you, effortlessly. This is a critical point, to understanding what is in this book. We'll make it again, in other ways.
105   P. 186, *The Ringing Cedars Series: Book One: Anastasia*, Vladimir Megre.

Consciousness begins with self reflection- the awareness that we are who we are, where we are[106]. We converse with the Universe in a waking dream, where questions are answered symbolically, and also in everyday ordinary experience[107].

Once you understand that everything unusual in your life is a dream message to you, a form of dowsing response, you can begin experiencing the fluid, dreamlike quality of waking life.

You can ask questions about unusual things that happened, such as *what does this mean for me,* or *what was I thinking about her,* or *what I have asked for, that this happened*[108]? When you pay attention, you notice that important messages are always showing up[109]. Synchronicities are actually reality shifts[110].

E. Practice: Intuitively measure people and situations

1. Relax, breathe deeply for a while, and enter a deeply relaxed heartspace.
2. In a non-judgmental state, concentrate on a person, or situation.
3. Notice what you notice, without judgment.
4. Concentrate on what grabs your attention.
5. Notice images, feelings, and so on. Whatever comes up is correct.
6. Write down what you notice.
7. Recognize that this is only one channel of data. However, see how it works out for you, as you move forward with it[111]. This may feel something like a waking dream.
8. Recognize that this is dowsing. The image you got is from your personal scale of images. It has meaning to you.

---

106 P. 239, *Reality Shifts: When Consciousness Changes the Physical World*, Cynthia Sue Larson.
107 P. 231, *Reality Shifts: When Consciousness Changes the Physical World*, Cynthia Sue Larson.
108 P. 232, *Reality Shifts: When Consciousness Changes the Physical World*, Cynthia Sue Larson.
109 P. 233, *Reality Shifts: When Consciousness Changes the Physical World*, Cynthia Sue Larson.
110 P. 236, *Reality Shifts: When Consciousness Changes the Physical World*, Cynthia Sue Larson.
111 Pp. 221-2, *Dr. Judith Orloff's Guide to Intuitive Healing*, Dr. Judith Orloff, and Laura Day's books. Laura discusses dowsing in fascination ways, however she calls it intuition.

This book is about playing with intent, patterns of light and information, and representational effects and systems. This book offers ideas that are beyond what was taught in most colleges when I was of that age, because it deals with the heart, the creative part of the mind, the part of consciousness where *you and others are already whole.*

This is the fun part of consciousness, and it lacks the separation-driven fear of the conscious mind. It feels really good. The better you get in this, the better you feel. You measure this area with feelings.

Disease- dis-ease- is a symptom of blockage, of fragmentation, of forgotten unity. Healing literally means becoming whole, or being restored to wholeness. One mythic model for this is Osiris, who was dismembered, the way consciousness in our culture has been.

Isis, a personification of deeper mind, recollected the pieces, and re-membered them. Reconnecting includes the physical, emotional, mental, and perhaps spiritual bodies. We become whole by recalling unity, and allowing something beyond the smaller self to reunite with us, into a new wholeness.

Seeing images of perfect systems operation is seeing in wholes, remembering at the physical level[112]. Renaissance art is an example of this. Modern art can be as fragmented as modern consciousness. Art imitates culture, which influences art.

However, this wholeness is a new wholeness, in the now, it is not the wholeness of the past. Becoming whole is simply realizing your true nature, who you truly are. You are already healed, in one or more points of possibility in the zero point field, and you need only to go to those points, and feel yourself already healed. Thus, all healing is self-healing. Non-linear change does happen. Consider the butterfly effect, in Chaos Theory- that systems are so inter-connected that the beating of a butterfly's wing outside your window has an effect on the weather in Hong Kong. This is not a metaphor, this is literally true.

---

112 P. 27, *Healing Visualizations: Creating Health through Imagery,* Gerald Epstein, MD.

Solving Problems with Dowsing **38** A book for new dowsers ISBN-10: 1482688573

However, watching reruns of *Friends*, on TV, playing video games, and worrying about whatever the latest strange attractor of negative energy is on the news, may not be effective.

The Renaissance did not start because of a lot of new ideas. It started because the printing press shared the old ideas far more efficiently. Perhaps the Internet is our new printing press, opening up new opportunities by making information much easier to find. Dowsing also opens up new opportunities, in this way.

F. The dowsing journey

The dowsing journey is the story of life, of growth, of molting out of old self into new Self. What we call manifesting wholeness is the story of the Yang/Yin sine wave life cycle, of growth. This happens as a unified whole, at times in under a second of clock time. I break out the stages, for clarity. Understand that your journey may have these elements out of order, and some elements may never show up[113].

This is also the structure of the VisionQuest, as I have experienced it, of the hypnotic induction, and perhaps even of incarnation into the flesh, as well as college education, and some military and corporate training. The journey to wholeness is mythic, and your personal story, your myth. Myth comes from a Greek word meaning story, as I recall.

There are three major stages[114]:
1.   Departure/Separation, or dropping down
2.   Initiation, or setting intent
3.   Return, or letting go

---

113   This was developed primarily from Joseph Campbell's work, and also that of Phil Cousineau, Bill Moyers, Christopher Vogler, James N. Frey, and Dan Bronzite.
114   Just as there are three stages to the story arc, in movies and plays, which dates back to Aristotle. This may be an Aryan archetype. Native Americans like four stages, on a medicine wheel.

At the beginning of your dowsing journey's adventure, you probably:

are good, or are becoming good, at what you do for a living

are grateful, and loyal to friends and family

are motivated by ideals, principles, some higher idea, values

are or are becoming aware, clever, forgiving, observant, patient, resourceful

clarify your intent

drink more water, and breathe more deeply

focus your energy, more and more, on what you seek

give without expecting return

grow in many ways

have probably been wounded in some way

 have, or are developing, one or more special talents

have or find courage, living from the heart

help others, when possible

know you are here for something more than just sucking up oxygen

live by your own code, or grow into that

persist

remain open to something being better than the best you can imagine

respect others, and larger systems

seek what gives you more energy

spend quiet time, to let spiritual awareness bubble up into consciousness

take action, based on inspiration and intuition

take the lead

you move away from, or don't:

act cruelly, or in a way that lowers your energy, or the energy of others

indulge in addictive behavior

quit

wallow in negativity

whine

win by luck

1. Departure

a. Some would start this with a miraculous birth, or hero's lineage. This is actually a symbol, a device, which tells the listener the story is actually about the listener. Stories are always about the listener[115], and the healing journey.

b. The *Call to Adventure*, the call of the heart, to create, to explore the unknown, to grow. Luke goes home, sees his adoptive parents dead, and knows he has to enter the unknown[116].

c. *Refusal of the Call*, or lack of confidence, or procrastination, or denial. Some called to dowsing don't respond right away. The hero tends to rot, in this state. Heroes and adventure, dowsing, and manifesting, go together like Yang and Yin.

d. Mentors, miraculous aides, books, awareness, tools, helpers, and counselors show up to help. This is the stage you are in, with this book. The classic example of this is Theseus being given the ball of string, and a sword, before entering the labyrinth. This is the dowsing tool stage.

e. The *threshold is crossed.* In the movie Star Wars, this is the stage where Luke is in the *Millenium Falcon*, as it takes off from Tattooine. There may be a threshold guardian who warns one not to enter. This is leaving the zone of comfort, and entering Yin, the unknown. Luke was blindfolded, and trained to dowse in fencing with his lightsaber, in this stage.

f. Enter the Belly of the Beast, as Luke was, in the *Death Star.*

In the course of the adventure of dowsing your way to wholeness, you will probably:
engage in conflict and its resolution
get a call to adventure

---

115 My mother used to love the TV show *Murder She Wrote*. Angela Lansbury stars as a very smart older woman, who shows the dunderheaded men the simple realizations only she is capable of making, and solves the case, in spite of the idiot men. Young children love the story of Rudolf the Red-Nosed Reindeer, because they identify with Rudolf. I used to love *MacGyver*. Women seem to enjoy novels like *Jane Eyre*, which for me drag horribly. I mentioned at work that I was getting married. The men looked off into space, bored, and the women leaned forward, as if it was the last minute of the Superbowl, and the ball had just been intercepted, with the possibility of an upset. All stories are about us. When I did storytelling in schools, the children were actually in the story, as the characters. I used to have children act out the *Three Little Pigs*, as each character, with some children as each house. They loved it. Anne McCaffrey's sci fi drags some, for me, but Edgar Rice Burrough's books I devoured. In Greek mythology, heroes were usually children of God and mortal, which means the listener is the hero. The Listener knows both seen and unseen qualities of self, but other people are only mortal, in the seen world, one doesn't see other people's unseen qualities. Jerry Seinfeld said that men see comic book superheroes as options, not as fictions. The movie *Pearl Harbor*, with Ben Affleck, is an example of a recent Hollywood innovation, the combination of the action movie, and chick flick, something both men and women could enjoy.
116   So, when were you called to dowsing?

may resist the call to adventure, and disintegrate in meaningless activity, till you respond

may consult with wise people, who give good advice

may get help from others

may have to go on the journey, even if you thought you didn't want to

may get a warning not to continue, from your own doubts and fears

enter the unknown, and what you fear

re-form your intent

grow in ways you didn't imagine

On your journey to wholeness, you will get an initiation, in the unknown, during which you:

may attend a celebration

may be betrayed

may be hurt

may be rescued

may change your appearance, clothing, or other external details

may encounter a Trickster, Elder, or other archetype

may encounter someone others think of as a fool, where only you see the wisdom

may find love

may learn dowsing, or parts of it, through direct download

may undergo solitude

will be opposed by embodiments of your doubts and fears, and negative emotions

will be tested, and overcome internal limitations

will change

will enter an altered state of consciousness

will find Grace helping you, perhaps when you least expected it

will find inner resources and strength you didn't know you had

will find limitations in your current belief systems

will have a death and rebirth experience of some sort

will have many of your idols and ideals broken

will help others

will learn new rules

will molt out of old ideas and beliefs

will show a willingness, or more willingness, to serve others

2. Initiation

a. *Trials and tests* occur. In Aryan cultures, these may be in threes, while Native Americans and Hawaiians would probably find them in fours. The classic example of this is Jesus, in the wilderness, tested three times by embodied negative thoughts. What is the mystery of the Grail? Whom does it serve?

The hero may get aid from advice, amulets, and agents of the wise helper. The hero/ine may find that a benign, if mostly invisible, power supports him/her, such as Aslan, or a dowsing system.

b. The *VisionQuest*. This is a seeking of truth, in the silence.

c. Meeting with the embodiment of love, or heart[117]. Campbell calls this meeting with the Goddess. This is a symbol of going to the heart. Dowsing is of the heart.

d. *Temptations* to leave the path show up. Perhaps that football game is more interesting than dowsing practice. Campbell cites this as Woman as Temptress, however this is all temptation, in the material world. This is Maya, or illusion.

e. Approach to the inmost cave of the dragon, or belly of the beast. The hero may reflect on the journey, and deal with more doubts and fears. The audience understands how great the ordeal is, and the tension escalates. Robert the Bruce, hiding in the cave, knowing he had failed six times to defeat Edward I, watches the spider, trying to swing. The spider swings, and fails, six times. Bruce watches intently. The spider makes it on the seventh try. Bruce, heartened, goes out, and succeeds on his seventh try, in a sort of fractal resonance.

f. The main ordeal occurs. This could be a dangerous physical test, a deep inner crisis, facing the worst fear, doubt, or deadliest foe[118]. The hero may be defeated at this stage, and retire somewhere to recover. The hero will win the next battle, or final battle.

g. *Atonement* with the father, or whatever holds ultimate power. This is the center point of the journey. Everything after this stage is moving out from this. This is where the higher self enters, and ego is subsumed into it.

h. *Apotheosis*. This is moving beyond opposites, to a state of divine bliss, compassion, knowledge, and love, to the

---

117   Galadriel is this, in *Lord of the Rings*.
118   This is the "does dowsing work?" and "does dowsing work for me?" stage, of doubt. Many dowsers go through it.

monopole[119].   Only through some kind of death can the Hero later be reborn. This is dying to the old self. This can also be the death of the wise companion, as when Obi-Wan, or Qui-Gon, or Richard Shimoda, dies[120].

i. The ultimate boon, victory, or resurrection. This is achieving what the person went on the journey to get. This might be attaining the holy grail, the elixir, the magic harp of the giant. This is grace, the imperishable, the light of illumination of the sage, or saint. The guardians only give it to those who have proven themselves.   This is the stage of getting to the mountaintop. This is the stage of being reborn, to the new Self, where the nevillized movie shows up in the world of the flesh, the answer to the dowsing question shows up. This is the ring cast into the fires of Mordor. I think this is what Aristotle means by recognition, in the *Poetics*. Those who have attained a higher state of consciousness generally exhibit genius, unusual gifts, lofty traits of character, and an expanded state of consciousness, which includes a highly developed intuition[121], perhaps expressing itself as enhanced dowsing ability.

When the healing initiation is complete, you:
may find you are no longer interested in what you thought you wanted[122], because something much better is available, and you could only have learned of it by entering the journey
realize dowsing is a beloved part of you, now
will be reborn as a new Self, having molted out of the old
will begin your return to the every day world
will burn in your new skills and abilities, in dealing directly with counter-intention and doubt
will get something of great value, possibly better than the best you can imagine
will have cleaned out a lot of negativity, even on your genetic line
will know your mission and purpose in life, in a deeper way
will overcome doubt and fear, perhaps in a confrontation

---

119   This may involve a download of dowsing ability and knowledge.
120   Neville compares this to what he calls the end of the procreative act. The story arc follows a similar trajectory. Spanish telenovelas follow this sequence addictively, playing it at length.
121   P. 170, *Heading Toward Omega: in Search of the Meaning of the Near-Death Experience*, Kenneth Ring.
122   Edgar Rice Burrough's *A Fighting Man of Mars* has Tan Hadron realizing Sanoma Tora has no value to him, now that he has Tavia, for example.

When you return to the every day world, you:
may encounter the same mythological, archetypal cast as during the initiation, such as the Fool, Trickster, Warrior, Elder, and so on. However, your dealings with them will be different
may have another death and rebirth experience
may have another encounter with doubt or fear, however you will be in this with far more strength, and confidence, and they will not be able to damage you
may keep tokens of the initiation
may re-experience some part of the initiation process
will notice that you have changed

3. Return, or realization
a. *Refusal of the return.* Some graduates of Tom Brown, Jr.'s classes in Wilderness Survival don't want to come back to the world, to teach what they learned. The only reason I came back was I had a daughter to raise. I've been in seminars I never wanted to leave. It is very difficult to get on the plane, to leave Hawaii, or the American Society of Dowsers' conference.
b. The *magic flight.*   It can be adventurous and dangerous returning from the Journey. Do you remember Frodo, and Sam, on the eagles, flying back from Mordor?
c. *Rescue from without.* The world may have to help the hero return.
d. The *crossing of the return threshold*, returning to the everyday world.
e. Realization of self as *Master of two worlds.* Tom Brown, Jr., talks about "walking the duality" of spirit and flesh, of being both in Medicine Place, and in the physical world, at the same time. For the dowser and manifestor, this is the stage of balancing the material and spiritual worlds.
f. Freedom to live, or living in the now.

Back in the every day world, you[123]:
may find no-one else cares, since they didn't do the journey, themselves

---

123 Adapted and expanded from pp. 230-6, *The Key*, James N. Frey, and Joseph Campbell''s work.

may find that the prize you brought back was not what you thought it was, and that you brought back more than you thought you did

may find yourself playing the role of Trickster, or another archetype, for others

may get a call to a new manifesting healing adventure, perhaps helping others

may know the strongest proactive drive behind your actions[124]

may know what brings you the greatest peace, by finding your place in life[125]

may know your greatest anxiety, as either a reaction to the unknown, or a wake up call[126]

may learn, from reflection, or a wise person, the meaning of your journey

will appreciate things in life, much more[127]

will enjoy each moment

will feel contented, and a sense of unity, with others, and nature[128]

will find dowsing and manifesting easier

will find more and clearer intuitive guidance

will find this whole experience gives your life meaning like nothing else can

will find you deal with people and situations differently

will find your heart more open, and flowing

will find yourself contemplating all that is, and notice the all that is contemplating you[129]

will find yourself far more skilled, with Grace showing up

will find yourself helping others as they start out on their own journeys, as an elder[130]

will find yourself joyfully helping others, for the sheer joy of it

will know your greatest joy, and whether it is compulsive or selective[131]

will know your most intense proactive desire and longing[132]

will live more from your heart

---

124 P. 125, *The Keys of Jeshua*, Glenda Green.
125 P. 125, *The Keys of Jeshua*, Glenda Green.
126 P. 125, *The Keys of Jeshua*, Glenda Green.
127 P. 104, *The Keys of Jeshua*, Glenda Green.
128 P. 104, *The Keys of Jeshua*, Glenda Green.
129 P. 105, *The Keys of Jeshua*, Glenda Green.
130 Perhaps by writing a book...
131 P. 125, *The Keys of Jeshua*, Glenda Green.
132 P. 125, *The Keys of Jeshua*, Glenda Green.

will lose interest in conflict, judging people, worry, and fear[133]

will notice and demonstrate your transformation

will notice more peace, love, joy, happiness, and other high grade feelings on the Hawkins scale[134]

will realize that gratitude manifests by itself[135]

will recognize that belief is essential for experience[136], and that beliefs can be easily changed out

will recognize that you have only one true need, to advance towards soul fulfillment[137]

will see the beauty and majesty in others, and in situations

will smile a lot, and enjoy making others smile

will tend to think and act out of intuition, and dowsing, not from fear[138]

G. Dowsing: integration of head and heart

In 1980, I had the good fortune to hear both the Dalai Lama, and the Hopi elder Thomas Banyacya speak, in person. The Dalai Lama is quite a teacher. I would paraphrase something he said, and say that *if you want to help others, help others. If you want to help yourself, help others. If you want to get out of depression, help others. If you want to improve your skills, help others. If you want to find happiness in life, help others. If you want to get better, help others. If you want to grow in just about any way, help others.* I add: *if you want to dowse well, help others.*

This advice sounds very mundane. However, as with most deep wisdom, it is very powerful, even while it is so mundane it is almost invisible. Manitonquat, the Wampanoag elder, says exactly the same thing. Mother Theresa said similar things. This is also my offering of service. I started gathering information for what has become this book, in 1971.

---

133 P. 104, *The Keys of Jeshua*, Glenda Green.
134 Of the book *Power vs. Force*; this will be discussed later.
135 P. 112, *The Keys of Jeshua*, Glenda Green.
136 P. 110, *The Keys of Jeshua*, Glenda Green.
137 P. 111, *The Keys of Jeshua*, Glenda Green.
138 P. 104, *The Keys of Jeshua*, Glenda Green.

Thomas Banyacya, as with most Native elders I've listened to, also seemed mundane. He said very simple things, in the same way. He discussed a rock drawing, from Prophecy Rock, which his people interpreted as showing both WW I and WW II, and later.

He pointed to a divergence, where people who live in their hearts- whose hearts are open- would enter a much better place, and those whose hearts are shut down, whose heads are separate from their hearts, will simply cease to exist. Of course he said the standard mundane things about how we can't keep crapping in our backyard, environmentally, and hope to avoid the stink. That is true, though most people, including those who do it in the worst way, seem to want to avoid understanding this.

Integrating head and heart offers many simple health benefits. Balancing intellect with intuition helps us accomplish our mission and purpose in life. When this balance is in place, we become open to endless creative ideas. We refresh and rejuvenate ourselves, expressing who we are, each time we turn these ideas into actions and events that help others.

The petroglyphs on Prophecy Rock in the Hopi reservation in Arizona suggest that we may have to do precisely this, if we are going to survive[139]. Dowsing may be necessary for survival- again, and soon.

Lynne Twist noted three major limiting beliefs in society: *That's just the way it is, More is always better*[140], and *There's not enough*. No matter how much evidence you put behind your observations, these are nothing more than belief systems. The word *fact* is taken from the Latin verb *facere*, from which we get our word factory. *Facere, hacer* in Spanish, means to make something. A "fact", then, is something that is made up.

If you like technical language, it is a standing wave form maintained, fractally, by belief systems. Facts can be discreated, or returned to the Void from whence they came.

---

139   P. 177, *The Human Hologram: Living your Life in Harmony with the Unified Field*, Dr. Robin Kelly.
140   This is one foundation of cancer, perhaps. Dowse the morphic field of cancer, using a proxy, and notice how hatred and resentment seem to fuel it. Oh wait, that's advanced, please disregard that.

Four people, working together, managed to topple a fact, the standing wave form of slavery, in the British Empire, by the 1830's.

The belief *There's not enough* could only exist in someone separated from the infinity of the deeper mind. If you live in a universe of infinite information, and possibilities, there is always MORE than enough. A Harvard graduate told me that this scarcity belief is the foundation of our economic and political system. If this belief alone vanished, our economic and political system would be transformed overnight[141].

Darkness is translated into light by love[142]. Humans are the otters of the Universe. We are here to play. Some seem to forget that. As you read this book, play with the ideas. This is fun. Children grow so quickly, because they know to play[143]. Their heads are hearts are not separated. We can learn from children.

H. Points about this book

I decided it would be useful to share my own compilation of ideas. This book started out by assembling notes from trainings and books, for my own use. I did not originally plan to write a book. Somehow, it emerged, as if it had a life of its own. Please do not come to this book to be taught. Come to be transformed, to transform yourself, to play with the buffet of ideas present, and to grow your own ideas from them. This book is not rational, in places, and cannot be, if it is going to help you access your deeper mind, where dowsing is possible.

---

141   One finds discussions of this kind of non-linear change here and there in literature. The final Narnia book, by C.S. Lewis, describes this. Some of Gregg Braden's videos on Youtube.com are quite interesting.
142   P. 130, *Dr. Judith Orloff's Guide to Intuitive Healing*, Dr. Judith Orloff, and every kahuna la'au'ao in Hawaii.
143   One of my college professors said education was the repetitive revelation of the obvious, to the as yet unaware. What better way to deal with repetition, than play? I can play computer games for 8 hours, and not notice the passage of time. Actually I had to quit, because it was getting too addictive.

Just look at what fascinates you, to start, and underline what stands out. Move slowly through this. We seek out problems for their gifts[144], because we grow as we solve those problems. You cannot solve a problem out of the same place it was created. You must go to a new level of order.

If we have great problems, it is because we are about to grow, greatly. Everything you see in this book, and every human creation, was sought out to solve some problem, by someone in a state of confusion, who didn't have the answer at first, and asked new questions.

Dowsing is the Law of [Resonant] Attraction at work[145]. You are always dowsing and manifesting what you are in resonance with. You are also manifesting according to the polarity you radiate. The question is how to have more control over this process, so it puts out more satisfying results.

I have sought to understand both, by studying my own life, and everything I could find. I sought what was common in all systems[146]. I had to simplify the wording of everything I read. Clarity in simplicity is power. I used the principles in the book *Crystal Clear Writing* for this.

To write the Quantum Mechanics section, I used about one sentence from every ~30 pages I read.[147] That was the only way I could make sense of it. I don't represent anything in here as anybody else's ideas. What you see here is only my interpretation of other people's ideas, and my own experience.

I have tried to list books, so that if you have a fascination with a certain area, you can pursue that through a book I found useful. Some editors of this book didn't like the long footnotes.

---

144   -*Illusions*, Richard Bach.
145   P. 84, *Butterflies and Dreams*, Dorothy Peltier-Fanchi.
146   This means I cannot advise anyone about religious beliefs. Those are very individual, and should and must be. Nothing in this book should in any way be construed as religious. This book is spiritual. The religious and spiritual may overlap, but they are not identical. Religious people have their own dogma. Spiritual people know each other across cultural barriers. I get along great with spiritual people, even if I don't speak a word of their language. We smile, and know we are on the same path.
147   Some people ask me which books would be useful for them. Personally, I think every book cited in this book is useful, or I would not have cited it. I suggest, however, that you read what you are attracted to, or muscle test strongly on. Muscle testing is a form of dowsing.

However, writers need to write for a wide audience. Some readers want only the most basic information, and won't read footnotes. Others want more, and read footnotes[148].

Footnote format is my attempt to balance these two kinds of readers. Having footnotes makes it easier for both groups. If you don't like footnotes, please don't look at them. The Quantum Mechanics material is so wild, I footnoted my sources, or some of it would be unbelievable.

You could summarize this book, and all of dowsing, in one word: Trust[149]. The Universe has benevolent intentions for you, and that is the most important belief system you can have, in dowsing. We choose our attitudes, our own way, in any set of circumstances[150].

Your default setting is peace, love, joy, healing beauty, happiness, forgiveness, satisfaction, comfort, contentment, unity, respect, kindness, and everything that makes life worthwhile[151]. The Universe has positive intentions for you. Resonate to this, and your dowsing will get better and better.

You already have, and are, everything you could ever need, want, be, do, or have, inside, in the field of possibility. Only you can change the default settings. You change them by invoking the Law of Resonant Attraction[152], or playing with polarities, with clear intent, which shifts energy.

---

148   The more important footnotes are this size. The less important notes are this size.
149   Why? The more you trust, the stronger the connection is to your true Essence. Your conscious mind hasn't hijacked your life with fear. This book is about reconnecting to who you truly are, and creating what you truly want.
150   *Man's Search for Meaning*, Viktor Frankl, cited p. 227, *Chicken Soup for the Soul: 101 Stories to Open the Heart and Rekindle the Spirit*, Jack Canfield, Mark Victor Hansen.
151   I first heard this, in roughly this way, from Paul Bauer, citing Abraham Maslow, on the experience of the deep self: "The moments were of pure, positive happiness, when all doubts, fears, inhibitions, tensions, and weaknesses were left behind. Now self-consciousness was lost. All separateness and distance from the world disappeared...", as peak experiences. Maslow said "They felt one with the world, fused with it, really belonging to it, instead of being outside looking in." Maslow saw these as moments of grace. Also described pp. 156-7, *Quantum Healing*, Deepak Chopra. This list is also cited at p. 103, *The Keys of Jeshua*, Glenda Green, and in similar form at pp. 14-15, *Thinking from the Infinite*, Carrell Zaehn.
152   *Be the change you want to see in the world*- Mahatma Ghandi- however this has the deep spiritual meaning of literally becoming it, at first at the vibrational level. What would it feel like, if you already had what you seek? Right now? I had a college professor who said that what he did was the repetitive revelation of the obvious to the as yet unaware. This is what the Universe does for us. The great truths are so mundane they are invisible, until we start paying attention to them.

Energy is another name for spirit. It is everywhere. It is the Quantum Wave Form of possibility, which you collapse or compress into form, with your intent, through observation.

Energy flows where attention goes. What you concentrate on grows. Energy follows awareness, which follows intent. When we learn a new skill, first, we practice according to the rules. Then we enter spontaneity[153]. This can be described[154], however it takes some practice to change perceptual habits. Eventually, you see this in a special way[155], you just catch it, it makes total sense, and you can do it.

The lawyers tell me I need to say that nothing in here is intended in any way to diagnose, treat, or cure any disease, or legal situation[156], and that the FDA has not evaluated anything here [and probably never will]. Science is based on the measurable and provable. Yet most experience is neither[157]. Nothing in this book is intended to help diagnose, treat, cure, or heal any physical disease. Physical disease, and disease management, in the U.S., are in the realm of allopathic doctors.

Also, nothing in here is designed to help you construct kit-built jet airplanes, from the parts; create latex masks of alien clowns, function as a Tilt-a-Whirl carnival ride operator, sew million dollar wedding dresses, Jet Ski from LA to Hawaii, dance the Hula, or skydive with experimental parachutes. If you need to deal with experts in those fields, please deal with experts in those fields. This book will inspire you, certainly, but it doesn't say how to deal with those fields directly.

This book is about having fun, playing with energies, and energetic patterns![158] Nothing in this book is intended to disrespect anyone or anything. This book has to be playful, to

---

153 P. 183, *Sound: Native Teachings and Visionary Art*, Joseph Rael.
154 P. 2, *Drawing on the Right Side of the Brain*, Betty Edwards.
155 P. 3, *Drawing on the Right Side of the Brain*, Betty Edwards.
156 *It is dangerous to be right in matters on which the established authorities are wrong.* -Voltaire
157 P. 2, *Touching the Light*, Meg Blackburn Losey.
158 How does one play with energies? Get out of the way. Stop trying to control. Let what appears to be a Higher Power of some sort, perhaps some aspect of deep mind, do it for you. We are not healers, we invoke a feeling of love and state of unity, and the Universe does the rest. Pp. 108, 114, *The Reconnection*, Eric Pearl.

Solving Problems with Dowsing **52** A book for new dowsers ISBN-10: 1482688573

accomplish its mission, so playful things are said from time to time, to help open up perception. Try not to have too much fun with it.

What do you do, to have fun?

How could you do more of that, now?

A book for new dowsers ISBN-10: 1482688573

III. You can start dowsing with devices

Dowsing is the invocation of focused intuitive awareness, with a readout device. The on switch is the carefully phrased question. You can use physical devices as that readout device. Dowsing devices are ideomotor response amplifiers, as our scientific friends like to say. They amplify responses from the subconscious mind. This is easy enough, because your physical body is a reflection of what is in your subconscious mind.

The classic dowsing readout device is the Y-rod, typically made from a tree branch. I don't recommend it, for beginners, because it takes longer to master. Bobbers are known, as well. Any switch, or thin branch, can be used as a bobber. I wouldn't recommend them for beginners, though they are fun to play with.

To start your dowsing- determine which device works for you. You could dowse this- which one feels better? I recommend the L-rod, to begin. Then move to the pendulum. I use L-rods, which are easy to make[1], and a pendulum, which can be made in a minute. Please note that devices only reflect what is in your consciousness, and have no power other than what you give them.

You can use an amethyst or gold pendulum, if you wish, if they make you feel good. You can also use a nut, a nail, a saint's medal with the Amazing Randi's picture on it, or anything else on a string.

---

1 Take a wire hangar. Cut it just before the hook, with wire cutters. Then cut it at the middle of the horizontal section on the bottom. Bend this to a right angle, as an "L" shape. Put the short end in your slightly open fist. You now have an L-rod. Let your slightly open fist tilt to the right. The long end moves. You now have feedback. For me, "Yes" is a movement to the right, "No" is a move to the left, and "wrong question/cannot answer" is a sort of quivering straight out. I prefer to get 3/16" stainless steel rod, from the hardware store, cut it into 3 equal lengths of about 16 inches [metric hardware stores sell something similar], with a hacksaw, and bend it in a vise, to an L-shape, with the shorter end about an inch, or 2.5 cm, longer than my fist height. I used a grindstone, or sandpaper, to smooth the ends. Then I cut a fist height length of plastic pipe, perhaps from a plumbing fitting. I now have a handle. I put the handle on the short end of the L, and bend the part sticking out of the bottom, so the handle won't fall off. This works very well. You could also go to a hardware store, and get brass rod, say 1/4", or about 5-6mm, about half a yard, or ½m, in length. A foot, or 1/3m, will do, but I like them longer. Look for plastic tubing that the rod will comfortably and loosely fit in. I use plumbing fixtures. You can also drill an inch or 25mm thick wooden rod, as a handle. Cut a length to make a comfortable handle. Use a vise to bend the rod so that the shorter end will fit into the handle, with maybe an inch or 25mm sticking out. Put the shorter end in the handle, bend the small part sticking out so the rod won't come out of the handle, and you have your L-rod. Some people find that brass is too sensitive, for them.

I use a pendulum to determine percentages[2]. You can use a chart for this- Raymon Grace has one at his website, or you can use the more complex chart of Walt Woods, in his free downloadable book *Letter to Robin*. I use a protractor, which costs me $1 in a dollar store[3].

You can use your fingers, rubbing them on a surface. For me, when I rub my fingers on a smooth surface, a smooth feeling is a no, and a "sticky" feeling where my fingers don't run smoothly is a yes. A confused feeling is the wrong question/cannot answer response[4]. I test before I start, as sometimes they switch.

There are those who like to use lists of archetypes, such as the Tarot deck. If you do that, be aware that you could also use a list of episodes or characters of *The Simpsons*, comic book characters, presidents, Darwin award recipients, military generals, comedians, baseball cards, and so on, to dowse with. They can be a scale just like any other dowsing chart. I wonder what a Celtic Spread of Simpsons and Flintstones characters would look like? You can do projective dowsing, with archetypes, also[5].

Learn to laugh, with dowsing, as you enter the spiritual realm, you will always be encouraged to grow, and learn more. I don't recommend this for beginners, however for some situations, I've found them useful. For those who disrespect the Tarot, read Dr. Carl Jung, on archetypes. The Archetypes he discusses are, interestingly enough, the major arcana of the Tarot.

Dowsing devices are a crutch. In time, you want to move to deviceless dowsing. I sometimes see a "heads-up" display, as in modern fighter aircraft[6].

---

2 When you are checking dowsing results against a machine, be aware that both have point in time measurements, which can vary greatly. Dowsing may or may not match the machine's results. As you play with Quantum Mechanics ideas, you'll realize that things can not only change greatly, from moment to moment, they can even vanish and reappear. Oh, wait, that's advanced, please forget I said that. No no, we live in the physical world, which is constant. Yes, that's it.
3 Robert Detzler's books have a staggering number of charts. I prefer to make my own, for whatever I'm dealing with.
4 My reference point for dowsing was entering a used car lot in Monterey, California. As soon as I crossed the property line, I felt like someone slugged me in the gut, I could barely breathe. The salesman came over, and I felt his hooks grab on. We went into the office. We wanted to stretch payments to 3 years; they told us that would be a bad idea, as after 1 year we'd need to be making another car payment. Hmm. They know their cars better than we do; they had just said the car we were looking at would last a year. I tottered out of the office, and off the lot, where I felt much better.
5 This is also called radionics, in one form.
6 The recent *Ironman* movies had a nice display. The movie *Top Gun* was my original inspiration. Thanks, Tom!

I cannot cover using portals to dowse, in this short book, though that is discussed in the books this came from.

A. Steps in learning dowsing

1. <u>Regular Practice helps</u>[7]. Dowsing starts by noticing energy flows, or feelings. Be aware of the energy flow where you practice. I suggest you find a place that is quiet, that feels good, that is available to you perhaps at the same time each day. This could be a room, a church, a quiet place in nature, a bathroom at work, any quiet place where you can be relaxed. Bars, bus stations, and sports games are not good places to practice in, to start. Their energy is dissipating. If you can only practice on the weekend, that's fine.

   Take what you have, do what you can, where you are, now. If you can work with an experienced dowser, such as, for example, at American, Canadian, or British Society of Dowsers conferences, that is very helpful, because their energy will entrain yours. There is no failure in dowsing. There is only quitting, or not paying attention[8]. If you keep at it, you will succeed. Failure is only a decision to quit, in this field. Sometimes there might be interference, from sunspots or some other energy disturbance. Stop, and go back to it later. This is playtime, be a little kid again, playing, in this time.

2. <u>Hydrate</u>. Drink several glasses of pure, clear water[9]. Dr. Feridoun Batmanghelidj's books on water are useful, if you need motivation. A dehydrated system will not get good dowsing results. Over 90% of Americans are chronically dehydrated, and don't know it. Let me observe that the Universe consists of light and information. Alcohol and drugs distort information, and so are not useful for dowsing. Dowse to confirm, if you like.

---

7 That won't be difficult if you work with what fascinates you.
8 Do you see kids giving up playing, because they "failed" at it? Of course not. They go right back to it.
9 By water, I mean pure, clear, preferably distilled water. I do NOT mean soft drinks, alcohol, vitamin water, juice, motor oil, olive oil, coconut oil, tea, or any other kind of liquid. I mean pure, clear water. Dehydrated people rarely do well with dowsing, just as your car doesn't work well without oil.

3. Take time to <u>relax,</u> into at least the Alpha EEG. When starting out, you could take a shower. You could breathe deeply, as many as 100 times. You could get some light exercise. Do whatever is necessary so that you relax[10].

4. It is extremely helpful to <u>use wide-angled vision</u>, or *hakalau*, in Hawaiian. Foveal, focused vision is tied to the conscious mind. Peripheral vision is tied to the subconscious. Breathe deeply, in and out, with no breaks for up to 100 times, paying attention to the breath, only. Let your thinking mind shut down, so that your mind is silent. If you have to, hum or sing a sound or note for 30-45 seconds, then stop, and notice your mind is silent. Maintain that silence for a time.

   a. Stand, looking straight out, and put your arms straight out to your sides, 180 degrees opposite, parallel to the ground.
   b. Look straight out. Wriggle your fingers.
   c. When you can look straight out, and see both sets of wriggling fingers, you are in wide-angled vision. This needn't take more than 10 seconds of clock time.
   d. You are now in the dowsing state, in heartspace, balanced between head and heart. In time, you will enter wide-angled vision, look up at 30 degrees, and be instantly in state. We will refer to this step, from now on, as: ***Relax, breathe deeply, enter heartspace.***

5. Statement of <u>intent</u>. I like intent statements more and more. To begin, I suggest saying something like: *"I am in the Universe, and the Universe is in me. We are one, together. Our purpose is service, transmitting Love from above. All dowsing responses are from my higher self, for the highest good of all[11]."* Use an intent statement that makes you feel good.

---

10 A massage, like what they do at the spas in Baden-Baden, Germany, would be a great way to enter state. If you only get the full massage once, you have a great reference state.
11 A devout Christian might add, "In the name of Jesus we dowse", I suppose. At least, those not swimming in fear of anything outside of their physical senses.

6. Now, take your dowsing device, which, if I've done the sales job well, will be an L-rod, to start out with. Hold the L-rod with the short end of the L in your dominant hand. Notice that when your hand trembles, the longer part of the rod swings. Say hi to it. Yes, I know, but say hi to it, like this: *"Hi L-rod[12]. We will be working together to help people, and we'll both grow. I welcome your help. Let's have fun playing![13]"* What the heck, you're just playing. This is a sensitive ideomotor response amplifier.

7. Let the L-rod hang with the long end to your front. Then ask the L-rod, *"What is my Yes direction?"* and see what happens. It will feel like you are making up the answer. That is perfect, because at some deeper level, you are. ALL intuition starts out just like this. Notice what happens. If you don't get a good response, you can let it go to your right, or left, and say, *"Let's agree this will be the Yes direction".* I recommend asking first, though.

8. Now ask, the L-rod, *"What is my No direction?"* and see what happens. If you get a clear answer right away, that is good. If you don't, you can let the rod swing 180°, or at least to the opposite of the Yes direction, and say *"Let's agree this will be the No direction".* I recommend asking first.

9. Now ask, the L-rod, *"What is my wrong question/cannot answer direction?"* and see what happens. If you get a clear answer right away, that is good. If you don't, you can let the rod go to a third direction, or aimlessly swing, and say *"Let's agree this will be the wrong question/cannot answer direction".* I recommend asking first.

10. Congratulations! You have mastered dowsing with a device. Let's play. You could ask a question like, *"On a scale of 1-100, where 100 is ideal, is my energy level above 50?"* Dowse- Yes/No. This is a very useful way to

---

12 The Boston newspapers refer to the baseball player Arturo Rodriguez as "A-Rod". I always wonder what sort of dowsing device one would use, in baseball. Could it be the bat?
13 Ok, ok, you are actually addressing the L-rod as a reflection of your subconscious mind, which loves to play.

get specific about areas you don't know well. If you get a No, you can ask whether it is above 40, above 30, and so on. If you get a Yes, you can ask if it is above 60, above 70, and so on. This is basic dowsing.

11. You can also take your pendulum, and ask it for its Yes, No, and wrong question/cannot answer directions, in the same way. You have the option for drawing an X and a Y axis on paper, and making the left to right direction no, and the front to back direction yes, or something like that. I prefer to ask. This is good training for later, when you realize you can't impose your will on phenomena, but you can work with them, cooperatively, for mutual benefit. Notice the forward swing of the pendulum, as that is your indicator. Later, you can get a protractor, and use this to measure percentages.

12. Notice what a strong and weak Yes, and No, feel like. This can be a great indicator of a question path, to pursue, to correct issues. Later, you'll use percentages, on a chart, perhaps a protractor, for more detailed feedback.

13. You can use the "sticky" method, which is used in Radionics. Rub your fingers on a smooth surface. Ask, "What is my Yes indicator?", and No indicator, and wrong question/cannot answer indicator. For me, a "sticky" feeling is a Yes, a smooth feeling is a No. Yours could be reversed. I feel something odd, for the "wrong question" response. Some use a direction for "I am ready for your questions".

14. Get comfortable with this process. Don't make any big decisions based on your dowsing, now, and never make a big decision based solely on dowsing, ever, unless you have an emergency. Use other methods as well. If you want to dowse stocks, dowse the Best of the Best, as Courtney Smith says. Don't waste your time on lousy performers.

If you use dowsing for monetary gain, always take a portion of it, say 5-10%, and give this to the source of your spiritual teachings, or to those serving others, in ways that feed your soul. If it feels joyful to do this, you're in the right place. In time, you'll also find that if you dedicate say 5% of your garden to pests, they will be there, and won't bother your other plants. This is a pattern worth noticing.

15. <u>Respect.</u> Traditionally, American dowsers asked permission as *Can I   May I   Should I pursue this dowsing?* You can dowse each of these, as Yes or No. That works. If you get a no, rephrase your question. If you continue to get a no, re-examine your motives. If you are trying to get personal information on your favorite actress, in a way that is not win-win, your system may not feel comfortable scanning for this. Respect that.

16. Raymon Grace suggests asking your dowsing system the question this way: Dowse: *Are you able and willing to do this dowsing?*   Yes/No   If you get a no, hydrate. Rephrase your question. If you still get no's, look at your motives, or maybe come back to it later.

17. Intent is a critical part of dowsing. It is very useful to program intent statements, for dowsing.

18. You might want to use some variation of the following: *All energies in my field not for my highest good are adjusted automatically for my highest good. I am a blessing to everyone and everything in my world, no matter what I feel, think, say, and do, and get regular feedback of this, in a delightful way. I am always at the right place, at the right time, with the right people, resources, and conditions, in the right way, saying and doing the right thing, in the best possible way, making as much money as possible, for the highest good of all. I am always connected to my subconscious and superconscious minds, working always for the highest good of all. I dowse from my higher self, perfectly, with*

Solving Problems with Dowsing **60** A book for new dowsers ISBN-10: 1482688573

always clear transmission and understanding. I am one with the Creator, and so is my dowsing. I deserve success in everything, and my success paves the way for the success of everyone else. I am totally safe in the world, the world is totally safe for me. I am always connected to the Creator, zero point field, and my heart field. I and my family and friends are blessed, guarded, guided, in bliss, optimized, protected, and totally aware, at all times. I deserve contentment, ecstasy, fantastic success, freedom, fun, happiness, health, joy, love, peace, prosperity, the opportunity to express who I truly am, vacations, and the best life has to offer. This is my normal state. I embody, fulfill, rejoice in, and understand my mission and purposes in life, which express as health, wealth, love, fun, and perfect service. I have more than enough time to do all I need to choose and do, joyfully, magnificently, and well, living in only that which is for my highest good. I run only positive attitudes, beliefs, feelings, intentions, thoughts, and words, knowing they create my world. My world is full of delightful surprises that I love to experience! My body is perfectly nourished by what I eat, drink, breathe, feel, hear, imagine, intend, see, and think at all times, in my ideal balance, condition, energy level, health, home, metabolism, place, size, and weight, effortlessly. Somehow, everything that shows up in my life supports the above, effortlessly. End[14].

19. Dowse [asking your dowsing system]: *Are you able and willing to install the above, now, in me, permanently, in total harmony with all other systems, until I change it consciously?* Yes/No   In the extremely unlikely event you get a no, examine your motives. For most people, the answer will be Yes. When you get the Yes, state:

20. [To your dowsing system] *Please do so, now, and give me a clear kinesthetic feeling response when it is done, so I know when it's done.* [I really like getting a feeling when

---

14   I recommend changing the words above to whatever you are comfortable with, and speaking the above out loud. I find that my own wording reinforces my personal morphic field.

a process is done. Feedback is useful.] Clear intent is always useful. Muddy intent gives muddy outcomes.

21. Now dowse: *Is that statement now installed in me, permanently, in total harmony with all other systems, until I change it consciously, with fully conscious intent?* Yes/No   You will most likely get a Yes. If you get a no, repeat the above till you get a yes. Repeated no's are probably an indication of lack of clarity, or motives that need re-alignment[15]. If you get an intuition of outside interference, just ask your dowsing system to scramble that.

22. You have installed a statement of intent regarding your dowsing program. This is useful. You can also Dowse: *Are you able and willing to install Walt Woods [or Raymon Grace's, or John Living's, or John of God's] Dowsing program and abilities, now?* Yes/No

23. When you get your Yes, say *Please do so, now, and give me a clear kinesthetic feeling response, so I know when it's done.*

24. Just for kicks,   Dowse: *Are you able and willing to optimize this system to perfect operation for me, in total balance with all systems, now?* Yes/No

25. When you get your Yes, say *Please do so, now, and give me a clear kinesthetic feeling response, so I know when it's done[16].*

26. It may be helpful to test[17]: Dowse: *Is this system now perfectly installed, clear and aligned, open to change at my request?* Yes/No

---

15 Years ago, I worked with someone using Radionics, who couldn't get results. I asked who his teacher was, and sure enough, it was Charles Cosimano. I tested immediately, using dowsing, this question: *"Is the inability to get results due to the mismatch of Charles Cosimano's moral code with yours?"* I got a very strong yes. Charlie is gifted, yes, but he is amoral at times. So we worked on balancing and alignment, and he started getting results.

16 Just so you know, you can install the Jesus, or Buddha energy, or the energy of any Saint, or master of any skill, in the same way. DON'T do these all at once. A woman I know who installed the Jesus and Buddha energy together had to take bed rest for 3 days, as her system recovered. Negative masters have energies that may fry your neurology, that they kept at bay with elaborate safeguards that you will not be able to replicate, because they are extremely situational. I can't believe anyone reading this would need that warning, but just to be sure, I will say it.

17 Be aware that asking questions like this is also a form of intent, suggesting that your system may not work perfectly. Having said that, when starting out, you may want to test. If you get a No, then run your intent sequence again.

27. As with a computer program, once you have a statement programmed in, you don't need to repeat it. For those who still want to repeat it, use a one word trigger to run the intent sequence again.

28. There is a $2^{1/2}$ page programming intent in the book this book was adapted from, if you want to get very specific. It is more detailed than anything anyone else uses. If you just want a short intent program, John Living and Walt Woods use a statement something like this:

This program is in effect until I change the intent. This program always works to the highest good of all involved, and automatically corrects to that default, no matter what my other intent might be. I request a most benevolent outcome for all my work with dowsing and energy shifting. My intent and results are always aligned with, and coming from, the Creator. My conscious mind is passive, and leaves the communications alone. Communication and operation are run by my higher self- my superconscious- in cooperation with the rest of my being, and the Creator, and beings of the light. Whatever is not in alignment with that simply cannot enter my system, or otherwise affect me, or my world, in any way. Answers, insight, and other offerings are given in understandable symbols, hearable sounds, and umistakable feelings, such that I understand and act on them easily, effortlessly, and perfectly. What I need to accomplish my mission and purpose in life shows up with me, at the right time, place, way, condition, energy state, with the right people, with the outcome of the perfect results serving the highest good of all, in a beautiful way. When I ask my dowsing system, "are you able and willing to..." this means, do I have the ability and permission, to measure and improve the situation, and are you able and willing to help me with it? This is part of my dowsing program. Measures of energy, templates, potential, probability, time, space, phenomena, and beings are given perfectly, in ways I understand. My dowsing devices will have clear, correct responses, clearly indicating yes, no, percentages, wrong question/cannot answer. I may make temporary adjustments to the system, as appropriate, and the system will revert to default status when that serves the highest good of all. End of program. This system is installed now, perfectly, in my being.

29. If you still want to play with doubt[18]: Dowse: *Is this system now perfectly installed, clear and aligned, open to change at my request?* Yes/No

30. You may have specific intents you want to add, such as skill in particular areas. If so, Dowse: *Are you able and willing to install this?* Yes/No and so on.

31. Note that you can also program statements of intent into your yard, your house, your community, and so forth. Why? Because you share a subconscious mind with them, the "Ku", in Hawaiian. Oh wait, that's advanced, ignore that.

32. You learned to drink from a glass, or ride a bicycle, and now they are in your subconscious. These skills are now installed in the same way.

---

18 Neville Goddard noted that doubt was the only Satan that ever existed. Think about that, whether you accept it or not.   Be aware that asking questions like this is also a form of intent, suggesting that your system may not work perfectly. Having said that, when starting out, you may want to test. If you get a No, then run your intent sequence again. I may have said this twice- for emphasis. Be aware of counter-intention.

B. Intent to supercharge map dowsing

The map is not the territory, right? So a map is a metaphor. You can use all kinds of metaphors- an L-rod, a pendulum, a phone book, a map, a Tarot deck, a listing of *That's all she Wrote,* or *That 70's Show* episodes, Michael Jackson or Weird Al Yankovic videos, baseball cards, to measure aspects of a situation on a scale. Map dowsing is useful[19]. Basically, you need a map, perhaps an acetate or clear plastic cover, some kind of pen, and a dowsing tool, or sensitive hands.

1. You may want to install a program like this: *I intend that my metaphor and map dowsing program now works harmoniously with all my other systems, for the highest good of all. It is in place until I consciously change it. When I use a map, drawing, or other metaphor, and tools, with my dowsing, I am automatically guided to the correct location/symbol. End intent statement.*

2. Dowse: say *Dowsing System, are you able and willing to install this in me now?* Yes/No

3. If yes, say *Please install it now, and give me a clear feeling when installation is complete.*

4. You can use a ruler, sliding it across the map. Dowse: *Dowsing System, are you able and willing to show me the location, on this map, of _____?* Yes/No

5. If yes, *Please indicate it as I work, and give me a clear feeling when I'm on it.*

6. You can run your ruler, or hands, across the map, till you get a sticky feeling. You can triangulate for more accuracy. You can also run a pendulum across the map, or let L-rods guide you.

---

19 Tom Brown, Jr., uses a very interesting map dowsing method, in locating lost people. He becomes the person, walking the ground, noting the contours, using a Geological Survey map. With his tracking experience, he knows what decisions the person will make, based on the land. Sometimes his intuition takes him straight to the spot where the person is, just by looking at the map.

C. Useful dowsing intent statements

Drilling for drinkable water
You may want to change this to your own wording.

This intent is part of my dowsing intent statement, and is optimized for maximum benefit to all. I may change it with conscious intent. Drinkable water is to be less than 600 feet/200m deep [adapt this to local conditions], easily reachable by drilling, able to supply a minimum of 20 gallons per minute/75 l/minute [or whatever you seek], year round, of drinkable, sweet water. End intent statement.

1. Dowse: *Dowsing System, are you able and willing to install this in me now?* Yes/No

2. If yes, say *Please install it now, and give me a clear feeling when installation is complete.*

3. Once this is installed, your questions are simpler:

4. Dowse: *Is a useful source of water attainable inside this plot of land?* Yes/No

5. Dowse: *Please indicate the best place to drill a well, to get the perfect supply of water for this house/building.*

6. If you are onsite, you will notice your attention attracted to an area. Notice what you notice. You can also hold 2 L-rods, and walk in the direction that feels right, till the L-rods cross.

7. If you are using a map, you can find the correct vertical and horizontal lines, and note where they cross, perhaps using a rule as your dowsing device. You may want to triangulate, for accuracy. If you map dowse, confirm onsite if possible. If you cannot openly dowse in some situation, you can use the "sticky" method on a table, or use a virtual dowsing device, that is, one in your imagination.

Solving Problems with Dowsing **66** A book for new dowsers ISBN-10: 1482688573

Dowsing and shifting energy intake

You may want to install something like this:

This intent statement works harmoniously with my entire system, and remains a standing intent until I consciously change it. Everything I ingest, to include at least air, food, water, medications, and everything else, is optimized to its highest energy level consistent with my good, and the good of all. As soon as my system can handle it, I feel strong feelings of delight about food, etc. that is good for me. I cease noticing food, etc. which does not serve me.

1. Dowse: *On a scale of 1-100, 100 being optimum, how useful is this food to me[20]?*

2. Dowse: *On a scale of 1-100, how effective is my respiration?* Intend improvement if necessary.

Noxious energies

You may want to install something like this:

This intent statement works harmoniously with my entire system, and remains a standing intent until I consciously change it. I may change it consciously. Noxious energies refers to any energy that is not 100% to my benefit, and the benefit of others, to include unbalanced energies that are otherwise beneficial. These are all balanced, effortlessly, in a 100 yd/m radius around me, such that I and all energies are aligned, flowing in harmony, benefitting all. Where possible, this balance continues operating, dynamically, and automatically. End statement of intent.

A question chain might look something like this:

1. *Are there any noxious energies affect me [my family, business, community, country, planet, solar system, etc.]?* Yes/No   Assuming you get a yes, Dowse:

2. *Dowsing System: Are you able and willing to shift, balance, and phase conjugate them, so that they are now beneficial?* Yes/No

---

20 Test soft drinks, aspartame, canned goods vs. fresh, to start with. If it's something you have no choice but to eat, as with MRE's in the military, Dowse: *Dowsing System, are you able and willing to optimize this food for me? Yes/No If so, please do so now.*

3. If you get a Yes, you could say: *"Please do this now."* You can also put this on automatic, to run at specific time intervals, or contingent, so that it starts working when necessary, like a virus scan on a computer, in this way:

4. *Dowsing System: Are you able and willing to put this balancing process on automatic? Yes/No* If you get a Yes, you could say: *"Please do this now."*

5. If you get a no, on being able to shift energies, you may want to test for effect of the energies, and any safe places you could be, or safe "windows" of time. I have not yet ever gotten a no, however[21].

---

21 Be aware that your subconscious will feed your interests. If you show a lot of interest in an area, you will start getting spontaneous downloads of useful information, without asking for it at that time.

I wonder what it would be like, to live in a fantastically beautiful Universe, full of wonderful surprises that you loved to experience, full of joy, peace, love, satisfaction, pleasant growth, ease, grace, contentment, and all that makes life worthwhile?

What if the world we live in is that world, right now, and the only thing keeping us from it is not yet knowing the right questions to ask, or how to open our awareness to it?

What other neat stuff could you notice in your life, that you haven't previously noticed?

IV. Playing with your new toys

A. Energy levels: dowsing and shifting them

During your playtime, whip out your dowsing device, and perhaps a protractor, or dowsing chart. I have held an L-rod upside down, to use it on a protractor, to get percentages. Dowse:

Dowse: *is my energy system at an ideal level?* Yes/No

Dowse: *What percentage of ideal is my current energy system at?* This is a way to get specific about something not measurable by other means. This is a reference point. It doesn't even matter if you got a wrong answer. Say you got 40%.

Dowse: *Are you able and willing to raise this to 70% of ideal?* Yes/No

If you got a no, then try 60%, and 50%. Respect this, there may be a good reason to not raise your energy level a lot right away, you might blow out some circuit breakers in your neurology.

When you get the Yes, say *"Please do do now, and give me a clear feeling when this process is done."* Wait for that feeling[1].

Dowse: *Are you able and willing to optimize this system to perfect operation for me, now?* Yes/No

When you get your Yes, say *Please do so, now, and give me a clear kinesthetic feeling response, so I know when it's done.*

You can run this same sequence on your house, place of work, community, church, and so on. You can trust your subconscious to take care of business, once it has clear intent, and you've cleaned out the trash of counterintention. If you can't trust your own subconscious, whose can you trust?

The subconscious mind does NOT like to be tested with meaningless foolishness. It very much likes to support useful work, that advances humanity, and all beings.

---

1   We live in a culture that watches slasher movies, because people are so separate from their feelings. Cut off the TV, radio, and other sources of noise. Spend time in quiet places, in nature if possible, thinking very little. Cut back on the coffee and other drugs. Your feelings are there, they have just been drowned out. It is better to let really bad feelings out, if possible, so they don't function like backed up sewage, in your body.

© 2013 All Rights Reserved Solving Problems with Dowsing **70** A book for new dowsers ISBN-10: 1482688573

One of its prime directives is to keep you alive. You could survive with your current energy level, however more energy would be nice. This is a good place to start.

Pick small things that are inside your belief system comfort zone. I could tell you that cancer has a certain energy level, and that, since it is energy, it can be shifted, however that means you deal with the morphic field of cancer, the belief systems around that disease, which isn't your job, and which is way beyond your abilities. You are not trained or qualified to deal with that.

I could also tell you that you want to play with patterns of light and information, as this is much easier. I am not a doctor, nor could I offer any kind of medical advice, however you might enjoy playing with such things, down the road.

You can also test the percent useful for you, of the outcome of taking, for example, a one day fast, or eating raw fruits, vegetables, grains, nuts, seeds and spouts, for a week.

Get friendly with your subconscious. Think of it as a mischievous 4 year old, who believes everything you say, and likes to have fun and play, and has infinitely rich parents it can call on, at will. In all cases, move quickly. This makes it so your conscious mind cannot interfere. Remember in school when the teacher said to go with your first answer? And then you changed it, because you worried, and it turned out the second answer was wrong. It is ok to test doubt, just understand that doubt is an intent. If you seem to not be getting good results with dowsing, it could be because you are not playing enough.

Dowse: *On a scale of 1-100, what percentage is my dowsing free of interference, and accurate?*

It's ok if you get only, let us say, 40% to start. Being right 60% of the time on the stock market is enough to make one a millionaire. Intend improvement, wipe out negative belief systems, and continue. Ideally, you would get to 100% free of interference.

Solving Problems with Dowsing **71** A book for new dowsers ISBN-10: 1482688573

B. Other points

After you've played for a little while, you'll notice dowsing is a point in time phenomenom. For tests like this, it is useful to test, for a period of time, as in:

Dowse: *On a scale of 1-100, 100 being ideal, over the last month, to what percentage is my dowsing free of interference, and accurate?*

100% accurate, and free of interference is a good place to be at. With intent, getting to 100% doesn't have to take long. In fact, be there, here, now. Feel it real, now.

Check for limiting beliefs and conditions. Here is an example:

Dowse: *On a scale of 1-100, what is the percentage of my desire to fail, in dowsing?*

That will wake you up. Ideal is at least 0, or even -100%, aka total desire to succeed.

To me, dowsing is like learning a new language. I practice, it gets easier, and fun, I get into the energy state of the language, and in time I'm speaking freely. Sure, some days aren't great, perhaps, but so what, that's true in any field. If you plan to enter a specialized field, such as the stock market, DO NOT BET THE FARM on your dowsing. Use at least one other system, if not two, and triangulate. There is a lot of emotional and morphic load on the stock market, generally, in the morphic field, and in you[2].

Jill Bolte Taylor had an experience that caused her to feel what she called the left and right sides of the brain. Her metaphor was that the conscious mind was like a bottle, and the right side of the brain was the genie, released from the bottle. Genies tend to answer requests literally, don't they?

---

2 The first woman I taught dowsing to immediately tested it on lottery numbers. She didn't get a winner, and dismissed dowsing, because it "didn't work". I can't begin to tell you all the limiting beliefs around the lottery. It is not a place for a beginner to start. It will give you quite an education in layered, cascading limiting beliefs. Keep in mind that service is important. Generally, people are paid for their service, as filtered by belief systems. If you want to increase your income, start by increasing your service, and awareness, and understand that income can come in as gifts, from places you least expected it. What are the infinite possibilities for new ways money could show up, in your life, in fun ways that benefit all, I wonder?

Solving Problems with Dowsing 72 A book for new dowsers ISBN-10: 1482688573

Especially when they are forced to respond? Enter a cooperative partnership with your larger self, working for the highest good of all.

Dowsing is basically asking questions, of your deeper self, and getting a response via intuition, sometimes in a way you didn't expect, or even realize was an answer, at first. *Dowsing and Manifesting* has a number of pages about questions, and how they work. Questions shape your Universe, you are the crystallization, even the interference pattern, of the questions you ask. So structure your questions carefully.

1. When starting out, <u>write down your questions</u>- and write the answers you got. For important questions, it is helpful to have two or more experienced people asking questions in their own way. Question chains usually take unique paths, even when the same person is working one. You will want your questions chains written down, so you can find what works for you, and use it again. You will probably modify your question chains regularly.

2. At the same time, you want to remain in heartstate, and relax. Play. The more serious you get, the more you are in your head, not your heart. Speak to the pendulum or device as if it were a person. If you have no device, speak to your dowsing system as if it were a person. This is a proxy method, which keeps you objective, and separate from unpleasant energies[3].

3. Always leave an "other' category, when you ask questions. This is why you have a "wrong question/cannot answer" response. It is even better to use a scale. A 70% yes is very different from a 100% yes, for example. Be very specific about your intent- what you want to know, or influence. What were the five questions they told you in school- Who, What, Where, When, Why, How. Each of these helps you get more specific[4].

---

3 I loved Star Trek, as a kid. A real navy, though, sends ensigns and sailors out to take risks, never the Captain or first officer. In the same way, you can send out proxies, which could be thought forms, or other graphical user interfaces, into areas you don't know well. The bridge of the Starship *Enterprise* is you, with aspects of your deeper mind.
4 The following is a format I've used, to evaluate people in a business setting. A standard form like this would be very

The military uses the SALUTE format for reports, for the same reason[5]. My father had a format for reporting geological conditions. Develop what works for you.

4. If there are ambiguous words, phrases, or conditions, install what you mean by them, in your dowsing program. Did I mention your dowsing program becomes your dowsing system? If you want to have some fun, dowse the name of your dowsing system[6].

5. Do NOT ask for opinions. Only your conscious mind can form opinions. Asking "would it be best for me to buy X Stock?" is bizarre, for your subconscious. Best for what? Wiping our your capital? For enriching your stockbroker? For X Stock to continue what they're doing, that will wipe out the value of the stock?

6. The classic example Raymon Grace gives is dowsing whether your car needs gas. Well, it does need gasoline, regularly, and also oxygen, which is a gas. A better question would be what percentage empty, or full, the gas tank is, or at least testing the accuracy of your gas gauge. Ask for clearly definable information that exists, somewhere in the Void of All Possibilities. Once you do this, you define its shape, its unique vibration, and your superconscious reaches it fractally, through scalar waves. Whoops, that's advanced, forget that.

7. Comparisons are important. A piece of quartz is hard, compared to mud, right? Compared to diamond, it is soft.

---

useful for your dowsing. My brother uses a more detailed format. Date of observation, customer name, address, telephone, birthdate, place, town(s) grew up in, estimated height/weight. Fascinations/hobbies/major areas of interest/what they are proud and ashamed of, including problems, immediate concerns, and long range goals. Primary focus: self interest, company interest, larger interest? Present/future oriented? Professional/trade/community associations membership, honors. Year graduation of HS, College(s), which college. If not a college graduate, are they sensitive about it? College frat/sorority, college extracurricular activities, previous employers/positions. What are they sensitive about? What kind of humor do they like? Where/how does vacations? Sports interests: team(s) What kind of car do they drive? Whom does this person most and least want to impress? How does this person want to be seen by them? Use 7 adjectives to describe this person   What is this person's immediate concern, right now? Ethical/moral considerations? Does this person keep their agreements? What obligations does the person feel, and to what? What does this person highly respect? Disrespect? Political active? Party? Importance to this person? Active in community? In what capacity? Religion   Active? How? Sensitive info: Divorced, AA member,etc. Subjects person has strong feelings about. Health- medical history Diet Alcohol consumption: Yes/No, what, how much/how often   Offended by others drinking? Smoker? Offended by others smoking? Allergies Relationships of person with persons we know   Who? Quality of relationship? What habits/beliefs would have to change, to work with this person, on a specific project? You can repeat the above for spouse, adding anniversary, and perhaps children.
5 I remember this as S ize A citivity L ocation U nit T ime E quipment. S=SIZE of group, A=ACTIVITIES of group, direction and speed of motion, L=LOCATION, U=UNIT IDENTIFICATION. T=TIME and DATE of sighting E=EQUIPMENT carried. You could modify this for your dowsing situation. There is a checklist I use, at the end of this book.
6 Oh, never use Ouija boards. There is something about them that is low energy. You can use lists- of letters, numbers, conditions, people, etc., but don't use the Ouija format.

This is why we use scales- how long is this, IN RELATIONSHIP to my measuring device- the ruler, or other set of conditions, on a linear organizing pattern? If you say something is long, you imply that it is long in relationship to something else in your experience. 50 hours to write a book is long for some people, and very short for others. They have different frames of reference. This is why some questions get a no, and other questions that superficially appear to be similar, get a yes. Another way to look at this is that everything in existence can be summed up in numbers.

8. The number Pi is interesting. It keeps repeating. Everything in existence will show up in Pi, sooner or later, as a sequence. If you precisely define your question, you have your metaphorical phone number, and you can dial it. If you leave off the last 2 digits, say, by asking imprecise questions, you won't get through, or you may get more than one response. If you dialed 7 of the 11 digits necessary to place a long distance call, and didn't get through, would you give up on using telephones, because they don't work? No, you would get the last digits, dial through, and make your connection. If you couldn't get through one day, would you give up on using your telephone? No, you'd wait till another time, when the lines were clear, or something like that.

9. Consider the question, "Is there water on so and so's land?" You will get a yes, in most cases, because there is water. There is water on the moon, and on Mars, for that matter. The question, *"where on this land could I find a vein of water capable of providing 20 gallons/75 l per minute of pure, drinkable water, at all times, including drought, at a depth of less than 1,000 feet/300m, where the septic system or other pollutants would not be able to affect it?"* is a very different kind of question. It is helpful to ask questions using different wording, to pick up any problems. Ask the question twice or thrice, using different wording, to triangulate.

10. You may want to use a proxy, for dowsing. You could have one of your multiple selves step out of you[7], and scan an area which has unpleasant energy. The Remote Viewing people always used a proxy in scanning UFO's, for example.

11. Some people want to be sick, and some conditions may be beyond your ability. If you get a strong feeling to avoid an area, or question chain, respect that. Generally, prying in private areas, unless invited, or where knowledge of private information would not serve the highest good of all, is best avoided. Consistent abuses in this area may lead to a cutoff of all ability. It has happened. Be advised[8].

12. You are not a doctor. Do not give either diagnoses or prognoses. You are interested in the playground of possibilities between diagnosis and prognosis. Dowsing is playing with patterns of light and information. Playing with energies is very different from playing with the physical, so you cannot give accurate diagnoses. If you or someone needs medical advice, get it from a medical professional. Even those medical professionals I've met who use dowsing confirm what they get with medical protocols.

13. Materialistic people are rarely open to the spiritual. Feed interest only. Do not talk about spiritual matters with those who aren't open to it. It's a waste of time.

14. You don't know everything, and never will. Nobody does. Look to improve constantly, and learn as much as you can. I had many strong beliefs when I was 16 years old. I have abandoned almost all of them since that time. Sometimes your greatest learnings and blessings are hiding behind your fears and prejudices.

15. Keep it simple and fun.

---

7   If you remember the comic book character the Flash, you remember all those multiple selves, in the drawing of the Flash, running. Just pull one of them off, and give it instructions.
8   People who have undergone near death experiences note that the "life review" consists of being every person one ever affected, and feeling exactly what they felt, as them, all at once. I don't know if that's what happens, but it would be absolute justice, both for a Mother Theresa, and an Adolf Hitler. Service to others may have more rewards than meet the eye, in other words... It could be service to oneself.

C. Playing more

You might want to keep some record of the intent statements you use, as you program. Or not. Once your system understands intent statements, you can start downloading them directly from Source. Sometimes I like to reach into a portal, and grab intent which I know is useful, where I don't know exactly what it does. Quantum physicists say you cannot ever see a Quantum Probability Wave, because in doing so one collapses it, according to one's expectations, into something real.

Yet the Quantum Wave Form is a metaphor. One can see metaphors. Sometimes I reach into a portal to get a QWF, to collapse it into an ability. They feel kind of rubbery, in a very ethereal way. It is useful to have intent statements programming the dowsing system. This helps you get specific about that which is beyond your current belief and modelling systems.

It is useful to narrow down areas to work with. You can dowse:

1. the average energy of a specific area for a period of time,

2. the worst area of a larger being

3. the best area to work with first, in energy shifting

4. the hinge points, which when shifted, will cause the most spontaneous other shifts for the better

5. any need for recurring energy shots, in steady flow or pulsating

6. energies that would be useful to you, but which you don't know how to name, or ask for

Once you identify an area to play with, you can Dowse:
Dowse: *Are you able and willing to shift this for the better?*
Yes/No   Y   *Is there any reason not to?*   N

When you get a yes, ask: *"Please do so now, for the highest good of all, and give me a definite kinesthetic signal when done".*

ISBN-10: 1482688573

You can use your dowsing device to track progress. I like to use a pendulum over a protractor for this. Be in a very relaxed state, where you just don't care about progress, you're just looking at the numbers as if you were lazily lying in warm, dry grass, on a summer day, watching clouds. It actually doesn't matter if this is accurate, or not- how would you confirm, anyway? In this attitude, you get accurate information.

You might add an intent statement to your foundation dowsing intent statement, as follows:

Balance means balancing and aligning all energies, including noxious energies, so that they are beneficial, for the entire area under consideration, including anything it is connected to, including all beings, for as long as is appropriate for the highest good of all. This may include asking the appropriate intelligences and beings to remove any unpleasant or unbalanced energy, to take it to the light, where it cannot return. This activates automatically, when I ask for help balancing an area, and at any other time it would be useful. End.

I also sometimes ask my dowsing system:

Is there something beneficial you would like to do, or download? Yes/No

If I get a yes, I say *"Please do so now, with grace and ease, for the highest good of all".* I may not get any feedback, which is ok with me. This does require trust. I don't necessarily know what is being downloaded. It's all been good, so far.

D. Summary of initial training:

1. Ask the device for its yes and no directions, movements, or indications. If you have to, you can move it in a specific direction, and say, "this is yes", another direction, say "this is no", and a third direction, for "wrong question/cannot answer".

2. The subconscious makes no assumptions, and does precisely what you tell it, generally. Once you have programmed the Yes/No/wrong question directions, it is useful to have intent statements. Install them in whatever way works for you. Speaking words silently is most effective for shifting the unseen world. If you can do so, it is better to speak out loud, for intent in the world of form, that we see, hear, and feel.

3. You may want to expand the intent statement to what you are working on. For example, I don't do much with water location, but I am extremely interested in cleaning up energy flow in cities. My intent statements precisely define that area. Always start this with *Are you able and willing to program in the following?* Yes/No Think of your subconscious as a partner, that works better when treated with respect, and patience.

4. Start playing. Start by determining useful information. If someone called you on the telephone, to ask you the time, how receptive would you be? Perhaps not much. You can use a clock for this. On the other hand, if someone asked you for very specific help, that you could give, you would probably help out, right? It is the same way with the subconscious. The subconscious loves to play, and to help people. You can play with having it give you the time of day, though it might want to play with you, and give you the time of day on the other side of the world.

E. Force Multipliers to help you be more effective

There are significant force multipliers for this work[9], I mean play, that will significantly increase your power. Some of these are repeated from before. This is part of your spiral learning.

1. Commit to helping others whenever you can[10]. The Wampanoag elder Manitonquat says we are all here to help each other. This at least gives life meaning. If you do things that only benefit you, you only have the power of you. If you do things that benefit many people, you have the power of the higher selves of all the people you are benefiting. Don't do it for any moral or religious reason, do it because it is fun! *The Universe helps those who help others.* This is the most important intent you can have, in all of this work. Without this, your work simply will not be as effective. <u>Nothing activates abilities faster than questions about how to help others.</u> The one quality all successful people share is persistence. If you do nothing else from this section, do this. One reason is that it leads you directly to the second absolutely necessary force multiplier, the heart:

2. Find the fun! The Wampanoag Nation elder Manitonquat, aka Medicine Story, notes that the creator put fun on the earth to mark out correct solutions. This sounds good to me. I like that idea. **Get playful.** It pays off. Have you noticed that kids can play for hours, with full energy? If school was more fun for them, we'd have much better students. If half the energy put into video games went into solving the world's problems, we'd all be living in paradise. *How could we play, as we solve the world's problems? Could you pretend, just for a second, that you have already realized your goals?* Pretending changes everything[11]. Celebrate loudly! Sing! Dance![12]

---

9 By force multiplier, I mean something that makes you far more effective, in everything you do, that boosts the power of what you do, that makes your work and life easier, that improves the accuracy of what you do, and causes more useful information to download or show up for you. Force multipliers are often among those truths that are so mundane they are almost invisible.

10 In a holographic universe, the achievements of every individual contribute to the advancement and well-being of the whole. P. 54, *Power vs. Force*, David Hawkins. When you improve yourself, you make it easier for others to do the same. When you help others, you help everyone, including yourself.

11 Go crazy, in a respectful way. Have more fun. Celebrate everything. This means you have more to celebrate. Fill in a mock calendar, with dates of cool stuff. Overpay your revolving bills, even if only by a buck. Talk about a fictional fantastic life, with friends and family, maybe about your Rolls Royce and LearJet. Play! Use scrap books and vision boards to inflame you with excitement. Use speech bubbles on pictures of famous people, with words that encourage you. Write about yourself as you are fantastically successful, 30 years in the future. Write letters and checks to yourself from admirers.

12 I met Brooke Medicine Eagle, at a Tom Brown, Jr., training. She noted that in the old days, you could tell whether a

Kindness and gratitude are fun.

3. Find the joy first. **Always get into a high energy state, before you do anything**[13]. Creating a healthy lifestyle is not easy, if you feel a gnawing fear in your guts, about lack. First, get into the state of feeling healthy, just like tuning your TV channel or radio station[14]. If you want anything, be in the joyful state of already having it, so you aren't needy. Practice appreciation, gratitude, and kindness, to raise your energy level[15]. Forgiveness is really helpful for this[16]. Be happy now[17]!

4. Flow Appreciation, and Gratitude, something like: *Thank you [God][Universe] for all the blessings I have, and am receiving!* Feel it in your heart! Having abundance, control, freedom, love, safety, and unity are not the problem. The problem is craving them, which translates as lacking them[18]. Appreciation, gratitude, generosity, and play all clean this out. The daily practice of gratitude is one of the conduits by which what you seek comes to you[19]. Resisting small things is resisting everything; appreciating small things, and showing kindness, is appreciating and benefiting everything[20], because the Universe does not discriminate; you do.

5. When I was a lad, they said we used maybe 5-10% of our brains. I knew I wanted to get into that other 95%[21]. I found out how to do that. Get out of your head. Be in your heart. Relax, breathe deeply, stop thinking, and feel.

---

native community was happy or not from the quality of the women's singing as they worked. She has some beautiful native worksongs out, on CD. What does it say that women in white man culture do not sing at all as they work? To quote an old Southern maxim, If momma ain't happy, ain't nobody happy. Henry Ford actually fired employees for laughing on the job, or telling jokes. Whose bright idea was it that fun, joy, singing, laughter, and dance shouldn't be part of daily life? We need to change that. We need to find the fun, in everything.

13 One of my favorite cartoons showed Edgar Allan Poe in a very depressing office, with skulls on a shelf, dungeon implements, and bones. He was speaking to someone else, saying, "I just can't seem to write comedy, and I don't know why!"

14 If you don't know how to do that, yet, you picked up the right book.

15 *I am aware, happy, harmonious - loving, perfect, and joyous - powerful, whole, and humorous; strong, whole, and healthy - radiantly happy, and wealthy - a blessing to all, in ways stealthy.* Charles Haanel had an affirmation that covered everything. This is what I use.

16 It restores transparency to your life, and freedom to your spirit. It resolves problems. It begins with a change in viewpoint. It is release. Pp. 174-5, *The Keys of Jeshua*, Glenda Green. It really helped me to realize that most people do the best they can, with what they have at the time.

17 The moment you think, "I am happy!" a chemical messenger, neurotransmitter, communicates this to every cell in your body. Every thought affects every cell in your body through neurotransmitters.

18 P. 27, *The Reality Creation Technique*, Frederick E. Dodson.

19 *The Science of Getting Rich*, Wallace D. Wattles.

20 P. 64, *The Reality Creation Technique*, Frederick E. Dodson.

21 That question of how to get into that other 90%, which is actually the other 99.9999999%, has guided my life, and gotten me into dowsing.

Enter the Alpha brainwave EEG state, at least, get out of Beta[22]. This opens up 99.999999999% of potential experience to you[23].

6.   One great way to do this is meditation[24]. **Meditation** is like an oil change, tune-up, and recharge for your being. It's like taking a 5 or a 10 minute vacation in place. It puts you in the Now, which is where all power is[25]. I used to know a woman[26] who built a business up from nothing. I asked her what her secret was. She told me she meditated 10 minutes per day, and she "downloaded everything" she needed to know that day, during that time. Another thing you'll notice is that your manifestations will start showing up more quickly. Why? Your resistance to them tends to dissolve, in meditation. Meditation helps you allow your desires to flow into your concrete experience. If you can't do 5 minutes, do just 1 minute. If you can't do that, do half a minute. If not that, 10 seconds. Try not to enjoy it too much, though.

7.   Another major force multiplier is finding ways to **increase your energy**. How do you do that? *Stop doing what lowers your energy, and do more of what raises your energy.* Energy is your most valuable asset[27], and all your other assets are only crystallizations of your energy. The more energy you have, the more you can do, the more money you will make, the more effective you will be, the more good stuff you will attract. When your energy is low, it is hard to manifest, everything is a chore. Self-doubt[28] and feelings of neediness reduce effectiveness[29]. You can change anything in the world, by changing its frequency, or creating an opposite frequency[30].

---

22   From the viewpoint of power, the physical heart forms months before the brain, in the fetus, and it has around 5,000 times as much magnetic force as the brain. The heart also has a toroidal torsion field around it, which extends out perhaps a meter/yard or so from your body. The difference between the head, and heart, is more than the difference between a D cell battery, and a lightning bolt. The classic Indian metaphor for head and heart is the elephant boy on top of the elephant, except it would be more like several thousand elephants.

23   Metaphorically, the tree of the knowledge of good and evil is clearly the conscious mind, which makes that distinction. The angel with the flaming sword is your own higher self, which you chose to separate from. Enter your higher self, from your heart, and mind and heart are in balance. Then you enter the garden, of the zero point field, of heartspace. I had intuited this, however it is also at p. 225, *You the Healer*, José Silva.

24   *Meditation is the dissolution of thoughts in Eternal awareness or Pure consciousness without objectification, knowing without thinking, merging finitude in infinity.* -Voltaire

25   Eckhart Tolle has a whole book just on this point. This is worth learning.

26   Who was, by way, very conservative religiously, I was amazed she knew what meditation was.

27   P. 50, *Reality Transurfing IV*, Vadim Zeland.

28   If you feel doubt, as Neville would say, reestablish your harmony by imagining your desired state. In fact, if you want to get a message to a friend, imagine yourself visiting, and give him your message, and see his eyes light up with the pleasure of your words. Whoops, that is an advanced method, please forget I said this.

29   P. 114, *Manifesting your Heart's Desire*, Fred Fengler and Todd Varnum.

30   Dr. Ben Johnson, cited at Pp. 137, 138, *The Secret*, Rhonda Byrne.

8. Cut off all energy drains, as quickly as you can, starting with the TV news. Don't read beauty magazines, they will make you feel ugly[31]. A very effective test in this area is *"How will I feel tomorrow?"* I personally do not use alcohol, or drugs, nor do I smoke cigarettes, and the reason is because each of these noticeably lowers my energy level.

9. The Universe consists of light and information, or modulation, and resonance. These substances tend to distort information, and so are not useful. They do not serve me. While I love a good steak, I've become almost vegetarian. The reason is that when I eat fresh, unprocessed raw fruits, vegetables, grains, nuts, seeds, and sprouts, I have much more energy. Some people set up rules where they get all the energy they need from anything they eat. That's fine. Freeing up energy is so important, however you do it. If you aren't at a high energy level, start by releasing anxiety, doubt, guilt, worry, and the other energies below 200 on the Hawkins scale of *Power vs Force*, discussed later. Skepticism and apathy indicate low energy levels. Ask your body what it wants to eat. Dowse your choices, or get a direct download. You may be surprised.

10. **Forgive** anyone and anything that has ever harmed you, and forgive yourself. This clears you like almost nothing else. It's not for them, it's for you. When I finally forgave the last person who had hurt me, I found a $6,000 check in my mailbox from a place I never expected to get a dime from. You will feel better, if nothing else, and you will have more energy[32]. Bless people, too. Hawaiians are really good at this.

11. Breathe deeply, at least five minutes per day, and as often as you can, otherwise[33].

---

31 – Mary Smith, a Chicago newspaper columnist, cited P. 250, *Dr. Judith Orloff's Guide to Intuitive Healing*, Dr. Judith Orloff.

32 I met a hypnotherapist, at a National Guild of Hypnotists conference, who asked all potential clients if there was someone in their lives they couldn't forgive. If there was, he told them they weren't ready for hypnotherapy until they had forgiven everyone and everything. Lack of forgiveness sets up blockages to flow. If you want to improve your dowsing, and manifest better, get into forgiveness.

33 I took a course with Robert Winn, the breathwork teacher, which was fascinating. If you breathe into a feeling, it transforms. If you breathe through your heart- imaginarily- this will clear out blockages. Huna breathing is fascinating. I look forward to his books, when he writes them. *Breathe Deep, Laugh Loudly, the Joy of Transformational Breathing*, Judith Kravitz, is also helpful.

12.   All things work better with love[34]. If you are having mechanical problems, try sending love to the machine. Put love in the machine oil you use. Someone where I used to work would have me turn on her computer. She swore her computer worked better if I turned it on. Never curse a mechanical object, or a person, as that is not beneficial energy. Love is a monopole that heals all problems[35]. If you have a jar lid, or a nut, that just won't come loose, imagine the joint nicely oiled. Play with it.

13.   Respect people, their boundaries, and the world. From respect grows rapport, from rapport, trust; from trust, communication; from communication comes cooperation[36]. Cooperation is how humans survive. Cooperation always gets better results than competition. This is also part of tapping your larger self. All you need do to tap the power of intention is to be in perfect harmony with the Source[37]. You are not the condition in which you find yourself[38], or others. When you help yourself or others to become whole, you are not doing, and cannot do, the healing yourself. The healing energy comes through you[39], on the tracks of your intent. Intent is choice. You are always running energy through yourself. Choose to run a higher and better kind.

14.   All problems are the result of blockage. Dowse the blockage, send intent to remove the blockage, and the restored flow heals the problem[40].

---

34 The resolution for each character, at the end of the Harry Potter series, involved love, or its lack. Voldemort came apart, without it. The Malfoys left, because they loved their son. Harry did what he did out of love, shortly after meeting otherwise invisible relatives in love. Luna and Neville came together, as did several other couples. Love is all there is, as the Sufis say. It is also a critical part of manifesting, as Carnelian Sage's *The Greatest Manifestation Principle in the World* notes.

35 Love is a state of being, a powerful force in the Universe. It is the portal from the immanent world to the world of form, from the spiritual to the emotional realm. The effortless way to manifest is to let go of your attachments, and focus on love. Pour love on all of your endeavors. You may get a different outcome, and it would be much better than the best you could imagine. P. 68, *The Greatest Manifestation Principle in the World*, Carnelian Sage. Love is who we are. Love is unconditional, it fits anywhere, and supersedes everything. Nothing is more powerful. It is the divine, mystical power that creates and sustains live for the joy of doing so. In its purest form, love is where creation creates itself. It is the pure essence of being. It refines and clarifies innate potential, and allows one soul to support and enrich another. It knows no boundaries. Whatever is transmitted by love is forever. It permeates, resolves, and unites as it moves to fulfill life. Pp.2-4, *The Keys of Jeshua*, Glenda Green. Love, if it finds you worthy, directs your course. Love has no other desire but to fulfill itself. -*The Prophet*, Kahlil Gibran.

36   Koichi Tohei was a Japanese officer in China, in WW II, at a time when Japanese troops were not kind to Chinese. He said that he had to impress his troops with his bravery, first. Then he told them there was no reason to hurt their prisoners. Their Chinese prisoners were taken back to their own lines, after dark, and released, unharmed. Chinese troops were not as aggressive with his troops, as they were with others. -*The Magic of Conflict*, Thomas Crum. *Silent Night*, by Stanley Weintraub, tells of the unofficial Christmas, 1914 truce, in the trenches, between German, French, and British troops. The soldiers traded food, played soccer, and for the most part the truce held. The generals didn't like it, and of course moved troops to get the war going again.

37   P. 247, *The Power of Intention*, Wayne Dyer.

38   P. 34, *The Keys of Jeshua*, Glenda Green.

39   P. 158, *Sound: Native Teachings and Visionary Art*, Joseph Rael, Dr. Richard Bartlett, Tom Brown, Jr., Vianna Stibal, Jesus Christ, and many, many others.

40   Stated differently, underlined: meaningful information heals. Cited also at p. 107, *Leadership and the New Science*, Margaret J. Wheatley. That is the essence of dowsing.

15.   Use what works. Conventional Newtonian Science is the realm of the flesh. This is maybe 10% or less of existence. Provable data, and repeatable experiments, simply aren't available for over 90% of experience. The only proof for what is said here is experience. If it works, it is correct.

16.   While you may get immediate results, **practice each sequence and idea for at least 21 days**[41], if you can. You can also use Quantum Questions to generate new sequences, and to put yourself in new possibility points in the Void.

17.   Use a journal, if you can. Regularly connecting with thoughts, feelings, frustrations and real life experiences can be helpful. Reflecting upon these experiences can help you. It allows you to be in the moment - the only moment we have. It is very useful to track gratitude, and successes, to measure your dowsing sequences. You could do it daily, twice a week, weekly. It is better to do it regularly, even if only once weekly. The key is to regularly get in touch with how you are feeling. This will help you understand your Dreams, your fears, or any energy that may be "stuck", and what worked. Even if you only write down your goals, feeling them done, three times per day, as recommended by R.H. Jarret's book *It works!*, that is very useful. It is a way to be present. It can be useful for noticing trends and patterns. You may notice that how you feel affects your dowsing, for example.

18.   Inspiration is a high energy level. Inspired people generate useful ideas, find brilliant solutions, and create masterpieces[42]. If you feel really crummy eating a certain kind of food, get it out of your diet. You may want to continue by eating fresh, live, raw, unprocessed foods, sprouts, raw organic fruits, vegetables, whole grains, nuts and seeds, and drinking more water[43]- or not. Meditation helps[44].

---

41   P. xxiii, *Psycho-Cybernetics*, by Maxwell Maltz.
42   P. 58, *Reality Transurfing V. Apples Fall to the Sky*, Vadim Zeland.
43   Dehydration builds acidity in body. This is not useful. Manifesting works much easier in a slightly alkaline body. Water, as a conductor, discharges the polarized mind.
44   Pp. 56-58, *Reality Transurfing V. Apples Fall to the Sky*, Vadim Zeland.

19. Avoid processed foods, especially refined carbohydrates[45], unless you find they make you feel good. Use natural mineral sources, where possible, including organic molasses, sea salt prepared by evaporation in salt flats, green powders, &c. Cut down on or eliminate animal products[46]. Eat an alkalinizing diet, as much as you can. I pay careful attention to how things affect my energy level, and I avoid those things that lower my energy. **Do more of what makes you feel good, and do a lot less of what makes you feel bad.**[47] Look at, and observe, only WHAT YOU SEEK in life, as already having it. This will be different for different people. José Silva loved a good steak, for example.

20. Spending time in nature raises one's energy level[48]. Being around anything beautiful raises one's energy level. Listening to soothing music raises one's energy level. The right kind of exercise raises energy levels. The higher your energy, the faster what you seek to manifest becomes reality[49]. Kind thoughts and deeds increase your energy[50]. A cosmic order, or a good dowsing question, illuminates the corresponding sector in the Void of all possibilities[51]. When you are above a certain energy level, it manifests immediately, even as healing.
Become one with your layer of the world, and you can shape it the way you control your body. In fact, be a particle of the world, and in its quantum waveform, at the same time[52].

---

45 There are so many useful books in this area. I like *Bragg Healing Lifestyle*, by Patricia Bragg, because it is simple. Her father started the health food store concept. And for those irritated by health food stores, what, do you want to shop in disease food stores? I mean fast food outlets? Will you have chemotherapy with that? Beyond that, Dr. John Christopher and Dr. Richard Schulze's books are useful to me. There are many others also good. I don't get anything for saying this, this is just what I like.
46 All externally administered hormones cause cancer just read the package inserts, and animal products are full of hormones and drugs. Factory farm raised animals are fed reprocessed manure, and you are what you eat. Maybe that's why so many people are full of....
47 Notice that the mass media seems to want to lower your energy, to keep you enthralled, which is a way to say enslaved. When I was in the military, I noticed that the constant, unnecessary harassment of the troops kept them in a lower energy state. I see the same thing in corporate America. Stop bitching, and start raising your energy level, so you can get free. Corporate America is abandoning its workers to their own devices. You have a book full of useful stuff here, and it starts with raising your energy. I have met people who live totally from manifestation, they have no regular jobs, and no desire to, they are blissfully happy. The only quality they share is high energy levels, they don't even necessarily know how they do it. They just feel it real, and it is real, for them.
48 If you take all of our great thinkers who formulated religious teachings, why is it that before formulating them, they went into solitude? This includes Moses, Jesus, Buddha, Mohamed, Orpheus, St. Francis, St. Anthony, many Native American medicine people, and others. P. 33, *The Ringing Cedars Series: Book One: Anastasia*, Vladimir Megre.
49 P. 59, *Reality Transurfing V. Apples Fall to the Sky*, Vadim Zeland.
50 P. 25, *The Power of Intention*, Wayne Dyer.
51 P. 59, *Reality Transurfing V. Apples Fall to the Sky*, Vadim Zeland.
52 P. 60, *Reality Transurfing V. Apples Fall to the Sky*, Vadim Zeland.

21. Become conscious of your thoughts, and upgrade them. Meteditate regularly, even if only for a minute or two at a time . This is like an oil change for the brain, a free tune-up for your dowsing system.

22. Test the energy level of music. Listen to music that energizes you. Test the flow in your home, what the Chinese call *Feng Shui*. If something in your house makes you feel bad, get rid of it. Post photographs taken in moments of happiness and love, and post them in your apartment. Be around people with a high energy level. I find that **having animals and plants around** somehow helps my energy level, and dowsing[53].

23. Visualizing, in heartspace, with feeling, is the least you can do, to get the most results. Pretend your dreams are already true. Feel what it would feel like, if you already had your dreams. Be what you seek.[54]

24. Be mindful[55]. Stay conscious. Notice the good stuff. Pay attention to your fascinations, what attracts you positively. You never know where your interests will lead you[56].
This also means letting go of certainty[57], and closure, and being open to what shows up. If your mind has taken your attention to the past or the future, you are not looking out the windshield. Mindfulness opens you up to the 99.99999999999999% of possibilities you cannot be aware of, using only the conscious mind. Dowsing is mindfulness in action.

---

53   Dogs and cats can be particularly useful in helping people maintain their energy. Both dogs and cats transmute negative energy in a household, to a certain extent. Sometimes dogs and cats will actually take on illnesses to lessen the burden on a stressed-out owner. As with anything else, don't believe me, check it yourself, with your own dowsing. This is another good reason to increase your energy level, it will help your pets.
54   There is a field of all possibilities, without limits. Some call it the quantum field, zero point field, the Void, universal mind. Everything you could ever want is already in this field, as potential. We are one with this field, though some of us have forgotten our connection, due to the ego, the judging mind. You can manifest anything when you are in alignment with this field. Your ego does not make things happen. It does not attract anything. Get out of your ego, let go of your desires, and exist in harmony with this field. Your desires will manifest into existence. Paraphrased from pp. 5-6, *The Greatest Manifestation Principle in the World*, Carnelian Sage.
55   Eckhart Tolle and Thich Nhat Hanh have written entire books on this, so this is clearly important. This is basically being present in the moment.
56   There is a Sufi story which illustrates this, and you are precisely at that stage of development where this story would be useful. A princess was shipwrecked, on an island. She was rescued by sailors, and taken to live with them. She learned how to make rope, and sails, and how to work with ships' spars. Later, she was taken in a raid, and eventually sold as a slave to the king of China. The king of China was making war, and needed a way to house troops on the move. Up to that time, the troops had slept in their coats, but they needed more. The princess, now a slave, said she could do that. She was invited to demonstrate, and she made the first tent. As a reward, she was married to the king. Did this actually happen? Maybe not, but it precisely demonstrates that circumstances that don't seem to make any sense may simply be preparation for something larger. In the original story, she was taken 3 times, learning from 3 separate peoples how to make rope, canvas, and poles. Much of life is like this. This book is itself a "tent" of my own experience.
57   P. 80, *Butterflies and Dreams*, Dorothy Peltier-Fanchi.

It also means seizing openings, and opportunities, in the moment. Perhaps you see a reference to an idea that fascinates you- google it. Perhaps you mention an interest in something, and a friend notes a great book, or course, on it. Write down the title immediately, and follow up that day.

Much of this book came from ideas my subconscious shared with me at times, during the day, which I then wrote down. If something relates to your passions, go for it, just do it, plunge. My daughter was invited to help during the Christmas rush at a store in town, when she was 16. She followed up, quickly, and was offered a regular position, because they liked her work. The Universe likes speed in followup.

25.   Choose words that energize, excite, and thrill you. Your spoken words are the invisible seeds that will crystallize in your world as things most quickly. When you encounter words, thoughts, images, and feelings that aren't helpful, use the Switchword "*cancel, cancel, cancel, cancel*".[58] See the world as an abundant, providing, friendly place, and the more you get, the easier it is for others to get what they seek[59]. Be aware of your thoughts in the moment, and raise their energy. Be generous. It feels better.

26.   For feedback, it is useful to have a before and after measure, such as a scale of 1 to 10. Your body can talk to you about outcomes[60], actually it already is, though you may not be listening. One of the best measuring devices you can use is the question, "*How do I feel?*" and then, "*How do I feel about that?*" or "*What am I noticing right now?*"

This is basic dowsing, basic intuition[61], learning to pay attention to the sensory information we normally ignore[62]. Intuition is paying attention to how you feel now[63].

---

58   Switchwords are described in *The Secret of Perfect Living*, by James Mangan. This one is cited at p. 101, *You the Healer*, by José Silva. The Three Fingers technique of the Silva Method, described at p. 111 of this book, can also be used for this purpose, as noted at p. 129 of this book. I have limited space, and some people always want more.
59   P. 183, *The Power of Intention*, Wayne Dyer.
60   P. 69, *Manifesting your Heart's Desire*, Fred Fengler and Todd Varnum.
61   What is intuition? It is a nonlinear, nonempirical process of gaining and interpreting information in response to questions. P. 83, *Practical Intuition*, Laura Day.
62   Consciousness can be aware of many levels outside of consensual reality. Just tune your awareness to that place beyond where information and potential cohere into matter.
63   P. 155, *Reality Transurfing I: The Space of Variations*, Vadim Zeland.

Many people use intuition, though they may not call it that[64]. If you have a brain, a body, memories, and you sleep, then you are intuitive[65]. Many heart phenomena cannot be modeled in language, or thought.

27. The conscious mind simply cannot perceive even 1% of what is going on. The conscious mind can hold 6-8 thoughts in mind at a time. This is one reason telephone numbers are 7 digits long. The subconscious[66] mind can process at least 60 million bits of information per second. We get far more information than we could consciously process. 99.999999% of this information is invisible. You can still feel its effects. It affects you. This information may give you the feeling you are being watched, make the hair on your neck rise in a certain place, or give a 'gut feeling' about ideas, people, possibilities, or situations. **Intuition is based on billions of times as much data as rational thought**. *Which do you think is more accurate, and has the better foundation?* Which one is more likely to come up with the answers that will help us solve our problems, and the problems of the world? When working with intuition, work quickly, before the thinking mind can interfere.[67]

28. Ceremony focuses the mind, and keeps the conscious mind occupied[68], but the power is in the mind and heart, not in the device. The pendulum is a crutch. Know when to quit using crutches. Objects have the power of belief in them, and no more.

29. Be aware of the Universe, the model, the domain you are working in. The model of the world a four-year-old uses is not the same as the one a 12-year-old uses. Their parents' model of the world is, of course, quite different. Whatever you do in the world is based on your model of how it works. If a particular technique quits working for you, this means it is time to

---

64   Troops on patrol in Vietnam who had a sudden feeling to get down, just before a mine blew up, or gunfire, were using intuition. Those who do well on the stock market all use intuition to one extent or another. They may not recognize it, but they do.

65   P. 174, *Reinventing Medicine*, Larry Dossey.

66   If you want a reference for how the subconscious works, note that deeper self-hypnosis is similar to lucid dreaming. P. 11, *Lucid Dreaming*, Robert Waggoner.

67   P. 146, *Practical Intuition*, Laura Day. Also, intuition supplements good judgment, it does **not** replace it, as noted at p. 157.

68   Ceremony is the hair, that keeps the genie, or conscious mind occupied, and out of harm's way, in the child's story *The Genie and the Hair*, which I think is now in book form, on amazon.com.

ISBN-10: 1482688573

download a more effective technique. This is part of growth. By way, the scientific model is only a model. It is far from complete. No model is, or can be, complete. The map is not the territory, it is only a model, a reflection in symbols. There is more out there than exists in our models.

30. In the tunnel that near-death experiences involve, one goes the speed of light, or even faster. One sees brilliant, beautiful white light. The light communicates instantly and absolutely clearly, with a feeling of absolute pure love. You are suddenly in communication with absolute and total knowledge. You think of a question, and you immediately know the answer to it. Light is the answer. It is the atmosphere, the energy, total knowledge, and pure love[69]. This is the purest dowsing. People can travel thousands of light years in an instant[70], in this dimension. Ultra consciousness, or cosmic consciousness, has the following characteristics: dazzling light, supercharged joy and rapture, illuminated perception, transcendental love and compassion for all living beings, fear of death vanishing into the enhancement of life, appreciation of beauty and what is important in life, flowering of genius, a sense of mission involving service to others, radiance, intuitive gifts. These transformations do not depend on having near-death experiences[71], though that can inspire them. Why say all that? Pajama people consciousness, the consciousness of the sleepwalking multitudes, is limiting. Expanding your awareness helps you grow, and really helps your dowsing.

31. Take inspired action, from intuitive guidance. Show up. 80%+ of success is just showing up[72]. Never defeat yourself before the battle, because that is someone else's job.

32. There are people who enjoy being victims. Do not rescue these people[73], as they will not forgive you. Many Native

---

69   Pp. 57-9, 116, *Heading Toward Omega: in Search of the Meaning of the Near-Death Experience*, Kenneth Ring.
70   P. 77, *Heading Toward Omega: in Search of the Meaning of the Near-Death Experience*, Kenneth Ring.
71   Pp. 227-8, 222-3, *Heading Toward Omega: in Search of the Meaning of the Near-Death Experience*, Kenneth Ring.
72   Woody Allen, a somewhat misunderstood modern philosopher.
73   If you take away their persecutor, they may decide to turn you into their persecutor. At some level these people take pride in creating a really insoluble problems. The most loving thing you can do for them is to say "Wow, that is a staggeringly difficult problem. I have no idea how it could be solved." When you admire their creations in this way, you give them space to turn around the polarity, and to start solving their own problems. Their solutions may be much better than yours. Also, you will save effort.

American Medicine People will find out what a person plans to do with their life, once they get over whatever is bothering them. If they aren't going to make some major changes, and serve the larger self of the tribe, at least, sometimes the Medicine person won't take any action. Challenges are often created [by ourselves] to cause us to grow, to get into the larger Self. Someone who refuses to grow, and get into the larger self, may just recreate their problem, when you're done. Why waste your energy?

33. Use strong emotion when visualizing, or using intent. Usually, it is better to be looking out through your own eyes, and hearing with your own ears, or at least alternating between being a participant and a viewer. One exception to this might be calling up memories of severe trauma, in which case it is better to be the observer[74], as you won't feel the pain nearly as much.

34. A good intent, or prayer[75] before you start is "it is done". It is useful to have an intent that everything you do is for the highest good of all.

35. When you set a goal, deal with details, and do it. There is no possible way to lose, because you will either get it, or get useful feedback. Don't know that you can't do it. Set your intent, set your goals, visualize with emotion, take action however small, persist, celebrate all small victories.

Working with metaphor[76] to dowse and solve problems, or even just to have fun discovering what your imagination[77] and intuition

---

74   The Observer is described at p. 94, *Lucid Dreaming*, Robert Waggoner. Basically, it is the part of self that is real, not wrapped up in extraneous detail, which observes everything. You can identify with it, and simply observe. This state is above 600 on the Hawkins scale, and is an ideal dowsing state.

75   Dowsing and praying, for religious folk, are almost the same thing. Both of them intensify and focus thought, as intent. One could use rhyming statements of intent, such as "From my hand shoots an energy beam, to heal my foot with power supreme!" P. 163, *Lucid Dreaming*, Robert Waggoner. What counts in dialogue is not what is said but what is meant, the intent. Dialogue shows rather than tells a story. - P. 218, *The Complete Idiot's Guide to Screen Writing*, Skip Press.

76   Metaphors are hypnotically powerful. The Newtonian metaphor for the Universe was a clockwork. It is still with us, even though it is very wrong.

77   You do not have to be rich to be happy, but you must be imaginative. Neville Goddard tells the story of one woman, working as a waitress, to support her family. She took the streetcar home from work, on Christmas Eve. She felt really restricted. It was raining. She tasted the salt of her tears, and said to herself: "This is a ship, not a streetcar, and I am tasting the salt of the sea in the wind. Isn't it a heavenly night!" In her imagination, the rail of the streetcar was the rail of a ship, entering Samoa. Two weeks later a check for $3,000 showed, up, from an aunt. Within one month, she was on a ship, to Samoa. A ship left a wake, of salt spray, which touched her face, and someone standing near said: "Isn't it a heavenly night." From Vadim Zeland's Transurfing point of view, she went to the Samoan address, in the Void, in her imagination, nailed it down with feeling, and her physical body had to follow. This is projective dowsing at its finest.

can do for you, is both an ancient human technology, and the cutting edge of mind-body technologies[78]. Metaphors connect the world around us with the metaphysical, which gives us a window on the infinite. Metaphor is energy in the state of action, breathing life into ceremony.

We work with metaphor to find the essence of everything we encounter in the material world in perceptual reality, and trace it back, through metaphor, to the one[79]. This is a domain of virtually limitless potential, that is easy to access, which comes naturally to most people. You can attract bad or good, they're both energy.

36. Everyone and everything in your life is only a mirror, metaphor, or placeholder[80] for what is inside you. What is outside of you is effect, and it reflects cause, which is inside you. When you are shaving, do you put your razor up to the mirror, to shave? Are you sure? If so, how could you hope to change your outer[81] world, without first changing your inner world[82]?

37. Your hands are exclamation points for your consciousness. When you do imaginary work, use your physical hands. You can move your hands around, to feel your consciousness[83], your energy fields, thoughtforms, sacred geometry energy forms, both as they are, and as you would like

---

78   In fact, people crave metaphors. P. 27, *Metaphorically Selling*, by Anne Miller.
79   P. 40, *Sound: Native Teachings and Visionary Art*, Joseph Rael.
80   A great demonstration of this is placebos. Placebos work better than many pharmaceutical drugs, in blind tests, though no-one will ever tell you that. My favorite placebo story, though, is the woman who, just after WW II, sent small packages of food and clothing, including *Lifesavers* brand candy, to relatives in a European country devastated by the war. The relatives were glad to get this, and asked for medicine. She couldn't find the medicine they wanted, and felt bad. She got a letter from the relatives, thanking her profusely, noting that the medicine she sent worked very well. She asked about that. They weren't native speakers of English, and so had to use dictionaries to read labels. The label on Lifesavers says *"Lifesavers"*. They checked the dictionary, which defines a Lifesaver as something that saves lives. They were delighted at how well the medicine worked. I lived in Southeast Asia as a child. A servant asked one of my mother's friends why she took saccharine tablets. The friend said it would keep her from getting "fat". This was when birth control pills had just come out. Later, the maid said that her friend was pregnant, and didn't want the baby. My mother's friend wasn't sure why she was being told this. Later, the servant came back, and reported that the medicine [Saccharine] had worked, the woman was no longer pregnant. My U.S. History teacher in high school recalled that his pediatrician kept 4 colors of sugar tablets, in his office. He would give detailed instructions on their use- "take 2 yellow ones twice a day, and a red one at lunch". His cure rates were as high as any other doctor's rates. One sees the story about a man whose cancer vanished in a day, due to Krebiozen, only to return when he found out it didn't work. In my Anthropology classes in college, a survey was cited showing the shamanic practicioners got higher cure rates than medical doctors. This is actually not surprising; shamans see the whole person, in a community context. Doctors are not allowed to go outside of their specialty. Belief plays a massive role in any healing, and all healing is self healing anyway, or so I am told by most people I talk to, who work in that field.
81   Young people focus on external events. However, at some point, experience is no longer valued by the nature of external events, but rather by internal and subjective standards. P. 227, *The Keys of Jeshua*, Glenda Green. The great journey of life is from outer to the dimensionally greater inner world.
82   All that you behold; though it appears without, it is within, in your Imagination, of which this World of Mortality is but a Shadow. -William Blake, *Jerusalem*
83   P. 30, *Beyond Human: Claiming the Power and Magic of your Limitless Self*, Jaden Phoenix.

them to be. Move your body.[84] Put a holographic, or imaginary, model of your dowsing area of interest in front of you[85], and feel it with your physical hands. If you find an imaginary blockage, pull it out, with your physical hands.

38. Know that it is possible to make money at this. There is no reason to exploit people. At the same time, whoever dreamed up the idea that spirituality and money don't mix did the world a major disservice[86]. You can charge money to help others, dowse for what is appropriate[87]. You may also be paid from some other channel. If you want to be rich, solve more problems, increase your energy level, and your awareness.

39. There is no one manifesting or dowsing sequence that works for everyone, since everyone is unique[88]. You will see multiple sequences cited here. Determine your own[89]. If you want it in a nutshell, energy, or attention tuned to a particular sector of the matrix, or information field, illuminates that sector, which is then realized in material form[90].

40. When in doubt, show up early. Expect the best. Persist. Smile, and live as if your success was inevitable. It is, because all events in your life lead you to that success, sooner or later. You don't have to know what will happen, for it to be great. Recognize fear as your friend.

Often your greatest gains are on the other side of a fear. When I feel fear, I notice that, and get curious about it. Sometimes fears

---

84 I read a book once, entitled something like *Ecstatic Body Postures*, which stated that certain body postures made certain kinds of energy work easier. Buddhist mudras, and Christian hand signs, as portrayed in medieval art particularly, have an effect. Be aware of the blessing gesture or statement in every culture you deal with. That has a powerful morphic field behind it. Use it, with love.
85 This could be a city map, if you are clearing energy blockages. It could be an anatomical drawing, if you are doing the Silva method. It could be the site plan of a house. It could be a child's drawing of the beach. Don't discount children's drawings, they reach deep parts of the mind.
86 Raymon Grace notes that Hannah Kroeger, one of the best healers in the world, said you can use dowsing for personal gain. We all have bills to pay, at least under the current economic system, and related belief systems. Unless you prefer to live in a cave, eat wild herbs, and bathe in streams, as some Mexican healers do.
87 You can earn money, and you can charge the money you spend with healing energy. Both meanings are intended.
88 There is no one path. However, manifesting and healing do tend to follow the "monomyth" described in Joseph Campbell's *The Hero with a Thousand Faces*, in that one ventures forth from the common day into a region of supernatural wonder, fabulous forces are encountered, and a decisive victory won, and the hero comes back with boons, for self and others. In the course of this journey, the hero dies symbolically, and is reborn to a new consciousness. -Neville Goddard. Every great work of fiction has such a transformation. -p. 2, *The Key, How to Write Damn Good Fiction using the Power of Myth*, James N. Frey. In other words, the manifesting journey has common elements, but it is always unique.
89 There are five stages to manifesting, however. They are: play and pleasure, manipulation, power and purpose, reflection and cocreation, and experiencing pure awareness. This is discussed in another context at Pp. 102-105, *Lucid Dreaming*, Robert Waggoner.
90 P. 148, *Reality Transurfing I: The Space of Variations*, Vadim Zeland.

help me get ready for a trip, imagining the worst reminds me to bring things I need. New York City, prior to Benjamin Bratton doing what Rudy Giuliani claimed credit for, was a fearful place for me to live, yet I lived there for a year, and nothing bad happened. Fear is useful, it may be a marker for something I'm about to learn.

41. Use dowsing charts and scales, and other such templates. It speeds up target identification. The Hawkins scale, from the book *Power vs. Force*, is useful[91]. Charts are actually a metaphor.[92] Single persons, and large groups of people, can be calibrated for their energy levels[93], preferably as an average, over a time, such as a week or month. As you transform your lower grade energies, you can get feedback on your energy level, on the Hawkins scale. This feedback is incredibly helpful, something missing from *The Secret*. <u>When you have transformed all or most of the energies below 200, on the Hawkins scale, in your being, and your average energy level for say the last month is over 600, on this scale, you will be able to dowse and manifest effortlessly, with one wish, and it will show up quickly.</u> From now on, test the energy of any book, course, or teacher you are considering, for usefulness to you.

Test the average energy rise in a class after teachings by that teacher[94], and projected increase, after you go to it. If they don't test out as useful, move on. Some books, courses, and teachers are perfect for some people, and not for others. Bless them, and go to those you have a high energy on. Your soul already knows how useful these are to you; you're just getting feedback.

---

91 The chart is a metaphor. Metaphors are powerful. Prior to the 1920's, roads were for short distance travel. Then a powerful new metaphor came out- road maps. Road maps showed those short roads connected in long roads- people could suddenly make long trips, in a car. Not an inch of roads was added by road maps, but the new metaphor had major effects on tourism. My mother went from Illinois, to Florida, in the 1930's, on vacation, with her family, based on that metaphor. A good chart makes many new things possible, with dowsing. I have used charts designed for children, from the dollar store, when I felt like playing. I wonder if Dora the Explorer might have some ideas on how to improve Congress, for example. Chinese acupuncture charts can be fun to play with.

92 Let's think of alchemy. You need a container- and metaphor means container; you need something you want to change, and then the energy/consciousness/awareness to change it. You have things you want to change, already. The metaphors in this book are useful containers, and you will also find ways to use your energy to change those things you want changed. You could use a trip, a workshop, a talk, a magic circle, art, and any form as a container. Come to think of it, magic circles were considered as being between worlds, where the regular rules did not apply. In every case, what you are changing is simply the pattern of light and information that supports what it is you don't want. Think of a hologram. What you perceive is only a holographic projection of an interference pattern of light and information, of energy. If you change this pattern, you change how reality is projected. Energy is easily shifted with intent.

93 P. 104, *The Power of Intention*, Wayne Dyer, citing *Power vs Force*, David Hawkins.

94 The highest increase after a training that I've noted in myself was after Raymon Grace's training. I also got major increases from Matrix Energetics, Theta Healing, Psi Seminars, and Silva training, particularly. Test also for usefulness; breathwork training was been extremely useful, though the numbers weren't as high. That is my experience.

42.   Attention is your ability to dowse and create, to learn anything. It is awareness. Focus it on anything. Then focus on something to get into its vibration, and notice you become it, even if only for a moment. Maintain that for just 70 seconds, and you vibrate at the same rate. Then focus it on nothing, which is, by way, a very powerful Buddhist meditation. In this silence and serenity, many problems fade away. This is heartspace. New and creative ideas arise from this space. Stop thinking about what you don't want, and are trying to avoid. Instead, think about what you do want, and are seeking[95]. Attention charged with relaxed intent collapses the quantum wave form into what you seek. Attention charged with resistance collapses the wave form into what you don't want. Attention without charge is a weak quantum measurement, a form of dowsing, which does not collapse the wave form.   In this space, a vast Universal intelligence takes over, and does the dowsing and creating for you. When you are in pure joy, in the now, fascinating stuff happens.[96] Plugging the cord into the outlet, metaphorically, gives you real power. So, let's put attention on attention. Let's notice what we notice.

43.   *Where is your attention right now? Where could it go? Where would you like it to be?*[97] This is your ability to create. This is essentially what the rest of this book is about. Let's play with that. Focus on something you don't want, in your life. Now focus on something you have no charge on. Go back and forth, till your attention is freed from what you don't want. In this state, focus attention on information you do want, until it manifests. This is creating wholeness. Yes, it really is this easy, and it happens all the time. Words have only the meaning of intent in them. Connect with love to change anything, this is often the missing piece. Thought stops the flow of energy. Don't understand it, just do it.

---

95   P. 25, *Reality Transurfing V. Apples Fall to the Sky,* Vadim Zeland.
96   Thank you, Andrea, Helen, Rissa, and Xine, for teaching this lesson by the example of your lives.
97   Thank you, Keith Varnum, for this lesson. The Sedona Method questions: *Could you release attention/bad feeling? Would you? When?* Are very similar.

44. Drink at least a quart/liter of pure water, preferably distilled, every day[98]. Drink a quart/liter of freshly made fruit and vegetable juice every day, made with a Juicer[99]. Cut back on or eliminate legal drugs, especially alcohol. Quit illegal drugs cold turkey, if you can, or as soon as possible, with medical advice. All of them stress the liver and kidneys. Legal drugs are the 5th cause of death in the U.S., killing over 160,000 people each year that they know of. The Universe consists of light, and information. Drugs and alcohol distort information. This is not useful. We are created of light[100].

45. Clean out your bowels. The average 50 year old American has five pounds of rotting meat in his/her diverticulated intestines. Use natural soaps, shampoos, detergent, cosmetics, and toothpaste. All of them end up in your bloodstream[101]. Wear natural fibers, such as cotton and linen. Avoid synthetics, at least for clothing next to your skin.

46. Walk some every day, and breathe deeply, for at least 20 minutes per day. This helps your circulation. Exercise more, sweat an hour a day if you can. This really helps your circulation. Alternate hot and cold showers, up to seven times, with 30 seconds or more, per instance of cold or hot. This will improve your circulation, and it was and is used by numerous health spas for serious issues. It removes blockages very well. Get rid of 1/3 of what you own- throw it out, give it away, get rid of it. Do this at least once per year, perhaps in Spring.

---

98 Dr. Feridoun Batmanghelidj, mentioned earlier, recommends up to 6 liters/quarts of pure water, per day.
99 After 1 hour, juice loses 80% of its nutrition.
100 P. xxvi, *Touching the Light,* Meg Blackburn Losey, and numerous indigenous creation stories.
101   Odors and artificial dyes stress the immune systems. Aluminum based deodorants are absorbed through the skin, and aluminum is a toxin. Some fingernail polishes contain lead-based paint. Many cosmetics have toxic materials in them.

47. Stop watching TV[102], especially, and at least, the news[103]. Follow your fascinations. Express yourself in positive, creative ways, whether through hobbies, dance, singing, or whatever turns you on. Find activities that make you feel better, and do them more. Do less of activities that make you feel bad[104]. Follow your spirit, meditate, pray, do whatever you need, to express your spiritual side, to experience peace, joy, satisfaction, love, and happiness. Find ways to love yourself, through affirmations, treating yourself better, or whatever it takes to feel good. Help someone else every day, however small the way. This is the most important single thing you can do, in life. Learn many jokes, and laugh uncontrollably, at least once a day.

48. Be aware of *morphic fields[105]*, as defined by Rupert Sheldrake, in his *A New Science of Life,* and *Morphic Resonance.* This is a useful idea. A morphic field is basically a track, a metaphorical footpath, with tracks of thought and feeling built up over time. The morphic field of computers has changed and grown drastically, since my mother saw the second computer ever built, in college, for example. Any structure shaped by thoughts is a [morphic field] pendulum.

---

102 If you are feeling like influencing the garbage the media puts out, figure out who the advertisers are, for the junky shows. Write letters to those companies, saying you felt like throwing up throughout the show, and now you can't buy their products, because they make you want to throw up. Some of us remember Phil Donahue, the pre-Oprah talk show host. A dentist, in Dallas, decided Phil's show was too racy for the afternoon. So he used a typewriter, to write letters in this way. He cost Phil over 10% of his advertising revenue- Phil would never say how much. Phil wanted him on the show; the dentist refused, saying he didn't feel like being demonized. One guy with a typewriter did that. Nowadays we have e-mail, e-response at websites... we could shut down the flow of garbage into the mass consciousness, if we all wrote just one e-mail per week, on what most disgusts us. Just a thought. The networks are tottering; the Spanish cable network Univision actually beat out NBC, in ratings, recently, so our letters now would be even more effective. So the next time someone complains about all the junk on TV, you can empower them with a way to affect it. Empowerment feels good, whether through dowsing, or other means.

103 Your eyes eat images like your mouth eats food, and in both cases you become what you eat. Watch only what builds you up. Commercial advertisements are designed by very smart people. You will be healthier without all that subliminal manipulation. Comparing yourself with fabulously rich people, or viewing violence, will not help you feel better. Stop viewing or reading any media that makes you feel bad. The average age of a female print model is 17, and most models are thinner than 95% of the female population. Images in women's magazines, really all magazines, now, are photoshopped. Men must now have washboard stomachs. Over 75% of American female high school graduates are extremely dissatisfied with the weight and shape of their bodies, though few are actually overweight. This is a mass culture hallucination. Americans are willing to feel incredibly bad, to look good, in comparison to these unreachable standards. Americans wear clothes that are too small, with tight belts, where they can barely breathe. This is blockage at a physical level. Latin women are comfortable in their bodies, because they have their own definition of beauty. All men and women look great when they are comfortable in their bodies, even if they are overweight. Even the most classically beautiful look bad, if they loathe their bodies. A study in a women's magazine a few years ago noted 100% of the respondents were unhappy with the size and shape of their breasts, and the placement of the nipple. Is it really a surprise that breast cancer is the number one cancer, among women, in the U.S.? When you are comfortable in your body, you breathe freely, with an air of confidence and ease, and your true self shines through. What makes you feel good makes you look good. Pp. 38-39, *The Breathing Book*, Donna Farhi, and also Dr. Richard Schulze. Feeling good, in your body, is a foundation to dowsing and manifesting.

104 Know that you can say no. Most people say "no" to prevent an experience, instead of saying no from within the experience, once they know it is not desirable. Know you can say no at any point inside the experience, and you can open yourself up to life, and receive without expectation. P. 75, *The Keys of Jeshua*, Glenda Green.

105 These may simply be the repositories of Plato's invisible, perfect forms, that can't be subdivided.

Morphic fields are energy-based information structures[106]. Low-grade morphic fields are like pendulums swinging wildly[107]. High-grade morphic fields swing much less, until one finds more dynamic balance, above about 600 on the Hawkins scale. Morphic fields depend on the energy input of attention. They have an inherent memory, given by morphic resonance. Our own memories may depend on morphic resonance[108].

If no-one on Earth ever thought of killing, no potential future about murder would exist [in the morphic field], and no actualization of murder would be possible[109].

49. Low-grade morphic fields access your energy by getting you out of balance, to vibrate on their frequency, particularly through fear[110], and other emotions below 200 on the Hawkins scale[111]. You can change anything in the world, since everything has a frequency. Change the frequency, or create an opposite frequency[112]. Intermittent high-pitched sound is much more upsetting than the constant loud din[113]; if you need to intend an energy flow, you could intend it as pulsating, rather than continuous.

50. I have good news and not so good news. First the good news: we have access to all the tools and information we need, through dowsing, to fix every problem humanity and the planet face, and to make our lives magnificent.

---

106 Pp. 29, 38 Reality Transurfing I: The Space of Variations, Vadim Zeland.
107 One classic study of large low grade morphic fields, or pendulums, as Vadim Zeland calls them, is Extraordinary Popular Delusions and the Madness of Crowds, Charles MacKay, originally published in 1841. Bernard Baruch highly recommended it. Advertising companies study it carefully.
108 P. xxii, Morphic Resonance: The Nature of Formative Causation, Rupert Sheldrake.
109 P. 77, Change your Future through Time Openings, Lucile and Jean-Pierre Garnier-Malet. The TV News, then, is a form of programming which encourages all sorts of crimes, then, isn't it, by putting attention on the negative.
110 P. 39, Reality Transurfing I: The Space of Variations, Vadim Zeland.
111 Your energy level is critical for manifesting. Use dowsing to test yourself for your average energy level on the Hawkins scale, for a period, say the last month.
If it was below 200, you don't have the energy to do anything except maybe survive, and run and hide.
If you are between 200 and 300, you can manifest, with a lot of work, and careful planning and evaluation along the road.
If you are between 300 and 400, you align your thoughts, emotions and energy with your intent, and it's a lot easier to dowse and create what you want.
If you are between 400 and 500, you start to use finesse. You still need repetition and practice to make things happen primarily by feelings.
If you are 500 to 600, you are in the cosmic ordering service realm. All you need is focused intent, a clear decision, and it happens.
If you are above 600, you are so much in bliss that manifestation is not that interesting anymore. This is wholeness at its finest.
You can see, from this, why it is important to start every process in a great state, and to clear out your energy blocks.
112 Dr. Ben Johnson, cited at Pp. 137, 138, The Secret, Rhonda Byrne.
113 P. 49, Animals in Translation, Temple Grandin. because you can't simply adjust to it. Pulsing energy can be much more useful than a constant stream. Maybe that's why we live in a quantum, not a continuous universe.

Now the not so good news: We may not have realized it yet. This book will help to remedy that. Before you work with anything or anyone, enter the space where you have the power to dowse and do good, where the good is already done. This is heartspace[114].

51. Be very aware of your *transparent beliefs*, core beliefs[115] that affect everything else. An example of this is the belief that life, or dowsing, is hard. People with this core belief find life, or dowsing, hard, no matter what else they do. This is not a useful belief to most people. Why not remove it? You could just as easily have a core belief that life, and dowsing, are easy, effortless, fun, and joyful. I have met people with this core belief. Their lives are easy, effortless, fun, and joyful, though not without the occasional challenge, to keep them growing. Why not get curious- asking quantum questions, or questings, such as: gosh, this stuff worked for others, *what could I change to get better results myself?* Why not install a core belief that *everything you do works, that useful change happens, for the highest good of all, even if you don't know what you're doing, do it wrong, have negative thoughts, or don't believe it is possible- or that nothing happens, when people are in the best possible state already?* That is useful, as you don't have to clear out limiting beliefs first. Every time a limiting thought comes up, you can flip it to a useful core belief. This means you can welcome monkey mind, and negative chatter, as an opportunity to improve yourself[116].

52. Everyone has an imaginary protective invisible energy sheath. You can strengthen this. Stand comfortably. Imagine energy coming up from the ground, and entering your body, approximately at the perineum, moving up the spine, going up to the sky. Note that sky energy descends through your body, from the top of your head, moving along the spine, and exiting into the ground. You could imagine the rising flow coming out of your head, and spread over your head like a Fountain.

---

114 The ideas in this book came from over 2,000 other books, and experience. The goal, usually unexpressed, of every one of those books, was to get people into heartspace.
115 These are called Meta-rule sets, at p. 13, *Beyond Human: Claiming the Power and Magic of your Limitless Self*, by Jaden Phoenix. I heard about them also from Harry Palmer, and Vianna Stibal. This is a major force multiplier.
116 We deal with this later, however, you could check whether you are good enough, deserve love, are safe, and so on, as these are common transparent beliefs. If you say you need to work hard, you will have to. If you say you aren't very good at it, that will show up. Discussed also at p. 45, *The Art of Conscious Creation*, by Jackie Lapin.

The descending flow does the same thing under your feet. The hemispheres connect to form an energy sphere[117].

This is similar to the lesser circuit of Chi Kung. Another way to do this is to find your blazing heart center, just inside your chest. Take that down deep into the earth, and then bounce it back up to your heart, bringing good red energy with you.
Native Americans use this for healing. While holding state, send your blazing heart up to the Sun, and bounce it back, to bring back brilliant white light, with tinges of gold. When they mix in your heart, they form either pink, or green. You can let this love energy spread over the entire Earth. Both of these flows will gradually clean out energy blockages in your system, the more you pay attention to them.

The more aware you are, the more you are connected to the informational field, for dowsing. If you need to be centered, for example, in wrestling, you can increase the descending flow. If you need to jump, increase the rising flow[118]. Chi Kung Masters allegedly could leap as high as 10m, 30 ft, in the air. If you need to move something, play with its center of gravity. When you start flowing energy to others from the infinite, you will find you have great charisma, and you will help heal the earth.

53. The Hawkins scale is particularly useful for sorting out energy levels[119], as identified in the book *Power vs. Force*, by Hawkins, which is a book well worth getting. The following is how I understand this scale, which is expanded somewhat from his ideas:

> **1000** is lightspeed[120], anything above this level leaves this Universe[121].

---

117   P. 12, *Reality Transurfing III: Forward to the Past*, Vadim Zeland.
118   P. 17, *Reality Transurfing III: Forward to the Past*, Vadim Zeland.
119   You see a similar hierarchy at pp. 90-1, *The Amazing Power of Deliberate Intent*, Abraham-Hicks. Hawkins is more detailed, however. It doesn't matter if Hawkins is wrong, it is a useful model, which works. The Romans sailed all over the Mediterranean, using the model of a flat earth, for example.
120   Near death experiences involve accelerating, approaching brilliant light, that feels like pure love, total acceptance, forgiveness, and homecoming. The light communicates instantly, nonverbally, and imparts knowledge such that one can see and understand one's entire life, understanding what really matters in life. There may also be transcendental music, paradisiacal environments, and cities of light. -P. 83, *Heading Toward Omega: in Search of the Meaning of the Near-Death Experience*, Kenneth Ring.
121   Raymond Moody's book *Life after Life* describes the tunnel of light that people go through, as part of the near-death experience. I wonder if this is simply the effect of traveling greater than light speed, as shown in the first *Star Wars* movie? Let us imagine a person traveling into a wormhole. Light coming from our universe would be sped up. One would see our entire universe die; all of the universe's history would pass before that person in a flash. -P. 161,

The energy that creates all form, both concrete and abstract, is rapidly moving light energy, which slows down to a crawl to become matter[122].

700-1000 is a place so pleasant[123], you may not even want to play with intent[124].

600+ Peace, Bliss[125]. You can dowse and create instantly and effortlessly with intent, in this level.

540+ Joy, Serenity[126]

500±5 Love, Reverence

400±5 Reason, Understanding

350±5 Acceptance, Forgiveness

310±5 Willingness, Optimism

250±5 Neutrality, Trust

200 Courage   Anything below this level takes energy from you, rather than giving energy.   It is better to stay out of these levels, and to clear them when you find them.

175±5 Pride, Scorn

150±5 Anger, Hate

125±5 Desire, Craving

100±5 Fear, Anxiety

 75±5 Grief, Regret

 50±5 Apathy, Despair

 30±5 Guilt, Blame

 20   Shame[127], Humiliation

 18-22 are disease frequencies

There are negative levels, also, however, don't explore them if you don't feel led to work with them.[128] What I say about this scale is my own, don't expect to find it in his book. His book is

---

Parallel Universes, Fred Alan Wolf, much like a near-death experience. Hawkins didn't say this in his book, I'm extending his ideas.

122 P. 123, *Sound: Native Teachings and Visionary Art*, Joseph Rael.

123 Successful people tend to be unhappy, as they must achieve so people will notice. Happy people tend to be seen as failures, because they are on such good terms with themselves they don't care how others see them. -attributed to Agatha Christie

124 Your slightest wish will manifest, effortlessly, in pure creativity, in oneness with the power of God, you will become the miracle, in unity consciousness. You will become the grail, the diamond essence. Pp. 166-7, *The Way of the Wizard*, Deepak Chopra.

125 There is little difference between compassion and the highest consciousness. P. 39, *The Keys of Jeshua*, Glenda Green.

126 Be aware that these are relative. Vadim Zeland points out that Joy could actually be a limiting energy, if one sought to go higher.

127 One way to clear these is to stop denying these, and notice these feelings, in full awareness. P. 77, *The Way of the Wizard*, Deepak Chopra.

128 Those levels are for advanced shamanic clearing work, as portrayed, for example, in the paintings of Hieronymous Bosch.

fascinating. It appears that as you improve yourself, you improve others directly, for example.

A first test in energy calibration:

Dowse: *Do I [the author] have permission to [Can I, May I, Should I] raise the energy level in the room you[the reader] are in, right now?* If I get a yes, I have the following sequence run on automatic for you[129], as a programmed contingent thought form, running automatically outside my awareness: I spin my pendulum, or bobber, Counter-clockwise [CCW] from my perspective.

I pile the gathered energy up in a corner, and let any intent[130], not for the highest good of all, fall out. I put a new intent of prosperity, success, love, and the realization of your fondest dreams, effortlessly, lovingly, and playfully in it, with ease and grace, along with an intent that you have already mastered everything in this book. I then spin the pendulum or bobber CW from my perspective, to put this intent back in. I also invoke this: what are the infinite possibilities of how this book helps you create massive changes for the better, in your life, better than the best you can imagine?

This book says some very simple things, in several ways, from different angles for different points of reference. One angle may not make as much sense to you. As you read, you'll find something, a story, a turn of phrase, an explanation, that makes great sense to you. You enter the Aha! State, of instant awareness. Those feel great. Those are healing beauty, to me. One hears people say something like *I'm going to go work on it now. I'm really going to get this.* Listen for the lie. This is from the mind, trying to convince us we don't already have it. The polarized mind causes all suffering, through separation.

Why not enter the state where you already have it? It feels better. What works for you? What do you already have? Give thanks, and notice that. You can spread that to what you seek.

---

129 P. 156, *You the Healer,* José Silva, discusses contingent intent, like this.
130 *God is not on the side of the big battalions, but on the side of those who shoot best.* -Voltaire, and U.S. Marines. Intent is more important than anything else. Intent means feeling it real, now.

Focus on creating value for other people, for the planet. Improving yourself is service[131] to humanity. We can heal every problem on the planet, with intent, through dowsing, and the Law of Resonant Attraction.

Have you noticed that having fun, and playing, in the moment, are very healing?

F. Intent is Creation

The goal and meaning of any living being's life is to control its reality.[132] Growing up, in our culture, usually means chaining oneself to low-grade, energy-draining morphic fields, of doing a lot of unpleasant things, to maybe, hopefully, someday get somewhere pleasant. There is a better way: <u>Enter into, and be, the state you seek, now.</u> Go where the goal has already been attained[133]. Enter into your dream, in your imagination[134]; do what you would actually do if it were physically true, and you realize that dreams are realized by the imaginative, not necessarily by the rich[135]. Use quantum questions. *How does it feel, being whole, and healed, with all the information you need, now? Right now?* Ask yourself that question often, during the day, and really feel the answer.

Unity of soul, mind, and heart turns potential into real[136], the dowsing question into the answer. You choose, with intent, through your dowsing questions, and your order is eventually fulfilled.

---

131 Here is a quiz: Name the ten wealthiest people in the world, the last ten Oscar winners, the last Miss Americas, or local equivalent, the last ten Nobel Prize winners, the last ten World Series or Soccer Cup winners. Can you recall more than one? They fade. Here's another test: Name three people you enjoy spending time with. Name three people who made you feel really good, appreciated. Name a friend who helped you through a difficult time. Name a couple of teachers who really helped you in school. Did you do better? The people who really make a difference may not be on stage, getting awards, or making the most money. They are those who care the most, and take action. There are some people only you can touch... Be Yourself. Everyone Else Is Taken! And quit worrying about the world coming to an end today. It's already tomorrow in Australia.
132   P. 65, *Reality Transurfing IV*, Vadim Zeland.
133   Pp. 59, *Reality Transurfing III: Forward to the Past*, Vadim Zeland.
134   My favorite book for expanding imagination is *Drawing on the Right Side of the Brain*, Betty Edwards, & anything related to Chinese Ink Brush painting, which depicts the energy of the subject, more than the material.
135   P. 15, *The Law and the Promise*, Neville Goddard.
136   P. 72, *Reality Transurfing IV*, Vadim Zeland.

The more indifferent you are to your order, the sooner it comes to you[137]. Clear your intent of craving[138], and attachment- and awareness and intent will let you get what's yours, without struggle[139]. Pure intent means thinking about, and feeling the goal, as if it has already been attained. When you go with the flow, everything falls into place, without extra effort[140].

Neville Goddard noted that YHWH[141] is the name by which all things are made, and without it there is nothing made that is made. This is the full expression of consciousness, and it is a formula of manifestation, and healing. It is the Law of Resonant Attraction in action. As such, it is a medicine wheel, a Ba Gua, a Mandala. The Medicine Wheel starts with the stirring in the East, the dawn that lights up awareness of the goal with desire, the element Air, which is movement.

Then comes South, the will, noon, the dowsing question, the element of Fire, which energizes, lights up the goal, and burns away limitations and blockages. Then comes West, the flowing emotions- feeling, dusk, Water, going to sleep knowing it real, or entering silence. Then comes North, the physical, Earth, the answer, perhaps in a dream; the goal realized, at midnight. This formula, in practice, is as follows, according to Neville Goddard[142].

The *first* step in projective dowsing, in changing the future, is the clarity of knowing exactly what you seek. The *second* step is to use open questions to define what you seek, to imagine an event

---

137   Pp. 58, 62, *Reality Transurfing III: Forward to the Past*, Vadim Zeland.
138   P. 63, *Reality Transurfing III: Forward to the Past*, Vadim Zeland.
139   P. 71, *Reality Transurfing III: Forward to the Past*, Vadim Zeland.
140   P.76, *Reality Transurfing III: Forward to the Past*, Vadim Zeland.
141   The Hebrew letters for the name of God were YOD HE VAU HE. Yod means hand. The hand fashions and molds both thought and physical. It also is what seeks. It is your awareness of being aware. In darkness, one puts one's hands out, and moves forward slowly. Yod forms all the other letters, and signifies omnipresence. It forms the world to come. HE means window. A window is to a house what an eye is to the body. It is imagination, and the ability to perceive something other than self. It means Look! Behold!, breath, revelation, light, and creative power. It combines the Aleph and Daleth, to mean God in the Human Heart. This is also the image of what one seeks. VAU means nail, tentpeg, or hook, which binds things together. It joins heaven and earth. VAU is also the word "and". This is feeling, and the ability to feel that you are now what you desire to be, to become aware of being what you were aware of, in the "heaven" of the dimensionally larger inner world. You nail it down, with intent [consciousness collapses the wave] from the waveform, into particle reality. The second HE, is another window, or eye. This is the realization of the dream of the first HE, in the physical world, the visible objective world, the mirror of thought, of what you are conscious of being, nailed down with the nail, or tentpeg, of Vau, of feeling it real.
142   Adapted from several books by Neville Goddard.

that would happen AFTER the realization of your desire[143]. You can simply limit this phase to asking open-ended questions.

The _third_ step is to relax, and induce a sleepy state, of an Alpha or Theta EEG[144]. Then, be inside that event, here and now, looking out through your own eyes, hearing through your own ears, doing it, feeling your feelings in your own body. If you use only the open ended questions, feel your subconscious lighting up neural nets, inside and outside of you, as it seeks the answer.

You participate directly in the imaginary action, in an associated way. This is not standing back and looking on, but FEELING that you are doing it, with the imaginary sensation feeling totally real[145].

If you wanted to get promoted, for example, you could pick a scene of being congratulated, having already achieved this[146]. Storyboarding was introduced in 1931, to guide the creation of animated movies[147]. Basically, a master picture for the scene is created, which guides scene development, in the subsequent frames. Neville discusses the creation of the master picture here, which the flow fleshes out.

---

143 Condense the fulfillment of the desire into a single event. If it is shaking a man's hand, then only do that. Do not shake it, then light a cigarette and do a thousand other things. Imagine actually shaking hands, and keep the act going over and over, until it feels totally real. Re-enact it until it feels real. If your attention wanders, bring it back. There is no effort or tension. It is like going to the bathroom in your house- you just go, there is no need to try, or strain, to get there, you just go, and you are there. Feel it real, and then, in a relaxed and drowsy state, repeat over and over again like a lullaby, a short phrase which implies fulfillment of your desire, such as, "Thank you, thank you, thank you", as though you addressed a higher power for having given you that which you desired. This is a "controlled waking dream." You are always an actor in this dream, never the audience. Be aware of polarization. You feel it real with as little effort as possible. If you "try", and tense up, and try to control it, you invoke the opposite polarity, of not having it. To desire or crave means you do not now possess what you desire, and because all things are yours, you rob yourself by living in the state of desire.Your attention seems to completely relax. You hold your attention within that feeling, without using force, and without using effort. There is no will power in this. If you can't run this movie, then reduce the idea, as a feeling, condense it to a single, simple phrase, I.e. _Isn't it wonderful_ or _Thank you_ or _It's done_ or _It's finished_. Three words work well. Repeat the phrase over and over like a lullaby. Feel it real. Breathe life into it. Know that the Universe has so many options that everyone benefits from your successes. Be so totally in state that you are shocked to find yourself elsewhere, when you open your eyes. There is no reason to worry about the how, when you already are it. Leave your three-dimensional reasoning out of this. Don't think it. You may observe a lovely liquid blue light, in meditation, like burning alcohol on a plum pudding. Huna breathing will take you to this space, as well.
144 This is a MASSIVE omission from _The Secret_. OK, they discussed it a little, but not enough.
145 Neville said he never saw Neville do anything, because he was never a spectator. He was always the the actor playing the part, looking out through his own eyes, hearing with his own ears, feeling feelings in his imaginary body.
146 José Silva might have a dark frame of the current situation, on the right, in imagination, and then a brightly lit frame on the left, of the desired situation, in what he called Mirror of the Mind, or even 3 frames showing a progression. Tad James would step out of the picture of it already done, and plant it at the ideal place on one's future timeline.
147 P. 82, _The Art of Walt Disney from Mickey Mouse to the Magic Kingdoms_, Christopher Finch.

Create a picture in which your goal or answer has been achieved, and you feel fantastic. Feel you already have what you seek. Keep playing the slide[148]/movie. Each time you do this you are nailing it down with the tentpeg, or nail of the letter Vau, or intent. Be aware there is lag time[149], which is hard to understand, because we get immediate results when we work in the physical world, on physical things. Attention must be fixated on already having it[150]. Gently follow the unfolding of events[151]. Neville says one must <u>enter into</u> the state, and not think of the state, to think <u>from inside it</u>, not of it[152].

The *fourth* step is when it shows up in the physical[153]. That is the law of resonant attraction. The rest of this book discusses calibration and variations of this process, and other ways to put it to use[154].

If this is too much for you, you can also use quantum questions, such as *What would have to happen for this to occur? What are the infinite possibilities for this occurring?* Just asking these questions invokes the process. If you can do this in a very relaxed, drowsy state, so much the better.

Neville Goddard notes that when you enter the state bordering on sleep, you are still able to control the direction of your thoughts. You are attentive, without effort or strain. Imagine a friend standing before you. You put your imaginary hand into his, feeling it solid and real. You speak and hear him speak, in an imaginary conversation, with the feeling of already having been promoted, for example. You do not visualize yourself watching this from a distance. The elsewhere is here, and the future is now. This is a great dowsing state.

---

148   P. 62, *The Magic of Believing*, Claude M. Bristol, uses the word "slide".
149   Neville used to say that no two eggs have the same lag time between fertilization and hatching.
150   P. 35, *Reality Transurfing V. Apples Fall to the Sky*, Vadim Zeland.
151   P. 37, *Reality Transurfing V. Apples Fall to the Sky*, Vadim Zeland.
152   As Neville puts it, spiritual discernment is when we get out of the evidence of the senses, and enter an invisible state, feeling it and sensing it, until it is real. The natural man receiveth not the things of the Spirit of God: for they are foolishness unto him: neither can he know them, because they are **spiritually discerned**. I Cor. 2:14 No endorsement of religion implied, however, wisdom is everywhere, when you are open to it.
153   Wong Kiew Kit, in his book *The Art of Chi Kung*, notes that a factory worker had his own factory in a year, using basically this method.
154   Consider this manifesting sequence: Make a list of 108 specific wishes. Clarify your vision, create a perfect day in your imagination. Believe you are worthy of receiving it, believe you can get it. Stretch your imagination, belief, and passion. Do what you can do now, even if you are afraid. Learn from experience, and be persistent. Pp. 53-59, 81, *The Aladdin Factor*, Jack Canfield and Mark Victor Hansen. It's the same thing, with a few twists.

The difference between feeling yourself in the center of the event, here and now, and seeing yourself as if watching yourself on an imaginary movie screen, can be the difference between success and failure[155]. If you watch yourself on a roller coaster, that is one thing. If you see yourself riding on the roller coaster, looking out through your own eyes, you get a whole different set of feelings. Ride inside the roller coaster, metaphorically, for this exercise[156].

G. The Role of Imagination

To start your own game, you have to let yourself be you[157], to let yourself fully show up. Let you be who you truly are, and let other people be who they really are; abandon control[158]. When you let go, the world becomes friendly[159]. When you get out of the way, and simply are, there is nothing to do, you are no-mind playing with no matter, so that everything is possible. Give death to what we think Truth is, so the real truth can come in[160].

You hold focused intent in mind, and a larger force or power manifests through that intent. A solid object becomes wavefront patterns, and then becomes a new physical outcome[161], your dowsing information, slightly later[162].

---

155   When you look out of your own eyes, hear with your own ears, and feel your feelings in your own body, in an imagined experience, you live it, and your subconscious mind knows it to be real. P. 40, *Wishing Well*, Steven Hall.
156   Here is another Neville method, for dealing your deepest wounds, or fears: Take your fondest dream. What is stopping you from having it right now? Can you take this through the chain of limiting beliefs to "I'm not good enough?" , as an example. What happens if you aren't good enough- what is the worst possible outcome? Could it be you would lose all that's important- and enter annihilation? Enter that now… feel it- and come out the other side. What do you see? Breathe deeply. This is crucifixion and rebirth. You could two point quantum measure this, to help fix it in your body, also. Thank you Robert Winn, for reminding me of this.
157   P. 66, *Reality Transurfing IV*, Vadim Zeland.
158   P. 11, *Reality Transurfing IV*, Vadim Zeland.
159   P. 12, *Reality Transurfing IV*, Vadim Zeland.
160   P. 68, *Sound: Native Teachings and Visionary Art*, Joseph Rael.
161   All good stories have a premise, a unified whole, what happens to the characters as a result of what they do, the changes each grows into. If you don't plan to change, don't play with manifesting, or seek wholeness. Both require change, and growth. Premise statements involve character, which will be tested and forged in the fires of experience. They involve conflict, a struggle to some resolution of polarities, with something at risk. They involve a conclusion- the final state of being for the character. This is summed up in Neville Goddard's outcome picture. They involve a conviction, a statement about life, and what it means. You can easily find the premise of your proposed manifestation. Start with the end of your manifesting story, compare it to where you are now, and ask how the change came about, and how you changed. Adapted from P. 104, *The Key*, James N. Frey. This is why many Native American healers will ask what a sick person will do, with the gift of health, before they do anything else. If the person has no plans to change, the sick pattern will simply come back, and any healing effort will simply be wasted. You are where you are now because you wrote the script for the story you are living. Manifesting means writing a new script, it means starting out where you are, entering "the woods", the unknown, learning the new rules, having a death and rebirth, confronting one's doubts and limitations, and returning to the world, transformed.
162   P. 96, *Matrix Energetics*, Dr. Richard Bartlett.

Solving Problems with Dowsing **107** A book for new dowsers ISBN-10: 1482688573

The wave function must be more real than merely a probability wave[163]. Quantum wave functions are different from classical waves[164].

Wavelike aspects remain, until we perform a measurement, and then it suddenly reverts to being a particle. There is a discontinuous and nonlocal change of state, a quantum jump, as we pass from the wave function picture, to the reality of the measurements. When a dowsing measurement is performed, the state collapses down to something localized. This instant localization happens no matter how spread out the wave function may have been, before the measurement[165].

Inspiration, the result, your dowsing information, comes from the infinite self, infused with the personal self. The physical body fuses itself to the heart, to the center of consciousness. Celebration occurs. When inspiration appears, awareness fuses itself with the self, the self fuses itself with the heart.

The heart fuses itself with awareness, awareness creates a radiance, a sense of light, that creates linkages, and fuses itself to a sense of reality with everything else. Everything is in its proper perspective, having come together as one[166].

We are composed of light and information, or consciousness[167]. The physical elements in our material world come into being when we observe them[168]. When you get your thinking out of its usual linear patterns, you can access and integrate new information directly from the Void[169]. You can know nothing while doing nothing, and access everything.

The mind does not have the capacity to develop a formula of success, in every case. That's okay, choose, and then stay out of the way of the world bringing it to you. You don't have to know how[170].

163 P. 520, *The Road to Reality, a Complete Guide to the Laws of the Universe*, Roger Penrose.
164 P. 514, *The Road to Reality, a Complete Guide to the Laws of the Universe*, Roger Penrose.
165 P. 516, *The Road to Reality, a Complete Guide to the Laws of the Universe*, Roger Penrose.
166 My understanding of something Joseph Rael said.
167 P. 46, *Matrix Energetics*, Dr. Richard Bartlett.
168 P. 46, *Matrix Energetics*, Dr. Richard Bartlett.
169 P. 33, *Matrix Energetics*, Dr. Richard Bartlett.
170 P. 132, *Reality Transurfing III: Forward to the Past*, Vadim Zeland.

Do not labor for the means to the end; rather, live imaginatively in the feeling of the wish, the solution, your dowsing question, fulfilled[171]. The flow always generates the most elegant and optimal solution[172]. The flow of life is always in the direction of what you have chosen[173]. Your life path is a succession of sectors of possibility in the Void, which you activated with your Intent[174].

Imagination creates reality[175]. Practice feeling things where your conscious mind cannot track the outcome[176]. What would it feel like if your life were better than the best you can imagine?
Facts are made up, they are compressions of information, which can be changed. If you change what you imagine, you change the facts[177].

Imagination is not tied to the senses, or enclosed within the body. Imagination is self[178]. You realize your dreams by imagining them already here, in the feeling of the wish fulfilled[179].

Attempting to change circumstances, before you change your imaginal activity, is only struggle. It's like trying to brush your teeth by putting the brush on your bathroom mirror. Abandon yourself mentally to your wish fulfilled, in your love for that state, live in the new state, and no longer in the old state. You cannot commit yourself to what you do not love. So combine absolute faith with love, and enter into the image in your imagination[180]. When you change your thought image, you enter a new lifeline[181], a new virtual address in the Void, of a new possibility.

Imagination is an art form. Mental images trigger many of the same information processing mechanisms active during ordinary visual perception[182].

---

171 P. 59, *The Law and the Promise*, Neville Goddard.
172 P. 95, *Reality Transurfing V. Apples Fall to the Sky*, Vadim Zeland.
173 P. 133, *Reality Transurfing III: Forward to the Past*, Vadim Zeland.
174 P. 14, *Reality Transurfing I: The Space of Variations*, Vadim Zeland.
175 P. 10, *The Law and the Promise*, Neville Goddard.
176 P. 136, *Matrix Energetics*, Dr. Richard Bartlett.
177 P. 135, *The Law and the Promise*, Neville Goddard.
178 P. 19, *The Law and the Promise*, Neville Goddard.
179 P. 30, *The Law and the Promise*, Neville Goddard.
180 Pp. 13-14, *The Law and the Promise*, Neville Goddard.
181 P. 105, *Reality Transurfing IV*, Vadim Zeland.
182 What you perceive comes from what you focus on with your attention. Most people are fixated on the physical. When you refocus your attention, whole new possibilities emerge, more of your potential becomes available, without needing external cause to make it happen. You might learn to be more open and curious when you notice an emotion,

Learning creative imagination is one of the lessons offered in life's school. Creative imagination is not exactly visualizing. Creative imagination brings, into this world, something that exists elsewhere, unfolding it from the implicate order into the explicable order, by compression. Creative imagination unveils what is real, but hidden[183]. For Sufis, the creative power of imagination is called *himma*, the power of the heart[184].

The imagined object is as real to the perceiver as the real object is, in the material world[185]. Active imagination guides, anticipates, and molds sense perception, and changes sensory data into symbols. It perceives the intermediate world to get better sensory data, and get more understanding of the knowledge of the divine[186].

In Sufism, the material world of the apparent and external, *zahir,* has its corresponding hidden side, *batin,* which is a world of idea images of subtle substances, and immaterial matter, where visionary images appear in their true reality. The organ of this universe is the active imagination[187]. The Sufi Ibn cArabi used active imagination, for spiritual work[188], as did everyone else who ever worked in the field of manifesting, and dowsing. By concentrating the active imagination, one is capable of creating objects, and producing changes in the outside world[189].

You create your own reality[190]. Once a pattern is selected and grown, it also serves as an antenna, that draws more of the selected energy back to it.

---

or particular interest. You might respond differently to an event, such as fear- perhaps you would examine it from another perspective, instead of running. When you know you decide how you experience the events of your life, you begin uniting inner and outer worlds, and coming back from separation. You select what you experience, with more clarity and certainty. You depend less on external stimulation. You accept life more. Evolution becomes the goal of experience. You respond to the movements of Spirit, and know them as the breath that gives you life. You find you don't have to do anything except relax, surrender, and allow the Spirit to move you, which frees you from attachment and expectation. Your ego fuses to your larger self. Unconditional reality is the now. One develops a great sense of humor. You become the Experiencer. Life unfolds in natural order, and you attain fulfillment not by directing it, but by BEING it. Pp. 227-31, *The Keys of Jeshua,* Glenda Green.

183   Pp. 127-8, *The Divining Heart: Dowsing and Spiritual Unfoldment,* Patricia and Richard Wright.
184   P. 221, *Creative Imagination in the Sufism of Ibn cArabi,* Henry Corbin.
185   P. 113, "Levels of Equivalence in Imagery and Perception", *Psychological Review,* 87:113–32
186   Pp. 239, 282. *Creative Imagination in the Sufism of Ibn 'Arabi,* translated from the French by R. Manheim; H. Corbin.
187   Pp. 4, 13, 78, *Creative Imagination in the Sufism of Ibn 'Arabi,* translated from the French by R. Manheim; H. Corbin. Neville Goddard would agree.
188   P. 32, *Portals: Opening Doorways to Other Realities Through the Senses,* Lynne Hume.
189   P. 237, *Creative Imagination in the Sufism of Ibn 'Arabi,* translated from the French by R. Manheim; H. Corbin. Neville Goddard would agree.
190   P. 97, *Matrix Energetics,* Dr. Richard Bartlett.

The energy of love and joy powers the spiraling force of life, but it is weakened when compassion and caring fail to flow through it.

We can choose- and dowse- what we want to grow more of, to draw into our lives, and use this information to influence evolutionary changes in our DNA, and create the lives of our dreams. Compassion and Love fuel the spiraling nature of all life, from the tiniest photons to the greatest galaxies. Sweet love and powerful joy drive the spiraling force of life through our hearts, to power our lives, when we act in harmony with our higher selves[191]. Objective reality is produced through imagination[192].

Visualize the intended change clearly, have total confidence, with focused and sustained emotional force behind the intent[193].

You make up the rules for how you experience reality[194]. What you can think and perceive limits what you can achieve[195]. We are made up of high energy photons. We are basically only patterns of light and information[196]. All you need to do is change the way you perceive and experience reality.

Live in the feeling of the wish fulfilled[197]. Nothing stands between you and the fulfillment of your dreams[198] except facts, which are the creations of imagining, that you've made up[199]. Change your imagining, and you change the facts[200]. When you change your past, you change your life. Your present problems are unrevised scenes from the past. Revise them[201], change your representation of them- and you change them, and yourself.

---

191 Pp. 111-2, *In the Presence of High Beings: What Dolphins Want You to Know*, Bobbie Sandoz-Merrill.
192 P. 11, *The Law and the Promise*, Neville Goddard.
193 P. x, *Matrix Energetics*, Dr. Richard Bartlett.
194 P. 51, *Matrix Energetics*, Dr. Richard Bartlett.
195 P. 39, *Matrix Energetics*, Dr. Richard Bartlett.
196 P. xix, *Matrix Energetics*, Dr. Richard Bartlett.
197 P. 18, *The Law and the Promise*, Neville Goddard.
198 In a lecture, Neville remembered an artist who had no food, or money to buy it with. She lay down on her couch, and said, "Lord, if I believe, all things are possible. I believe I am well fed." She got a sense that she needed to set the table, in her imagination, so she did. She went to sleep, in this state. Then the telephone woke her up. A friend of her mother's said she really wanted to re-experience a meal she prepared for her, some years ago. She asked if the artist would do it again, that night, if she brought over the ingredients. She showed up in an hour, and they had a great dinner, with leftovers. My brother does this with deals. His friends, and I, are in awe of his skill with this. He bought a VW Bug, in high school, for the price of the tires on it, and had it running the same day. He drove that car for some years.
199 P. 15, *The Law and the Promise*, Neville Goddard.
200 P. 15, *The Law and the Promise*, Neville Goddard.
201 "Though your sins are like scarlet, they shall be as white as snow". P. 16, *The Law and the Promise*, Neville Goddard. The word for sin in the New Testament came from a greek word that implied missing a target. What do you do when you miss? You refine, and throw again. In time, you hit the target. So it is with dowsing.

The past and the future are possible outcomes, which can be altered. Past and future are connected to the present as possibilities[202]. The problem is only one possible configuration of light and information, which can be reconfigured, based on how we choose to perceive[203]. If you have an injury in the past, revision it[204], recompress it to something more useful.

You can imagine a new outcome, in which the event or trauma never happened in the way you thought it did[205]. Live in your dream, until you live in it, as fact[206].
Relive your day, before you go to bed, as you wish you had lived it, revising the scenes so they conform to your ideals[207].

The goal of life in the process of serving the Creator consists of co-creating[208]. The Creator gave the freedom and power to every living being to shape its reality- to the extent of its consciousness. Everyone has freedom of choice. However, few use it[209]. The language of the Creator is creation. When you believe in your own abilities, you believe in the Creator, and realize these words[210].

Feel energy moving through your body. Don't control or force it, just notice it, allow it. It shows up when you ask the question, when you put your attention on it. The more you notice it, the stronger it gets. Notice it start to engulf a limb, then your body. Perhaps it is a tingling, a rush, something. Don't limit it with expectation or intent, or anything else[211]. Just notice it[212].

---

202 The Eagles Quest, Fred Allen Wolf.
203 P. 48, Matrix Energetics, Dr.Richard Bartlett.
204 Pp. 40, 41, The Law and the Promise, Neville Goddard.
205 P. 147, Matrix Energetics, Dr. Richard Bartlett, and every book Neville Goddard wrote.
206 P. 18, The Law and the Promise, Neville Goddard.
207 P. 33, The Law and the Promise, Neville Goddard.
208 P. 88, Reality Transurfing IV, Vadim Zeland.
209 P. 97, Reality Transurfing IV, Vadim Zeland.
210 P. 88, Reality Transurfing IV, Vadim Zeland.
211 Limiting the way your manifestation can come to you is extremely limiting. P. 47, The Greatest Manifestation Principle in the World, Carnelian Sage.
212 Wong Kiew Kit's book The Art of Chi Kung, among others, has exercises on noticing Chi. I am not discussing Chi Kung, however, for those who want more, that could be a useful path. This book is complete as is, however some people always want more.

Enter the gap between, the Void, no-mind, meditative space, the place where thoughts aren't. You may not notice anything for a time. Know that whatever happened needed to happen, it was appropriate. Drop it. Letting it go is your thanks[213].

I don't know, but when I do this exercise, or just enter the Void, when I come back out, I feel refreshed, as if I had been in a negentropic place. Perhaps we enter this state when we sleep, also. Perhaps energetic conditions appearing as what some might call diseases could vanish, in this state, I don't know.[214]

What one thing could you notice, right now, that would vastly improve your dowsing, and ability to solve problems?

---

213   For those who want more, congratulations- you completed a mini VisionQuest!
214   There is a scene in the *Lord of the Rings* where the elves leave Middle Earth, symbolic of the departure of magic. Yet Magic, and wholeness, never departed from us, we departed from it. It is delighted to return to us, if politely invited, respected, and welcomed. It was always with us, in our hearts.

Solving Problems with Dowsing **113** A book for new dowsers ISBN-10: 1482688573

H. Useful Sequences

Filling your own cup
1. Relax, breathe deeply, enter heartspace.
2. Think about the excitement of being with a great companion, a great friend, a lover, a beloved spiritual master. Really feel that. Let it expand.
3. Create a clone, a hologram, of yourself, across from you[215]. Let your excitement flow into that hologram, which is of course you. Imagine this hologram having already realized all its dreams, now, effortlessly, easily, playfully. Imagine it whole and complete, a radiant center of light. Enter your hologram, and feel all that energy coming at you from you.
4. Feel that energy continuing to flow to you. Feel what it feels like to be overflowing with love. Feel gratitude, feel so full you don't need anything. Move back into yourself[216]. In all cases, when you do sequences, or any exercise, you want to start in a positive state. This is a good state to begin exercises from. Mark this state, with some kind of anchor, so you can get into it in a second or two. This will also tend to blow out secondary intent, or counter intent.
5. If you have someone, or a situation, or an experience that keeps happening, that is irritating, or a problem, you can have that in front of you- in your imagination- and light this up, in the same way[217]. Note if you have any parts attached to them. Don't label or judge this, just note the pattern. The pattern may change all by itself, under your attention, or you might unravel it, or throw a pebble in the middle of it. It might dissipate.
6. Know that it is shifting, and changing, under your observation, in fact you can't stop the change. You will note that your attachment to this feels different, which means it will continue to change. The next time you encounter the person or situation, in the flesh, note the changes. Observe these.

---

215   Actually everybody else is a hologram of you as well, you just may not perceive this yet.
216   Keep the hologram around, it can do tasks for you, if you ask.
217   Discussed also at p. 163, *Practical Intuition*, Laura Day.

Think of a human being as an extremely sophisticated multidimensional organic autonomous computer. The heart is the CPU. We have short-term working memory in the conscious mind, and short term memory in the brain. Long-term memory is in the body cells, with a RAID backup array in the hologram. The machine language is frequencies, or information, transmitted by light. The primary programming language consists of images, sounds, and feelings.

The subconscious mind runs numerous operations in the background, even when the input devices of our senses are switched off. The subconscious mind does this because it runs programs, some installed by the manufacturer, and some installed later. Belief systems function as memory resident programs. Old programs that don't serve your current needs may simply not be useful. When you get rid of programs that you don't need anymore, the entire system works better[218].

Let us consider an example. Imagine someone was told they had an incurable disease, when they were younger. This is not a useful belief. Think of the EEG states as floors that you access with an elevator, or stairs. A belief installed when you were young, perhaps in the theta state, must be removed in the theta state[219]. Here is one sequence for doing this:

1. Relax, breathe deeply, enter heart space.
2. Scan. Notice what you notice.
3. You may be aware of a feeling. It may not feel very good. You may get an associated image of an adult figure in anger, or sadness, telling you that you have an incurable disease, and then the bad feelings of starting to believe it. It's okay if you don't get this image.
4. If you do get the image, change it, so the adult(s) is(are) in a very loving space, telling you how healthy and happy you are. Remember, you're in a very relaxed place, and you are creating this memory. So create it a little differently, so that it's more useful to you.

---

218   Pp. 47-8, *Simple ways to access your intuition on demand*, John Living.
219   Metaphorically, if you want to throw out old shoes, you have to start in the closet they are stored in.

5. If not, there's another way. In your imagination, look out through your own eyes, into a mirror. Smile at yourself. Really appreciate yourself.
    Make a heart-to-heart connection to yourself. Think of something that feels good, that describes you with outstanding ability. To overwrite this negative programming, you could say something like
    Every moment of every day
    I'm so healthy in every way or
    I [my name] am healthy in every way.
    Every moment of every day
    [your name] is healthier in every way
    Every moment of every day
    You [your name] are healthier in every way

6. When you say this, be in a very relaxed place. Say it as if you were simply exploring something. Some people say affirmations like this on top of subconscious resistance to the idea. This is not useful. Instead of allowing subconscious resistance, why not simply imagine yourself in the mirror, getting more radiant, brighter and brighter with light? That's a much better activity to keep your conscious mind in.

7. If you feel really good as you're saying this, you're doing it correctly. Recall that your subconscious mind does not know the difference between images happening outside you, and images run by your imagination. If you're in a deep heart state, it may only be necessary to say this once. If not, just do it until it kicks in. There's no need to get obsessive about it, because this is a suggestion that you don't have it. Just feel already having it. If you like ceremony, you could do this for four days.
    Also, keep these very simple, one thing at a time. Lengthy complicated statements can be generated by the conscious mind, but they simply don't go anywhere. Clarity and simplicity are power.

8. As you go through your life, perhaps certain incidents happened where you used to indulge in negative self talk, such as perhaps telling yourself you were less than totally healthy. Consider these incidents, and, say something like *oh it's so wonderful that I'm reprogramming myself to*

Solving Problems with Dowsing **116** A book for new dowsers ISBN-10: 1482688573

have a wonderful life. And this incident reminds me of how much better I'm getting, because I do not pollute my being with negative self talk anymore.

9. The statement of itself is of course an affirmation, and a reprogramming.

10. More importantly, when things happen that suggest you are quite intelligent, or some other useful state, be sure you put a lot of attention on those, and say something like *oh it's so nice to be getting brighter and healthier every day, now.*

11. Since the people around you are only acting out what's in your subconscious mind, you may be surprised to notice that the input you get from other people gets more and more positive, in a subtle, at first easily overlooked, kind of way.

12. If you find a need to listen to sad music or read sad stories, to drain out your pain, that's fine. Finish up with some very invigorating music and images to clean out all this energy when you're done. The Johnny Nash song *I can see clearly now* is a perfect example of this. You cannot be depressed listening to Sousa marches, with your fists high in the air, and your eyes looking up to the heavens. I also change lyrics on songs that are no longer useful. For the Rolling Stones song. *I can't get no satisfaction,* I changed the lyrics to *I get all my... satisfaction... In my life... from the people around me, and it feels so... very good Now!* And then I imagine the guitar riff. For a time I was extremely depressed. I still get those same extremely depressing thoughts from time to time, but now I just don't entertain them anymore. Negative thoughts are like cinders on a shirt. Brush them off quickly, and they don't do any damage. Depression taught me a lot. I've seen people whose lives were such that they never had any depression, and they don't know how to handle negative events. I do, and I can help others going through them[220].

---

220 Once you master this, try Eve Brinton's Energy Exchange technique, as described in her book of that name. This is how I do it. I identify a no longer useful belief. I say, "*I release and remove the belief that my dowsing is not effective or accurate*". As I do this, I put my thumb, index, and middle finger into my mouth, as if I was pulling out a balloon, of the fixed belief, from my mouth, and all of my existence. I put the balloon to my side, and pop it. I keep doing this until the belief is 100% removed. Then I say, "*I replace this with the belief that my dowsing is extremely effective and accurate, and done even before I ask.*" I then say, "*I give thanks that my dowsing is extremely effective and accurate, and done even before I ask.*" I then say, in a heart-felt way, "*Thank you! Thank you! Thank you! Thank you!*" This

If you want a more detailed affirmation process, here is an example. Let us imagine someone who has been told they are not aware enough times that the belief was installed. That person could say this:

1. *In every minute of every day, You,* [your name] *are aware in every way* Repeat three more times, for a total of four[221].
2. Then say this in the third person, four times: *In every minute of every day, [your name] is aware in every way*
3. Then say in the first person: *In every minute of every day, I* [my name], *am aware in every way*[222]

Dowsing is focused awareness, so this is a useful belief system. Donna Eden, in her book *Energy Medicine*, suggests that when you're done with the affirmation, you lock it in by placing your finger on your pelvic bone, and running it up to your lip, along your governing meridian. You can also intend this is locked in.

Can you think of some belief systems that would be useful for dowsing? Here's an example:

1. I [your name] am one with my dowsing system. I always get correct information, and act on it in the right way.
2. You [your name] are one with your dowsing system, always getting correct information, and acting on it in the right way.
3. [Your name] is one with his/her dowsing system, always getting correct information, and acting on it in the right way, with excellent results that benefit all involved.

Test for % correct, and aligned, and intend this up to 100%.

---

technique is very simple, too simple for most. Much of her book is devoted to supporting a belief system to make use of her ideas possible. I footnote this, because it is an advanced technique that is too easy for a beginner to doubt. Advanced dowsers, just like advanced Martial artists, can do a lot of things in a very easy way, however it is necessary to build the foundation before the roof, metaphorically. May I say it is well worth reading her book, and I get nothing for saying that. You can also dowse the percentage of which a belief is present, or not present, also, which is fantastically useful feedback.

221   Doing things 3 times is an Indo-European custom. Hawaiians and Native Americans know 4 as the number of power, it earths the other three.

222   P. 87, *Intuition Technology*, John Living, Professional Engineer.

Bill Askin, who introduced Raymon Grace to dowsing, uses a sequence something like the following:

1. Pour a glass full of water. If you want to calibrate it, for comparison later, taste it, and remember the taste.
2. Use a pendulum, or similar dowsing device, as a physical metaphor, or visualize this, and make counterclockwise (CCW) rotations over the glass of water with the intent that *all things that are not good for you, including all toxins, are phase conjugated at 180°, and removed from the water.*
3. Dowse: *Has everything, that is not good for me, been removed from this water now?* Y/N
4. When you get a yes, taste the water to calibrate it. It almost certainly will taste somewhat better.
5. Now use your dowsing device to make CW[223] rotations over the glass of water, with the intent that *Everything necessary for your fantastically good health, wealth, love life, and service to others, are entered into the water.*
6. Dowse: *is this process now complete?* Y/N
7. Taste the water again to calibrate. It may taste even better yet, and now it has some very interesting vibrations in it.
8. Drink it down, perhaps with a feeling of gratitude to whatever intelligence helped you to have such good water.
9. You could also have the intent that the water, now pure, now has the ability to empty the toxins out of other water it comes into contact with, and that this spreads, with no loss of signal strength.
10. Dowse: *Does the water now have the ability to empty the toxins out of other water it comes in contact with?* Y/N
11. Once you get a yes, you can pour it into nature somewhere, or spray it. You can load this intent into snow and rain, if you wish.
12. You can also load the water with the specific intent of clearing less than useful energy in a room.

---

223 Note this simple application of Torsion Physics- CW tends to amplify, CCW removes. Note that intent above 200 on the Hawkins scale seems to be CW, also.

You can spread it in that room with a spray bottle. You can load water for your pets, in the same way[224].

You might want to play with dowsing, and intent. Here's a sequence you might enjoy:

Dowse: *Is my health over 50% of my ideal level, of health*[225]*?* Y/N
Dowse: *Is my health at 100% of my ideal level of health?* Y/N
If you get a no,
Dowse: *Is my dowsing system able and willing to make changes to increase my health now?* Y/N
Assuming you get a yes, Dowse:
Is there any reason not to request my system to do this now? Y/N
Assuming you get a no, Dowse:
Is my dowsing system willing and able to make those changes now, when I say, please go ahead and do it? Y/N
Assuming you get a yes, Say, *please go ahead and do it now.*
Scan, notice what you notice. You may get some fantastic imagery, internal sounds or unusual feelings. Or you may get nothing at all.

You might want to make a list of those things that could cause you stress. Test if they are stressing you unnecessarily. When you get a yes, you may wish to consider removing the stressors from your life.

You might want to test food in the grocery store for the presence of toxins[226]. If you get a strong yes, you may wish to avoid these foods. If you need to calibrate on toxins, there is a certain fast food chain that uses a clown as its corporate symbol. You might want to test whether the joke is on you, when you consume their food. Will you have a colostomy bag with that?

---

224 Pp. 139-144, *Simple ways to access your intuition on demand*, John Living. He adds that his own ideal blessing for water is something like "*I bless this water with 'true holy love. Namaste', with 'Blessings 995' and with 'Healing 997'. I send my gratitude and love to all who help in the ceremony*". I really like his book, and get nothing for saying so. Gary Douglas notes that anything physical has consciousness, and choice. Mostly it also wants to help. Which means, if you are dowsing water, it is dowsing you. Think about that- what you seek is seeking you. You can even connect with it, and ask for its help in what you seek. This is a very advanced point, if you are a new dowser, please ignore this.
225 P. 101, *Simple ways to access your intuition on demand*, John Living.
226 P. 105, *Simple ways to access your intuition on demand*, John Living, also the Abbe Mermet's book on dowsing. Test artificial sweeteners and fluoride for toxicity. Test microwaved food for vitality.

You can use your left hand as an intuitive scale[227], if you left your chart at home. You can also use your fingers to open portals to useful information, or even reach your hand into a portal.

Statements of intent can be useful. You might like to try a variant of this: *All of my dowsing is to serve the light and the highest good of all. I welcome the help of the light for my intuitive team and my own dowsing system, ensuring that all answers are absolute truth to the maximum level I can understand, obtained from sources of the light. Thank you thank you thank you.*
Dowse: *is my intuitive team, willing and able to work with the light, to spread the light?* Y/N when you get a yes, you are ready to begin. The programs you install may run outside of your consciousness, especially when you really need them[228].

---

227   P. 118, *Simple ways to access your intuition on demand*, John Living.
228   Be sure you're totally focused when you do this, in a state of inner peace. I feel much more confidence when I avoid doubters. Doubters do not help you, or themselves. It is best just to avoid them. I find that images of violence in my immediate environment are not useful. You might want to clean up your environment of anything that disturbs you, if you can. If you can't, at least put a thought form veil over it. Structure your questions carefully, within clearly defined boundaries. Generally it is better to get percentages, and averages, than strictly yes/no answers. The subconscious mind is very literal. If you ask if your car needs gas, you will always get a yes, because it always needs gas in the form of gasoline, and in the form of oxygen. It is better to test if the gas tank is more than 50% empty, right now, for example. It is helpful to test energy levels as an average, over a period of time, say, for a week. Just as with the stock market, sometimes there are spikes. These even out, over time. Prying into other people's personal business, without a very good reason, is generally not a way to serve the light, and your abilities will tend to shut down, if you invest a lot of time in this area. This is self enforcing. Most people's minds are so full of garbage, that you would just lower your own energy level. Only look if you have to. A strong intent of service will protect you from low-grade energy. It is helpful to ask *can I, may I, and should I ask questions in this area?* Or you can subsume them in the question: *Is there any reason not to ask questions in this area?* If you get a no, and you still feel a strong need to enter that area, you could phrase your questions differently. If you ask questions about the future, you can only get probabilities. When you are first starting out, you might want to test. *Have I correctly understood the truth?* or, *what is the percentage of the truth that I have understood?* Another useful question is, *did I make the correct decision with regards to serving the light and accomplishing my mission and purpose in life?* A question like, *should I marry this person?* will result in an answer that is unlikely to be useful. What are you seeking, as a result of the marriage? Are you seeking spiritual growth that would result from paying out half your after-tax income in child support, for 20 years? Are you seeking a loving partner with whom you could grow greatly? Are you seeking a loving partner who will hold up their end of the bargain, and not harass you mercilessly due to resentments about your not being as rich as J. Paul Getty, or as good looking as Photoshopped images in magazines? There is an Arabic proverb, *look for the mother,* [which is to say the woman you would like to be married to in about 20 years], *and then marry the daughter.* This proverb reflects a deep understanding of patterns playing out. You might want to test for addictions, level of resentment towards your gender, willingness to hurt you, based on resentments or whatever, the probability of their continued interest in sex, their ideal level of retail therapy, their respect for marriage vows, and whatever else is important to you. If, for example, you would like to have a nice family, it would not be useful to marry a woman or a man who is totally dysfunctional around family. There are more and more of them, and not just in the United States. *Will this car last a long time?* is not a useful question. Last- as an exhibit in a museum of lemon cars, that is, cars that don't work? For a long time as a perfect example of poor design? It would be better to test for the average dollar amount of repairs likely over the period of a year. Test the percentage of health for engine, transmission, electrical system, and so on. Test the compatibility of the car with you. Start out by testing the possible sources for a vehicle for the ideal vehicle for you, even before you start looking at the vehicle.

Is this a good house? Is not a useful question. Good for what? Wiping out a bank account? It would be better to test for the probability of repairs over $500 in specific systems to include roof heating, electrical, and so on, over the next 10 years. Test the percentage of ideal condition for the systems. Test for compatibility of the house with your entire family. Test the percent that you can improve the energy of the house and lot. Test the energy level of the neighborhood, and how much you can improve that. There is an Arabic proverb that says, *look for the neighbor first and then think about the house.* This reflects a deep understanding of process. A neighborhood full of nasty people probably has low energy levels. On the other hand, houses may be cheap there. If you test for the extent to which you can improve the energy of an area, and it is high, you may get quite a bargain that appreciates considerably, as the energy of the area improves.

Questions like What is the minimum offer that the seller would accept from me, where they would still want to do business with me for this product? would be very useful. *What is the ideal offer for this product, that would benefit all?*

Solving Problems with Dowsing **121** A book for new dowsers ISBN-10: 1482688573

Perhaps you'd like to install a few contingent programs, to turn on automatically if there is a situation where they would be useful.

What if joy is at the core of everything we seek?

---

might also be a useful question. Setting an intent demands even more clarity. Setting an intent that you have a Mercedes-Benz might bring you one that is 30 years old and rusted out. Is that really what you want? You don't have to specify a specific model, but you would set an intent to have a Mercedes-Benz in excellent condition, which serves you very well as a vehicle. You might go to a Mercedes-Benz dealership to sit down behind the wheel of a Mercedes. Run movies in your mind, looking out through your own eyes, contentedly driving that Mercedes on the road. Feel the feeling of already having it. *How do you feel now that you already have it? What you see here and feel as you enjoy this, in the now?*

Make images, and load emotions into your desired result, or outcome. Never look at what Mike Dooley calls the "accursed hows". If you're asking for money, don't ask for $300, for now, ask for all the ingredients of a good life. Love and gratitude are also extremely useful in any kind of intent work. Emotions, of course, need to be high-grade, above 200 on the Hawkins scale. If you use only one emotion, make sure that one emotion is love, where your intent helps others, and not just yourself. You get a major boost in helping your manifestation. Looking out through your own eyes, see yourself enjoying the desired result. Notice how your life has changed for the better. Notice how others also benefit from your already having this. Feel the appreciation of others for the benefits you brought to them, through this. Here are other people congratulating you. Is there a special food or drink that you drink, to celebrate your success, perhaps? What does it smell and taste like? Having already achieved this, how exciting is it to think of other ways that you can benefit yourself and others? The best time to seed your subconscious is when you're half awake, going to sleep or awakening, and especially if you wake up for a short time in the middle of the night. You might want to pick a unique symbol, which holds, only for you, all of the meaning in already having this.

The above gets you ready to work with intent around wholeness. Sickness is often a call from the deeper mind, to grow, to shed no longer useful belief systems, energies, and so on. Wholeness for a 7 year old is not what it is for a 21 year old, nor is that wholeness for a 40 year old. Wholeness often involves better service to others. If healing was as simple as saying magic words, or popping some concoction, you would have already done it. Healing involves change, from within. You can get help, you can get professional help, however only you can heal yourself.

Solving Problems with Dowsing **122** A book for new dowsers ISBN-10: 1482688573

What if life was about finding joy, and sharing it?

What if solving problems was a joyful process for you? How would that feel?

What if the problem felt joy, as it resolved, under your attention?

V. Setting the stage for the dowsing play

This section is designed to expand your mental model of what dowsing is. Your dreams are the children of your heart, the voice of your soul, God/the Universe seeking manifestation through you. They are important, they are part of your wholeness. You came here to manifest your wholeness, with them. Seeking wholeness is the same as seeking positive growth, it is dynamic, and shifting. Wholeness for you, ten years ago, was probably not what it is today, for you. Dowsing takes you into wholeness, continually. It takes you out of the world of the solely material, and into a balance between matter and energy.

Start by asking yourself questions:

1. What do I seek from life? What are my top seven desires?

2. What will I see, hear, feel, and know, when I have successfully manifested or realized them?

3. What are my five biggest blocks, fears, issues, limitations, problems, shortcomings, or stories about why I can't have what I want?

4. What would my life be like without these?

5. If I had a book that had powerful dowsing tools, how could I have fun with that?

6. What would I love to create or experience, in wholeness, using the tools in this book?
I mean, what would make me want to dance in the street, if I got it?

7. What de-energizes me? How can I do less of that?

8. What energizes me? How can I do more of that?

Using your answers to the above, <u>write down</u> your main intent, maybe even on this page, for reading this book, and learning how to dowse. If your intent is to sample ideas, you'll get some benefit. If your intent is to doubt, you will have much to doubt.

If your intent is to totally transform your life into something better than the best you can imagine, you will get that. Intent is something like a GPS, you type in your destination, follow the path of awareness, through dowsing, and you get there. There may be no feedback, until you get the final leg, the home stretch, of the journey. Intuition- dowsing- could be called a sixth sense. Dowsing has four modes:

1. Pushing a message into conscious awareness, when the matter is important, even if the recipient is not usually open to it.
2. [Constantly] giving messages to people who are open to it.
3. Responding to questions asked by those who actively seek help.
4. Transmitting intent.

The first three are *reflective* dowsing. The last one is *projective* dowsing. All dowsing is opening up to awareness, or the flow of information.

The more aware we are of our environment, the easier it is to be aware of changes in our perception. It is very important to notice what we notice. When we are fully aware, we ask the question, and then note the changes to the environment. This is the shadow of intuition changing its point of attention, to give you your guidance. If the answer isn't quite clear, you can ask for clarification[1].

Start collecting pictures of what you want. In fact, do a Vision Board this weekend, for one of these areas: health, wealth, or love. Collect Internet images, and put them in a PowerPoint presentation, if you like.

---

1   Pp. 20-1, *Intuition Technology*, John Living, Professional Engineer.

It's time to start feeding your consciousness with images of what you seek. Find images that inspire you: scenes from nature, people having fun, houses, cars, things you'd love to have, and so on.

Find images that give you high grade FEELINGS of abundance, joy, love, peace, and any other high energy state you'd like. If there's anything that doesn't feel good in your house, get rid of it, if you can, or at least store it where you don't see it much.

Please say right now: *I request a most benevolent outcome from working with the ideas in this book, with results better than the best I can imagine.*

This is a useful intent to start with. You might even want to start every day with an intent like this[2]. We create our own reality, as our inner subconscious reality draws us into situations from which we learn[3]. So, every day, intend that your day goes well, that you're in the flow, see opportunities, have fun, and are full of vitality. Make this conscious intention as regular as breathing[4].

A. Why are we here?

People seek meaning in life, and turn to stories[5]. In New Mexico, descendents of the Anasazi, fundamentalists with their Bibles[6], and physicists and biologists seek order in the randomness.

---

2 Thanks to Tom T. Moore, for his book *The Gentle Way*, on this extremely effective, if subtle, tool.
3\ -Dr. Edgar Mitchell, P. 137, *Gamma Healing,* Chris Walton.
4 P. 136, *Gamma Healing,* Chris Walton.
5 The myth-making facility is inherent in the thinking process, and it satisfies a basic human need. *Myth and Modern Man*, Raphael Patai.
6 Dowsing is very much present in the Bible, if that matters to you. The world was created with an act of projective dowsing, of intent formulated, and then spoken. Exodus 28:29-30 notes the use of the Urim and Thummim, which were clearly dowsing devices, noted at Exodus 28:30, Leviticus 8:8, Numbers 27:21, Deuteronomy 33:8, 1 Samuel 28:6, Exra 2:63, and Nehemiah 7:65, as acceptable. Proverbs 16:33 and 18:18 notes dowsing devices. Genesis 44:5 notes that Joseph used a cup for divination- for dowsing. Jacob used projective dowsing to put branches in front of sheep and goats, so there would be ones that were streaked, speckled, and spotted. Harmful work was of course proscribed, as at 1 Samuel 28:3-15. Dowsing was used in the Qumran community, which produced the Dead Sea scrolls. This is no surprise. The Israelites got many ideas from the Egyptians, who got their ideas from the Babylonians. All of these practiced dowsing in some form. The Romans practiced dowsing. Note also that literate cultures, which the Hebrews were becoming, tend to move away from intuition. Their concept of God, and the Universe, is vastly different from that of non-literate cultures. There is variation even among literate cultures. When a telenovela soap opera in Mexico is planned, the entire cast and crew go to a church, to pray- to projectively dowse- for success of the telenovela. Interestingly, Mexican telenovelas are successful worldwide, notably in Russia. Can you imagine American soap opera production teams doing this?

Each seeks answers to the question of why we are here. Science and religion create creation myths, stories that give our lives meaning[7]. This must be important. Why are we here? Here are some thoughts, which you can dowse for accuracy:

We are here to find wholeness, which is a moving target.
We come here to experience choice, and to learn to choose love over fear.
We come here to experience joy, and to share it.
We come here to help each other[8].
We come here to help each other find wholeness.
We come here to manifest[9].
We come here to use and embody metaphor, and practice imagining[10].
Whatever you deeply feel demands to be given form, and released[11].
Without desire, you cannot grow[12].

We are here to become celebration and generosity, we are a portal where the Universe celebrates its existence. It constantly offers useful information, for those willing to tune in, through dowsing.

You already create your world, perhaps unconsciously. If you weren't, it couldn't exist. This book is intended to lead you to where you resonate with wholeness, so you consciously choose what you will dowse and create, and then become dynamically and effortlessly whole, in alignment with your larger self[13]. The Law of Attraction is very simple. It is really a Law of Resonant Attraction[14], or creation. Dowsing means asking the right question, which puts you into resonance with the answer.

---

7   P. 26, *Fire in the Mind: Science, Faith, and the Search for Order*, George Johnson.
8   Manitonquat/Medicine Story, the Wampanoag elder, told me this, well it's also in all religions. This is a very basic truth that is so mundane it is invisible, and yet extremely powerful.
9   P. 144 , *Sound: Native Teachings and Visionary Art*, Joseph Rael.
10   From many of Neville Goddard's books.
11   Pp. 146-7, *The Universe is a Green Dragon*, Brian Swimme.
12   P. 132, *The Way of the Wizard*, Deepak Chopra.
13   True happiness comes in looking from higher values. This is the only way we can shape shift through these times. P. 25, *Shapeshifting into Higher Consciousness*, Llyn Roberts.
14   This is not about deserving or working for it- though you might- it is about becoming the change you seek, identifying with it totally, like a moth in a candle flame. The delay between intent and manifestation allows you to fine tune it. Negativity and "bad" stuff allow for comparisons, so you know what you do like, and seek. This time lag seems to be shortening, have you noticed?

Basically, you change your energy to a frequency that is totally in resonance with what you seek- you feel already having it, now- and you are in the point of possibility in the zero point field where you do already have it. That is dowsing in a nutshell. If you seek to create something physical, with this process, there is a lag before it shows up in the physical.

You attract what you are in resonance with[15], you attract what you are. If you want to improve your life, stop believing, feeling, and thinking about what you don't want, and *start believing, feeling[16], and thinking about what supports you, and what would support your growth[17]*. If you think of what you don't like, you get what you don't want[18]. Align yourself with what you seek, to support dowsing.

Intent is pure love[19]. If you're feeling anything less than peace, love, joy, contentment, wonder, and so on, you're focusing on what you don't want, or judging[20], or wallowing in negativity. Feelings come from thoughts.

Ask yourself *"What do I want? What would I really enjoy, now?"*, and start concentrating on that, instead. You never want things as things. You seek the feelings having the things will bring to you[21]. You can create those feelings right now.

What would it feel like, if your dream was real, right now? What would you see, hear, and feel if you already had whatever you seek? Spend as much time as you can, in that state of being. 90% of success is having a clear intent[22]. Then, take action as you feel guided to do so.

---

15 So many people see manifesting and praying and LoA as basically pleas to, metaphorically, save the sand-castle from encroaching tides. This is driving by looking in the rear view mirror. It is better to look in the heart, to see what it seeks. Many LoA efforts, prayers, manifesting efforts, and so on, cannot be answered, because people refuse to receive. Pp. 61, 74, *The Keys of Jeshua*, Glenda Green.

16 Don't ask "What should I feel?" Ask what you do feel, and you will be on the right path. Let go of your preconceived ideas and expectations, and your vitality emerges naturally. P. 14, *The Breathing Book*, Donna Farhi.

17 Beliefs can be harmful as well as helpful. P. 180, *The Keys of Jeshua*, Glenda Green.

18 Pp. 21-22, *Reality Transurfing I: The Space of Variations*, Vadim Zeland, and all of Neville Goddard's books.

19 P. 26, *The Power of Intention*, Wayne Dyer.

20 Judging others puts a negative possibility in ourselves. P. 180, *The Keys of Jeshua*, Glenda Green.

21 So don't think, feel, like the Neil Diamond song said. The key is to release resistance, to feel your default state of happiness, lightness, joy. Trying to solve the problem is resisting the solution. Let go, and be what you seek. It is not enough to create, speak, draw, and focus on the vision. One must feel it as having already happened. -p. 84, *Butterflies and Dreams*, Dorothy Peltier-Fanchi.

22 When I made the decision to edit numerous notebooks, to create this book, somehow the entire Universe started helping me. It was as if books on my shelf jumped out at me, with pages opened to useful ideas. The idea of service-helping others- through my notes- energized this, also. The principles in this book made it possible for me to put this book together.

Some religions talk about killing out desire[23]. This is useful, if the desires don't support your growth. If your desires do support your growth, and that of others, the best way to handle them is to focus them, so you attract them into your life. Desires that support your growth, and that of others, come from the heart. You can dowse, change, or manifest anything[24], because everything is made of energy. You will find force multipliers in here, to speed up these processes.

One major force multiplier is creating for the highest good of all, of service[25]. Another major force multiplier is having fun. I read over 2,000 books, and attended a number of seminars, during 40 years of seeking, before I could write this book. What follows is the refined essence of some of what I learned[26].

As with all learning, I was confused when I started, and continued in that confused state. Eventually understanding crystallized. However, I still seek out confusion[27], so I can be sure I'm still learning. I grew up in Oriental countries, which are comfortable with ambiguity. Perhaps that helped me. That which is fixed, sure, crystallized, scientifically provable, detectable with focused foveal vision, and touch; and also definite, is less than 1% of life.

The vast majority of life, including everything we work with in dowsing, exists in the space between this space, between 100% present, and 0% probability of existing. What you seek to manifest is in this space between, also. Learn to pay attention to the space between, to what is not absolutely definite.

---

23 Neville Goddard would also say to kill out desire. He would say to ask yourself what it would feel like, if your desire was already real? The moment you catch that mood, you are thinking from inside it, not of it, so desiring it would be like desiring to have the body you currently have.

24 You will find, however, that manifesting what is aligned with your mission and purpose in life is far easier.

25 The 5th-century Pali text *Vissudhimagga*, or *The Path of Purification*, cites advanced abilities as the byproducts of advanced stages of mastery. However, it warns that these can actually be an impediment, if one lets ego get involved. Humility in service to others will take care of this. Also, it's more fun.

26 This work started out as a compilation of notes from seminars and books, and stuff I learned in college, dating back decades. It describes what I see as different ways people apply the wisdom of the heart, Systems Theory, Chaos Theory, and Quantum Mechanics, in their daily lives. This paradigm is growing rapidly. If you use any electronic device, you are using Quantum Mechanics, for example. Systems theory is transforming our society. It has already transformed our world, and it continues transforming it. Originally I wrote it for myself, I didn't think anyone else would be interested. Then my daughter asked me for it, then my mastermind group was interested, and it grew. It is a small introduction to the use of finesse, from a quantum paradigm. It is only a beginning. I took seminars, read books, and sought out wisdom because I had a lot of problems. I also, perhaps foolishly, set the intent that I would learn this material well enough to teach it, which meant I learned some lessons at a very intense level. What is in this book are my own ideas, my interpretations, and I do not represent these ideas as being theirs. I don't know of any teacher who offers all the ideas in this book, in one package. If you know of one, please let me know. Portions of this book consists of artistic parodies, as described at 17 U.S.C. 107, and several other places.

27 *Everything is a mystery. Once it stops being a mystery, it stops being true.* P. 197, *Dreamkeepers*, Harvey Arden.

Solving Problems with Dowsing **129** A book for new dowsers ISBN-10: 1482688573

This is where every creative person has pulled their creations from. It is a fascinating space. You will never get bored with it. It is an adventure to explore.

Perhaps a few poetic statements would set the stage best.

To my mind, there must be, at the bottom of it all, not an equation, but an utterly simple idea. And to me that idea, when we finally discover it, will be so compelling, so inevitable, that we will say to one another, "Oh, how beautiful. How could it have been otherwise?"[28]

If you learn how the world works, you get what some might call miracles. Not so. When you know what the magician knows, it's not magic anymore.[29]

God is a Comedian, playing to an audience afraid to laugh[30]

*The Universe, above, below
Tis but a shadow puppet show
The candle in the box, the Sun
Round which we phantom figures go*[31]

Imagination is greater than knowledge[32]

Sell your cleverness and buy bewilderment. Cleverness is mere opinion; bewilderment, intuition[33].

28   -John A. Wheeler, a Quantum Mechanics theorist.
29   Paraphrased from *Illusions*, by Richard Bach.
30   -*Voltaire*
31   From the *Ruba'iyat* of Omar Khayyam.
32   -*Albert Einstein*.
33   -Jalaludin Rumi, The *Masnavi*, Book IV, Story II, as translated in *Masnavi I Ma'navi: The Spiritual Couplets of Maulána Jalálu-'d-Din Muhammad Rúmi* (1898) by Edward Henry Whinfield.

Wean yourself, gradually, as you move on the path. An embryo's nourishment comes in blood. An infant drinks, a child eats solid food. The student seeks knowledge, the seeker, wisdom. Then there are hunters of more invisible game. Were you to speak with a fetus, you could say, "There is no reason to stay confined in darkness. The world you will soon enter, outside, is vast and beautifully intricate. There are orchards in bloom, wheatfields, and mountain passes. At night, one can see millions of stars, and in daylight, the beauty of friends, dancing after the wedding." And the fetus would say, "There is no other world than what I know from my experience. You are hallucinating. You are crazy."

God turns you from one feeling to another, and teaches by means of opposites, so that you will have two wings to fly, not one.

"How could you reach the pearl by only looking at the sea? If you seek the pearl, be a diver: the diver needs several qualities: he must trust his rope and his life to the Friend's hand, he must stop breathing,   and   he   must   jump".

The world is full of remedies, but you have no remedies until God opens a window for you. Though you are unaware of that remedy now, God will make it clear in the hour of need.

The thinkers are like pearl fishers, who seek to get to the pearls by bailing out the sea with buckets. There is a better way to get the pearls[34].

---

34   The above statements are attributed to Jalal al-Din ar-Rumi.

Solving Problems with Dowsing **131** A book for new dowsers ISBN-10: 1482688573

Fragmentation is everywhere. It confuses the mind, with problems, and muddies our perception so we can't see how to solve them[35].

As far as the laws of mathematics refer to reality, they are not certain, and as far as they are certain, they do not refer to reality.

Time and space are modes by which we think, not conditions which we live [36].

If one begins with certainties, one ends with doubts; if one begins with doubts, one ends with certainties[37].

The Universe consists of waves of motion, which spring from stillness and return to stillness[38].

---

35   -David Bohm.
36   The above two statements are from Albert Einstein.
37   – Sir Francis Bacon.
38   – Walter Russell

B. Dowsing uses finesse instead of force- it costs less, and is much more fun

The book *Lifetide* cites 35 known senses. Our senses include all of Gardner's "intelligences", and intuition. The subconscious processes at least 60 million bits of information per second. It is helpful to know something of how they are processed, and the three phases of consciousness.

Conscious mind, *Uhane,* sometimes *Kane,* in Hawaiian. This is the Yang thinker, and judger. The conscious mind deals with thoughts, and the outer world as perceived by the senses, which is the reflection of the inner world. Materialists, those who believe only what they can sense directly, know only this mind. It depends on the brain, for sensory input. This is the smaller self. It is the filter. It collapses quantum wave forms into reality, through attention. This provides consciousness, which collapses the quantum wave form into particles, and also creates intent. This is the Yang polarity. The conscious mind sets intent, it chooses. From a dowsing point of view, the *Conscious mind asks the question*.

Subconscious, inner, or subjective mind. This mind is the prover, and will prove that whatever you think and believe is real. It also works to keep you alive. It holds long term memories, including all trauma. The subconscious mind, *Unihipili*[39]*,* or *Ku,* in Hawaiian, is the Yin counterpart. It has all memory, and programmed behavior. The subconscious holds the template to construct your body, from a single cell, and runs all its systems, including breathing, digestion, and elimination, 24/7.

Compared to this, tracking down information, dowsing, healing a wound, or correcting a bodily malfunction, is a relatively insignificant task[40] for it. You don't control it, and cannot force it.

---

39   For those who remember the old *Kung Fu* TV series, Unihipili means grasshopper. For those who don't, Caine was called "grasshopper" by his Shao Lin temple martial arts master, for the way his untrained mind jumped around.
40   Your deeper mind was programmed to create a certain type of body, and to keep it functioning smoothly. It will do this as long as your conscious mind or emotions don't interfere. The subconscious does not reason, judge, or decide. It normally accepts what the thinker says, without question, like a four year old child. It will usually follow constructive suggestions, such as what we do in this work. The subconscious holds obstacles to flow, and when it drops them, the flow washes away obstacles. It will respond to questions. In fact, it shapes your life based on the questions you ask, the thoughts and feelings you habitually run, and the pictures you run in your mind, all of which reflect your intent. **You cannot do any healing.** All you can do is offer imagery to a subject's deeper mind, about opening up the flow, to remove blockages to flow. The flow, which is beyond you, does any and all clearing. The powerful deeper mind, which grew the physical body from one cell, and keeps it operating, can easily heal any issue, so long as there is no

You can only coax, or "sell" it, on an outcome, with vivid imagery, feelings, and exciting words. Placebos and Nocebos are examples of a sales job, here. The Subconscious mind will answer questions itself, and sometimes be wrong, or it can go to the Superconscious, and get correct information. You want to be happy when you get correct information, as the Subconscious learns from this.

From a dowsing point of view, <u>the Subconscious mind delivers the answer</u>[41]. It speaks a different language than you do. It speaks in the language of ideomotor response, symbols, signs, dreams, hunches, don't-know-why-but-just-do-it, and so on. The subconscious mind thrives on seeing service, and beauty created.

Henry Ford made the statement that if you think you can't, you're right. If you think you can, you're right. He referred to the role of the subconscious mind. If you seek success in life, which is more useful- the state of can't, or can? It's your choice.

Superconscious, higher mind, sometimes referred to as the soul. This takes the imagery from your subconscious mind, and weaves it into reality. The Superconscious mind, *Aumakua* in Hawaiian, is one with everything, and does not see divisions, or separations.

From a dowsing point of view, <u>this mind already knows all the answers to any question you could ask</u>. This is the larger self, this is you, outside of the bounds of space and time. The superconscious is the real self, the true Self[42].

interference. Causes may be an accident, or strain from lifting, or other things. Sometimes people will ask why the deeper mind doesn't just automatically heal problems. The deeper mind automatically guides all body functions, including clearing and growth. However, it also responds to suggestion, and programming, whether negative or positive. If you take all the FDA tests of drugs, not just the two best, placebos sometimes work better than drugs. Really think about that. This is saying the mind works better than drugs. The subconscious will present "black bags" of negative emotional complexes, to the conscious mind, as if asking "will you take out the trash?" This is why flashbacks occur. If you reject the trashbag, the subconscious takes it deep again, for storage. Negative emotion, stored in the body long enough, tends to show up as disease. Dr. John Christopher stated that Cancer was the result of storing hate in the body. By analogy, a car takes care of its own operations- you don't have to run the fuel pump manually. However, if you drive a car into a river, the car will not stop you. You can also notice that your car, your house, your community, rivers, mountains, the planet, the Sun, the solar system, and our galaxy also have a Ku, a subconscious mind, which is connected to yours. That is one reason dowsing is possible. Our materialist friends don't see this mind, so they cannot make use of it.
41   Through ideomotor response- by working your dowsing device- if you are using a dowsing device.
42   This part can shape physical matter and events more easily than your hands can shape wet clay. Whoops, that's advanced, ignore that. One can do projective dowsing, or intent work, in groups. Groups can invoke more, with stronger

The term deeper mind, or heart, used here, is the subconscious, with some elements of the superconscious mind. The divisions are somewhat arbitrary, and even metaphorical of themselves.

The Conscious mind is the "head" of the head/heart polarity. The Subconscious, and Superconscious, are the "heart" of that polarity. Balance of head and heart is power. Imbalance is weakness. Intent works when head and heart are balanced. Dowsing is a form of intent, in expression. Be one with the question. A properly formed question evokes the answer, as soon as the question is asked.

Use of intuition means working with the deeper mind. The conscious mind sees itself as separate from other things. The subconscious mind is far less separate, and the superconscious is not separate at all.

We recommend strongly that you commit to doing no harm, to doing good only, using these methods. If you feel the need to cause intentional harm, examine your motives, they are almost certainly inadequate to support this. If you just absolutely have to harm someone, use physical methods, do NOT work in the spiritual realm to cause harm[43].

The reason is simple: the harm you wish on others will come back to you multiplied, just as the good you wish on others also comes back multiplied. That sounds so mundane, and it is so very real. It is like standing behind a bazooka, and being burnt by the exhaust of the rocket as it leaves the tube. Kindness generally works much better than revenge.

Will Rogers made the comment that some learn from books, but not many; some learn from other people's mistakes, but not many; the vast majority of humanity has to learn by urinating on the electric fence[44] for themselves. In this case, learn from a book, ok? I strongly recommend committing yourself to service to others. This will power your dowsing like nothing else. The Universe likes and helps those who help others.

---

imagery, than one person alone can. This is a great invocation of the Superconscious in each person.
43   Self-defense and defense of innocents is allowed, of course.
44   I fell into a stream, as a boy, and walked into a live electric fence. I will never make that mistake again.

Some parts of this book are taken from discussions of Quantum Mechanics, to help entrain your belief systems, so that dowsing is easier. If you don't understand it at first- great! That is good. Confusion is good, because it means you are learning. Good dowsers are more often confused. Those who think they know everything are not learning, and are decaying.

Your choice: growth or decay. Which will it be, today?

Suspend your disbelief. Limiting yourself to solid reality is like driving, and looking only in the rear view mirror. Confusion is good, because it's part of growth. Which is more fun: talking to someone else about their vacation, or going on vacation yourself? Which is better, reading a cooking magazine, or having a really good meal?

Direct experience is usually preferable. With direct experience, one has a choice, to work solely with the physical, or to work with both the physical and non-physical, the world of energies. Actually, that choice is an illusion, since only energy exists,[45] but it is a persistent illusion.

Working with the physical world usually requires strength and _force_, over time. Working with energies requires only power, through _finesse_[46]. The more power you have, the less effort and force you need, to allow things to happen[47]. The Law of Attraction is another name for love[48]. Intent is pure love[49]. Finesse, also known as grace, or effortless effort, is how one works with and experiences the Law of Attraction, as dowsing.

---

45   Einstein, a modern archetype for wisdom, noted that mass was a special form of energy, E=mc squared. Everything is energy- P. 25, *Shapeshifting*, by John Perkins.
46   *It is not enough to conquer; one must learn to seduce.* -Voltaire   He speaks of finesse, really of sales theory, and this applies to a Quantum world.
47   P. 64, *The Reality Creation Technique*, Frederick E. Dodson, and Wayne Dyer, David Hawkins, and Wong Kiew Kit.
48   -Charles Haanel
49   P. 26, *The Power of Intention*, Wayne Dyer.

Solving Problems with Dowsing **136** A book for new dowsers ISBN-10: 1482688573

Working with energy flow[50] is a lot of fun, and it gets much better results than working directly and only with the physical. There are two kinds of energy in humans. The first is food digestion, and the second is free energy[51]. Life is nice when you move with the flow[52].

The flow moves on the path of least resistance. Thus, it has the best solutions to problems. As the *Tao Te Ching* notes, if you let the flow follow its course, the solution comes on its own, and it will be the best solution[53].

Every top level spiritual path, including most martial arts, moves into playing with energy[54]. Here, doing less is more[55]. One returns to playing, the way children do. It is fun! The key to dowsing, and the Law of Resonant Attraction, is not needing what you seek.

---

50   There are two major kinds of energy, for humans. The first is a sort of biochemical energy, from food, etc. The second is the Chi, the Force, Mana, the life force energy. The first kind is actually a stored up version of the second kind. Could you live totally off the second kind? Yes, some people do. I remember a story about troops liberating Dachau concentration camp, during WW II. A Pole, who was totally into the energy of love, had survived over 5 years of a diet designed to kill people of malnutrition in under 6 months. Tibetan monks imprisoned by the Chinese, with no food, lived for years, in total darkness. There are other examples. Raymon Grace has a friend who loads water with the second kind of energy, and has given up eating regular food. Fast food, in the U.S., is devoid of life energy, anyway. Freshly made raw juice loses 80% of its nutrition in an hour; the juice we buy in the store is flavored water, by comparison. If you eat a diet of fresh, raw, unprocessed fruits, nuts, vegetables, grains, seeds, and sprouts, your world view will shift unimaginably, compared to when you ate processed foods. Yoga, and Chi Kung, are examples of ways to increase that life force energy.

51   Pp. 3, 4, *Reality Transurfing III: Forward to the Past*, Vadim Zeland

52   P. 8, *Reality Transurfing IV*, Vadim Zeland.

53   P. 112, *Reality Transurfing IV*, Vadim Zeland.

54   There are stages to learning and mastery, of anything, especially manifesting.

1.   Not knowing. This is the state of innocent perception. This is unconscious ignorance, the state of a young child. This is beginner's mind. This is the state of having no idea how to drive a car, or ride a bicycle.

2.   The mechanical stage, of learning technique. This is conscious ignorance. This is the stage of thinking, calculating, judging, analyzing, research,and so on. This is the stage of driving the car, or riding the bicycle, thinking about every step.

3.   The next stage is conscious mastery. Parts of the skill are unconscious, there is less thinking. One absorbs what is useful, and discards what is not useful.

4.   The final stage is unconscious mastery, the stage of artlessness, or spontaneity, of effortless spontaneous action. -*The Warrior Within*, by John Little. Mastery at this level will show what the Japanese call *shibumi*, sublime excellence, or what the Chinese call *Gung Fu*, which can be similar to one meaning for graceful, in English. One becomes purposeless, and formless, like water. This state requires the return to beginner's mind, to innocent perception, to love, to essence. This is the stage of the book writing itself through you, of the dance becoming you, of you moving with the wave forms. This is the stage of no way as way, of adding your larger Self into the equation. You become water, without resistance, not resisting, just flowing, without trying. This is also the level of perfect manifestation. This is not a state of thinking, or analysis.

Morihei Uyeshiba noted we need to know who we are, our own patterns, values, intentions, dreams, and so on, for that is our center. Life will throw us off balance, but we can return to center when we know it. We participate and live in the moment, because it is so full of useful information about ourselves and the environment. We become curious about what's going on, what is happening, and spend less time in analysis.

55   From a Chaos Theory perspective, extremely minute variation over the course of time can produce profound change. P. 52, *Power vs. Force*, David Hawkins. Some call this the "Butterfly effect", because the flapping of a butterfly's wings outside your window literally affects the weather in Hong Kong. Things are that inter-connected.

The need and craving[56] drives it away, and lowers your energy. Be in the energy and resonance of already having it. Don't look for or try to become what you seek, **be it**, now.[57]

Nothing in here is intended in any way to diagnose, treat, or cure any disease, or legal situation. Do not fight with diseases, or medical conditions, or sick situations, because you tend to become what you fight with. From a Quantum Mechanics point of view, we recommend that you not think about disease at all, because if you do, you will make it more concrete, as you become entangled in it, in its morphic field[58]. Think about health, instead.

With Quantum Mechanics, and dowsing, you are playing with patterns of information[59], and modulation. What you do is rarely provable, repeatable, or even understandable, though you do get results. Authentic dowsers and healers put out their intention, and then surrender to some other kind of greater (healing) force[60], a point you'll see repeatedly in this book, and in life. The healer only actualizes a potential future of being healthy[61], as the dowser crystallizes a future of having the information.

C. Attention, Awareness, and Dowsing

All healing, nurturing, and prosperity are only an outward sign of love- the giving of it, and the willingness to receive[62], including receiving all that one is. All lack is the result of lack, or blockage, of love, and flow. Dowsers identify blockages, and in time find ways to break them up, to restore the flow, whether of water, or more subtle energies.

---

56   You can intend to sense something, with your senses, or you can intend to be it. P. 143, *Lucid Dreaming*, Robert Waggoner. In other words, you can look at it from the outside, or from the inside.
57   If you find a piece of music, recipe, dowsing sequence, or anything in a sequence, that is difficult to learn, here is one way to deal with that. One organ master had his students learn organ music one note at a time- they played the first note, then the first and second note, then the first, second, and third note, and so on. This can be very effective.
58   If you need to play in morphic fields, why not play in the morphic fields of great healers, and geniuses, instead? They won't mind if you borrow them.
59   The visible universe is a set of signals [information]. P. 123, *Quantum Healing*, Deepak Chopra.
60   P. 219, *The Power of Intention*, Wayne Dyer.
61   P. 44, *Change your Future through Time Openings*, Lucile and Jean-Pierre Garnier-Malet.
62   P. 261, *The Keys of Jeshua*, Glenda Green.

You will find contradictions here. That is intentional. The early bird gets the worm, but the second mouse gets the cheese, and he who laughs last, laughs loudest. Life has contradictions. One measure of intelligence is the ability to hold contradictions in mind, because this leads to higher realizations. Quantum Mechanics, and dowsing, are full of contradictions[63].

Let's talk about non-linear, unexpected change. Reality shifts occur with no direct physical action. The more you put your attention to the idea that reality shifts, the more reality shifts you will see. We live in a magnificent universe that gives us what we wish for, as if we were in a waking dream.

Attention creates our reality[64]. Even our own bodies are capable of miraculous transformation, because we shape reality with our thoughts, feelings, and actions. There is infinite health, information, inspiration, joy, love, and prosperity in this Universe[65], and it is freely available to all, through the magic genie of attention, focused with questions, through dowsing.

Reality shifts cannot be tested experimentally, because they do not occur on demand. They are unique, and not repeatable. However, dramatic reality shifts most often occur when they are needed, as they do in some dowsing situations.

You can choose to doubt that reality will shift in ways you are not aware of, and you can also choose to doubt that it doesn't[66]. I prefer to put my attention on those ideas that empower me.

Dowsing means connecting with your heart to get intuitive information, which helps you to remove blockages, to heal, by becoming whole. It is helpful for dowsing to meditate, to quiet the mind[67].

---

63   This is because they involve multiple models of how things work, of differing points of view, including the fractal resonance, through quantum entanglement, that makes dowsing possible. Stan Tenen has noted that the Hebrew, Arabic, and Greek alphabets are all shadows of the spiral of manifestation, from different angles. The letters- as viewpoints- are different, but they come from one place.
64   So dowsing, which is specialized attention, can shift reality. Some dowsers are surprised when they discover this, and some aren't.
65   P. 3, *Reality Shifts: When Consciousness Changes the Physical World*, Cynthia Sue Larson.
66   P. 25, *Reality Shifts: When Consciousness Changes the Physical World*, Cynthia Sue Larson, and of course Richard Bartlett's books.
67   P. 5, *Dr. Judith Orloff's Guide to Intuitive Healing*, Dr. Judith Orloff. When the lake is clear, you can see all the way to the bottom of the lake, metaphorically. Even just 2 minutes in the state is very useful.

Dowsing, and intuitive healing, is listening to your body's intuitive messages, which guide us to grow, and become more physically, mentally, economically, spiritually, emotionally and sexually whole, and to help others, and the community, to grow. Humans are manifestations and embodiments of different kinds of energy.

You can learn how to balance the energy of situations, including your body, for regeneration and repair into wholeness. Information and intuition are multidimensional.

Intuition- dowsing[68]- offers solutions that the mind cannot see or understand. Silence is very powerful. It is full of blessings and guidance, if you simply stop, and ask for them. Take some time to be still, to look inside[69].

Intuition also takes you into genius, where ideas, imagery[70], and dreams come together to create solutions and healing, even when science says it is impossible. Get ready to be surprised, and even delighted, by the solutions that come up. Start by noticing your beliefs, because they are what makes solutions and healing possible, or not.

Be present in your body, which means, in part, pay attention to the many intuitive messages already coming in. Be aware of your body's energy, which you can shift with intent. Ask for guidance, particularly in meditation. Meditation really helps dowsing.

You can simply follow your breath, in a quiet space, to prepare to receive useful information and dowsing awareness. You can use remote viewing to tune into the past, present, and future, or any person, place, or situation, or to picture the body's organs, and dowse useful information.

---

68   If you could solve your issues from your conscious mind, you would already have done so. Dowsing means opening up to awareness beyond limiting belief systems, judgments, and so on. The flow of information heals, in other words.

69   P. 143, *Dr. Judith Orloff's Guide to Intuitive Healing*, Dr. Judith Orloff.

70   *Let Magic Happen: Adventures in Healing*, by Larry Burk, MD, discusses this in more detail

Listen also to your attention, dreams, feelings, field of vision, hunches, musings, signs, symbols, the flow, your gut, and direct downloads of information, as all of these are the language of intuition. Also, have fun with it. Playing is a state of grace, which can only be entered through humility.

The heart offers clarity and peace. We become something greater than the small self. Don't compare yourself with other people. Your path is unique to you. The energy that flows through us makes a difference. You have a healing code, a template, inside you, that has useful information about ways to stay healthy, solve problems, and improve situations.

Illness sometimes brings learning, and maybe a message from a frustrated larger being telling you to open your heart to the deeper truths of life. Intuitive participation makes healing easier and faster, with fewer complications.

Your body runs energy, which in Chinese is called *Chi*[71]. Toxic job syndrome, which can generate many limiting energies, may bring illness[72]. When there are blockages in the flow of the energy, problems result.

Spirit brings to us experiences and people that will help us grow. Illness may be such an experience. Spontaneous healing happens when reality shifts occur in our bodies, which restore balanced and healthy consciousness. Dowsing situations come up in the same way. In some multidimensional way, each dowsing situation is a lesson in the classroom of life, a lab experiment in invoking wholeness.

Love is the power behind healing and health. Love can cross any distance or barrier, because we are all interconnected in quantum entanglement[73]. Love can break down any blockage or obstacle to the flow. Love is the flow. I see dowsing, and intuition, as focused love.

---

71   P. 7-29, *Dr. Judith Orloff's Guide to Intuitive Healing*, Dr. Judith Orloff., and of course any book on Chi Kung. The *Star Wars* movies called this the Force.
72   P. 34, *Dr. Judith Orloff's Guide to Intuitive Healing*, Dr. Judith Orloff.
73   P. 257, *Reality Shifts: When Consciousness Changes the Physical World*, Cynthia Sue Larson.

One can intend that healing happens by focusing awareness and intent, and channeling love. You can change how you feel, by changing what you say, and how you say it. Words spoken from love shift realities in fun ways[74].

Helping others energizes the helper. We heal those around us every time we share kind words, smiles, and feelings of love and kindness, and even our dowsing ability, for those open to it. Not everyone is ready and willing to receive help shifting their reality. Respect where they are.

Everyone has their own lessons to learn[75]. Injuries, dowsing situations, and illnesses may be a physical manifestation of unconscious conflicts[76]. Allowing universal life force energy to run through you provides the power necessary for healing and solution to occur. Remember that you don't do any healing, or solution. You only direct the flow[77], with intent. The difference here is between spitting, and using a fire hose, metaphorically.

All physical things can be dowsed and healed, with intent, even what we think of as inanimate objects. This includes airplanes, appliances[78], boats, cars, cities, neighborhoods, and even larger entities. However, we cannot force any change or initiate healing for someone who does not:

- believe it possible
- have a willingness to change, or cooperate with spirit[79]
- want to be changed or healed[80]

---

74 P. 266, Reality Shifts: When Consciousness Changes the Physical World, Cynthia Sue Larson.
75 P. 259, Reality Shifts: When Consciousness Changes the Physical World, Cynthia Sue Larson.
76 Pp. 261-2, Reality Shifts: When Consciousness Changes the Physical World, Cynthia Sue Larson.
77 P. 263, Reality Shifts: When Consciousness Changes the Physical World, Cynthia Sue Larson.
78 P. 285, Reality Shifts: When Consciousness Changes the Physical World, Cynthia Sue Larson
79 P. 284, Reality Shifts: When Consciousness Changes the Physical World, Cynthia Sue Larson.
80 How many healers does it take to change a lightbulb? NONE! Except that the lightbulb has to choose to change.

How much easier could my dowsing get, if what I was dowsing was helping me to find it, I wonder?

What if all problems really, really want to be solved, so they can grow, and they are eagerly awaiting the attention of a dowser seeking the way to solve them?

D. The spirit of dowsing: a reflection of what can't easily be put in words

I had finished this book, but something didn't feel right. I realized I hadn't talked about the spirit of dowsing, the dowsing that is beyond words and technique, the heart of dowsing, dowsing as pure intent, at least as I know it. I knew I had to say something that I've never seen in print before.

I asked myself the dowsing question, "What could I say, that would be fantastically useful, never before seen in print, on dowsing?" What follows came up, as any other dowsing response does. I do not claim to understand all there is about dowsing, some dowsers may disagree with me, and I'm sure many know more than I do[81]. That's fine. Take those ideas you find useful, and discard the rest.

We were taught a limited way of serial thinking, in school. We need to get out of that, into more effective ways of solving problems, that involve using more of our problem-solving capability. I do not want to talk over your head. I speak to under your head, to your heart, to your deeper mind, from my own heart. This is a different kind of language, and some may find it odd at first.

What is the source of all problems? Blockage. Remove the blockage, and the flow heals[82]. How do humans grow? Solving problems. What is the spirit of dowsing? Service. What does the dowser do? The dowser identifies blockages, with reflective dowsing. Some physical means may then be used to solve the problem. It may be possible to solve some problems with projective dowsing, or focused intent. Dowsing is empowerment to solve problems[83], to do good, to create healing beauty, in the world.

---

81   I wish the many dowsers who know more than I do would write good books, as I would happily read them.
82   The Yellow Emperor said this 5,000 years ago, in reference to physical healing, however it is also true metaphorically, for everything in life, especially those issues related to dowsing.
83   Those who are selling you on doubt, and other disempowering ideas, generally don't support empowering ideas like dowsing. Have you noticed this yet?

There are stages to reflective dowsing[84]:

- it starts with a context of <u>service</u>, in humility, which puts one into the larger self. Few dowsers welcome publicity, or glory. They are usually the kind of people who just want to get the job done. This is the foundation of dowsing intent.

- <u>asking focused questions</u> on what is sought, in a context of service. This is setting intent. A good dowser becomes the question, and notices that the question expands and enhances one's senses, known and unknown. For many, this may be enough by itself. They get answers, perhaps through devices, and they are happy with them. As one grows, there are new stages. This is the conscious mind phase.

- <u>grokking</u>, or becoming, or expanding, or entering. One shuts down thinking and analysis, enters quiet mind, ("no-mind", in Japanese) and goes into fuzzy focus, with wide-angled vision. This activates the subconscious mind. The dowser gets into what is sought, and perhaps becomes one with it. If one is dowsing an area, one becomes the area, feeling what is in the area, perhaps in one's body. A water dowser may actually feel himself/herself as the water, coursing through the ground, and/or as a lake, as rain, as clouds[85]. One doesn't think about the question, or try to rationally figure it out. This is the subconscious mind phase.

- Stepping out of self and other, to <u>see it as a dispassionate, super Observer</u>, observing the whole context, outside of both the observer and observed. Envisioning is a name for this. I've heard water dowsers talk about seeing down into the earth, as if it was transparent, with all the water veins clearly visible.

---

84   Adapted in part from p. 234, *Entering the Mind of the Tracker,* Tamarack Song. About half of what follows is heavily influenced by the books of Tamarack Song, especially that book, as they awakened my own indigenous dowsing consciousness.

85   Tom Brown, Jr., teaches water dowsing with exercises like this, though he never uses the word dowsing. Apparently indigenous peoples seek water in this way. If you lived in the Kalahari desert, or Death Valley, water dowsing would be a very useful skill, don't you think? Yes, they pay attention to patterns, and previous experience, and at the same time there is an element of dowsing in what they do.

- You may get a vision of events in time that created the current situation, and you may get a projection of the probable future, of the situation, with everything happening at once. This is the superconscious mind phase, which includes the other two phases, all as a unity. The superconscious lives outside the bounds of space and time.

The best dowsers are generally the best listeners. They leave preconceptions, beliefs, judgments, opinions, and analysis behind, and follow the question chain, by being the question. Consistently effective dowsers know that perspective guides and channels focus. One goes from the wave form to the particle, from the big picture to the small item. The song of what you are seeking is the quantum probability wave, its spirit.

Dowsers notice what they notice, and notice what is different. They get out of their judgments, and opinions, to get directly into the raw information, much of which is beyond modelling in language, or even understanding. They may notice that reality is very plastic, and can be transformed with intent, in the Void. Dowsers learn that all patterns and conditions can change, by shifting awareness, point of view, or consciousness.

Dowsers get out of the limiting mind set of the blockage, or problem, and go to potential, for something new. Dowsers, in time, work with the Creator, to bring immanent healing beauty into form. Dowsers use heart-centered awareness, and play with intent. Dowsers open up portals to new possibilities, new templates or patterns, to useful information, with well-structured questions, and intent.

Some dowsers may seem to be wizards- but it's not magic if you understand the process. Dowsers seem to have multi-dimensional awareness. Dowsers may use clairvoyance, or the kinesthetic counterpart, a sort of spatial or three dimensional clairvoyance, where they simply feel energy fields and flows, and get useful information. They may get information directly from the morphic field of what they seek.

The Office of the Holy Inquisition was born out of the Cathar revolt[86], in France. Simon de Montfort commanded the army around the city of Beziers. He asked the Pope what to do about all the women and children, in the city. The Pope said, "Kill them all, God will know his own." The Inquisition proceeded to kill out intuitives, and to snuff out intuition, generally, right up into the early 1800's.

They had to allow water dowsers, though, because water is so important to life. Even today, some drilling companies will note they have dowsers, or water witches, advising them, in the U.S. In the days of drilling wells with pick and shovel, dry wells were very costly. They are still costly.

Direct, aware experience trumps theory. Theorists will tell you that you can drill for water anywhere in New England, and get water[87]. Homeowners who paid for 14 holes, that all came up dry, develop a different theory[88].

Let's talk about water. Dowsing is as much in our blood as water is. Water is a singing of a song that has been sung since the beginning of creation. Dowsers tend to drift into a timeless state, when they are dowsing, a state outside of the bounds of space and time, where there is very little difference between the water, the dowser, the Creator, the track of the water, past, future, and present, and the land.

To understand water, I need to describe the spirit of water, which is, in a way, beyond words, but I'll do what I can. The Taoists note that water is humble, it seeks the low places. Perhaps not of itself alive, it yet gives life to all.

---

86 I don't believe in reincarnation, and I didn't believe in it the last time I was on the planet, nor the time I lived in Cathar France, either.

87 Let us imagine someone deaf from listening to rock music at 150 decibels all the time. They assure you that foxes make no noise, as they walk. Would you believe them, or would you spend some time in nature, and notice that they do make noise, as they walk? The people who say dowsing doesn't work have chosen to be deaf to it.

88 Addicts to theories, and conclusions or judgments, in the military, without paying attention to actual experience, get people killed. For example, the naval torpedo the U.S. had at the start of WW II was vastly inferior to Japanese and German torpedoes. The Admiral who had pioneered the torpedo trigger system simply could not hear the repeated reports of submarine commanders saying none of their torpedoes worked, so he would say that they were stupid, or incompetent, or didn't know how to use the torpedoes. Tests later proved what the commanders said was correct. The U.S. finally got effective torpedoes for its submarines- in 1943! So many companies have executives addicted to theories that don't work. The cartoon *Dilbert* does well, speaking about nothing else. How Dilbert-compliant is your employer? So when you hear theory addicts saying dowsing doesn't work, just remember, there is no cure for stupidity beyond direct, sometimes painful experience.

Blood in our bodies performs many of the functions of water on the earth[89]. Our blood chemistry is similar to that of an ancient sea.

Water is an old image for spirit, and deep waters of the deeper consciousness. We still say "Still waters run deep", of quiet people. We have all the water on earth we've ever had, which means that when you drink a glass of water[90], you get molecules of the sweat of a Pharoah, the urine of ten thousand dinosaurs, and rain that washed mountains a million years ago. Dr. Masaru Emoto has done interesting work with how human emotions and water interact. Lionel Richie has noted that creative ideas come to him in the shower. This is not unusual. Who among us does not enjoy the yin and yang flow of water, at the beach? Let's continue with selections from sections of the *Tao Te Ching[91]*:

8
Water mirrors emptiness
all the world, with self, to bless
Live in harmony with flow
with the Oneness, one may go

36
Rocks and water, force and form
each one from the other's born

63
Water cares not about the block
It simply flows around the rock
It worries not where channel goes
in the moment, it just knows

---

89   Dr. Feridoun Batmanghelidj notes that Americans are usually dehydrated, and that proper hydration relieves the effects of many diseases. Dr. Richard Schulze recommends drinking at least a quart/liter of pure water [which is not tea, not soft drinks, not vitamin waters, not any other beverage], preferably distilled, each day. He also notes that fresh fruit or vegetable juices are like a blood transfusion.
90   One mole of water is 6.023×10^{23} molecules, if I remember my high school chemistry. That is a lot of molecules.
91   The selections are mostly from *The Rhyming Tao Te Ching of Lao Tse*, by Cedargrove.

66
The ocean at its lowness lives
on the tribute that each river gives
in their emptiness they fill
with waters that, into them, spill

76
A newborn baby's soft and weak
a dead man's corpse is hard as teak
wet and tender, green plants spry
at their death they're stiff and dry
The hard and rigid slowly crumble
before the water's gentle mumble

78
Water very softly yields
yet power over rock it wields
The weak may easily subdue the strong
the flexible has life so long

Number 8, of the *Tao Te Ching*, can be rendered:
Virtue is like water, pure
It is good for all, a cure
It judges not, nor does it fight
It follows humble path, on sight
A house must needs have level ground
In thought, one needs depth, to be sound
Gift's spirit is the generous heart
For speaking, honesty, in art
Of government, just simple serving
of work, skill; and action, timing
No competition, and no blame
no guilt or fear, and naught of shame

Bruce Lee developed a "water" theory of martial arts, of acting in life as water acts in nature, based on these ideas. Water resists not, yet conquers, all; without taste, invisible like the Tao, it gives life to all. It drops its load when it can, and in movement, shows the pure reflection of beauty. It is flexible. When it meets a block, it cuts a new channel.

Polynesian sailors navigated on the open Pacific, without compass or sextant, in part by looking at patterns on the water.

Consider that creatures in the water exist as part of a continuum, sometimes as particle- the creature- and sometimes as waveform, or energy, or spirit, in potential. The spirit of Frog is one with water, and yet of itself. Each one shapes the other.

A dowser keeps asking questions, which keeps him/her open to the song of water, or whatever is sought. The dowser knows that life is continual learning. Dowsers know we see only a few pieces of the puzzle, that everything is in relationship to everything else, that we all have a path of growth to follow, that everything in life is a teacher. Dowsers tend to be generalists, with a broad base of knowledge and experience, that helps them in specialized tasks.

Dowsers ask their focused question(s), and do not think, or analyze, much. It is as if they cast a hook, the question mark, into the waters of the deep mind. When they hook the fish- the answer- they gently pull it into awareness, with little thinking, or analysis. At some point, the answers leap into awareness, as inspiration, or a download, or an awareness capsule, sometimes outside of the limitations of language.

A perfect example of this is dream dowsing. One considers all the aspects of a problem or situation, just before going to sleep. As one comes out of the dream state in the morning, several answers pop up. I did that just this morning, myself, to write this. People ask how you remember dreams. I use mnemonic pegs, as noted in the book *The Memory Book*[92].

Dowsing is often not a focused, find-the-answer-now activity.

---

92 I'll give you an idea how this works. You already know the numbers, in this case one through two. We assign an image to each number. The image for one is a tie. The image for two is Noah. So let's say I got ideas relevant to a book about dowsing, as I came out of sleep. I take the first idea as an image, and I wrap a ridiculously colored tie around that image. I concentrate on several details of the images, so they are compressed enough that they come back to me. The second idea is also made into an image, and I see two of those images walking up a plank, into Noah's ark, where Noah and Napoleon are spray-painting twos on the ark. I do not move my body position, or open my eyes, because both of these will erase dreams. *The Memory Book* has 100 pegs, and I've seen 1,000 peg systems. I never needed more than 64 pegs to remember all my notes for my exams, for my M.A., so unless you are dreaming a lot of information, 100 pegs will take care of just about anybody. Harry Lorayne memorized the Manhattan White Pages, in the 1970's, to show it could be done.

It's more like entering into, and becoming, the question, in the place of the question. You start out in a place in the grid, or matrix, of all possibilities, you formulate your question, and the question takes you to a new place in the grid of all possibilities, where you have the answer. Picasso said computers were useless, because they can only give you answers.

The questions are more important than the answers. The question tunes you to the [metaphorical] radio station where the answer is. Thinking you have the answer, or all the answers, shuts down the metaphorical radio, and the search. It is a dead-end street, metaphorically.

A properly phrased and structured question dies, and is reborn as the answer. However, you want to live in the question, as long as you can, to be certain that you have the complete answer[93]. Learning, and growth, and getting answers, are a journey, not a destination. Remaining in the question leaves the spigot of awareness on, and opens you up to new questions, that take you down fascinating paths that you could not have imagined when you started.

Lipan Apache scouts inflamed themselves with a question, which requires two questions in English to properly translate. They are: *"What is going on here?"*, and *"What is this telling me?"*. When I use these questions, I find my sensory range expanding considerably.

Remember, challenges are opportunities to grow, and life throws them at us when it wants us to grow. When you start out riding a bicycle, you have to think about the pedals, the handlebars, the front wheel, the path in front, your balance, and so on. At some point, you just ride the bicycle, thinking about your destination.

So it is with dowsing. At some point, you decide to be the experience.

---

93 Native peoples teach their children everything about a plant- its life cycle, its context, everything, and only at the end do they give the name of the plant. In our Western culture, we give the name first, and shut down or at least inhibit all that other learning. Native cultures are often very rich in ways Westerners cannot understand. Add to this being raised in a cradleboard, which causes children to pay attention first, before exploring, with a deep respect for life, and you have a culture with a strong foundation for dowsing, and no idiots in denial, addicted to harebrain theories saying dowsing doesn't work, because it can't work.

You stop speaking, and listen with your whole body, your whole being. There is no failure, there is only learning. Mistakes teach us what does not work.

If I see a rock in the woods, I leave it alone and stand back, so it can tell me its story, its song. The rock doesn't really tell me its song; its relationship to the circle of life tells me its story. By comparison, what would country music be without straying and faithful spouses, polarity, family, pickup trucks, hunting dogs, and clueless bosses? Without these relationships, there would be no country music.

The same is true of Opera, and all music. Music itself is about the relationship of the notes, as the spaces between the notes, and the listener. There's an old riddle, that asks, if a tree falls in the forest, with no-one around, does it make a sound? The answer is no, because there is no observer.

The observer maintains the relationships, by directly observing them, and by compressing them enough to keep them around. Water is in an intimate relationship with everything on the planet, including the dowser. The song of water is particularly rich. I can listen to a gurgling brook, or the waves on the beach, or rain, for hours.

Dowsers tend to have a great sense of humor, which is very useful, in exploring parts of the deeper mind, and deeper dowsing. Humor is finesse. You could say to someone, "Yo, wake up, you are half asleep, you fool, you missed something important!" or "Gee, I wonder if what that, over there, is screaming at us could be important? It's the deepwoods equivalent to a Las Vegas neon sign, possibly there is something associated with it?" Good jokes are also based on relationships, and they can trigger expanded awareness as well as good questions.

In Western culture, we have a lot of analysis paralysis. People aren't trained to enter into the question, without much thinking.

Thus, they overbalance into analysis, looking for a preconceived answer, sometimes so addictively that they shut out the larger truths, the way the Amazing[ly Disempowering] Randi does.

Courtney Smith, one of the best dowsers for tracking the stock markets, and Forex, has to train his students out of this kind of thinking. He tells them "follow the rules", and to stop thinking, and trying to second guess the markets. He tells them the markets know much more than they do, so follow the market, the flow, don't stand in the path of the flood.

Tamarack Song[94] calls this the Sherlock Holmes syndrome- the addiction to the single clue, letting only the clue talk, as if listening to only one instrument in the orchestra. Richard Marcinko's cure for this state is to back up, roll one's eyes clockwise and counterclockwise, look around, and go back to the big picture.

Charles Glass' book *Tribes with Flags* describes some archaeologists, in the Middle East, who tried to puzzle out the function of parts of 2000 year old houses. An Australian woman, who was smart enough to deal with the locals, pointed out that these parts exist in modern houses in the area, and one can simply ask the locals.

If you know the deer's lifecycle, dowsing their tracks is far easier, because you know something of the spirit of the deer, and how it flows in different seasons, and weather, and times of day. If you know water's habits, its likes and dislikes, it is easier to dowse for.

When you know both the particle and the wave, both head and heart, both matter and spirit, your dowsing will be much better. A good dowser is always learning, and combines head and heart, as question, and aware, patient wait for the answer.

---

94 If you want to understand something of what it is like to live in a culture of dowsers, Tamarack's book *Journey to the Ancestral Self* is the best book I've ever read on this subject. I get nothing for saying this. I got a B.A. In Anthropology and a language, looking for this information, and that one book is more concentrated than anything I read in college.

Animals do not have analytical minds. Can you imagine a squirrel, suddenly realizing a fox is stalking him, putting his head in his paws, and saying, "Woe is me! What is life for us, but a series of chases, I'm so depressed, what am I going to do with myself?" No.

The squirrel takes immediate evasive action, without thinking, operating out of intuitive awareness, ancestral memories, and sensory acuity. Animals think in images, rather like autistic people.

Humans thought in images, before language suppressed this, and original writing consisted of images, also. Language-thinking, and analysis- suppress this awareness. If you really want to develop your dowsing, spend a few days in the woods, alone, with nothing to read or distract you. Get to where a whisper sounds like a shout.

Like a muddy pond allowed to settle, your mind and subtle senses will settle, and you will perceive a steady stream of dowsing information, almost like a fiber optic cable with uncountable messages streaming through it. You use questions to tune into what you want, and stay quiet, in oneness with the question, as the program comes on the radio, metaphorically.

When we are presented with a riddle, a mystery, a questing for awareness, the entire body becomes more alert. Senses sharpen, and extend. Excitement infuses the body. Free association begins, scanning the many association paths of memory, for relevant information. It's like entering a movie 2/3 of the way through. One intuits what happened before, and where it will likely go. The rational mind is serial. The deeper mind is a parallel processor.

A cigarette butt on the ground- a piece of trash, and we walk on- or do we look closer? Is there lipstick on it? Was the smoker right or left handed? Was the person who smoked it relaxed or agitated, when they tossed it? Where did that person come from, and where are they going? What is their purpose there?

Intuition is listening to the whole story. Some things you see, some you don't see, and intuition fills in the gaps. If you only pay attention to what you perceive physically, you see only the musical notes on the page, you aren't listening to the live performance. Fortunately, we still have that wild, always dowsing hunter-gatherer side inside.

We can wake it up with attention, and questions. It starts by cutting through illusion, belief systems, judgments, hard facts, to see and perceive things just as they are.

The dowser enters the deeper mind. Other stuff largely ceases to exist, including one's own consciousness. Language, self-talk, mostly shuts down. A dowser's consciousness is something like a spider, who feels what s/he seeks on the Web of life, and moves carefully towards it. If you can find a spider in action, blank out your mind, become the spider, feel yourself as the spider. Their attitude is very much that of a dowser.

Then step back, and become the spider, the prey, the web, and the immediate surroundings. You are not a part of the story, the song, you ARE the story, the song. This is the spirit, the realm of the dowser. The song is sung somewhat outside of the bounds of time. Time- the now- is eternal, and every powerful, yet it is only a particle, ever changing, in the now. One must be completely in the now, to hear the song, for it is sung in the present, in harmony with the past, and echoing into the future, somehow all at once, yet in the now.

Daniel Boone was once asked if he'd ever been lost. He said, no, but there was a time when he was a little bit confused, for five days. If you are lost, or confused, or faced with a seemingly impossible problem, don't try to think your way out. Emotions cloud the mind. Intuitive indicators lead the way out.

If the spider caught everything it hunted, the first time, it would get fat and weak. It is always hunting, or dowsing, and it sharpens its senses each time. There is no failure, there is only learning. When you dowse, eat lightly. Hunger sharpens the senses.

Drink plenty of water, but eat lightly, perhaps fruits, vegetables, seeds. Avoid meat and carbohydrates, if you can, or at least consume them only lightly. You don't have to, but I've found this helps me. Wild edible plants have more nutrition in them than anything in the grocery store, by far.

Practice by playing. That person walking down the street- where do they work? What is on their mind? Where are they going? Do they enjoy their relationships? What is their primary dream?

Analyze less, learn more. Work the deeper mind, with questions on subjects that interest you. How would you dowse on the surface of the moon? A good dowser keeps asking questions, and shapeshifts into being the question, listening to the music of what s/he seeks. The good dowser sponges up everything in range. The good dowser steps out of the confinement of ego, and judgment, and into respect, and the joy of communion, with what is real.

A good dowser knows that unlearning is also important. Judgment, beliefs, and opinions shut down awareness. Questions open it up. When I analyze the financial statement of a company I might like to invest in, I don't analyze. I try to get a previous statement, so I can compare, and see trends, because numbers only have meaning in relationships. I don't think, much, I let the numbers talk to me. They always have an interesting, unique story to tell. A good Profit and Loss statement is like a medical chart, to me.

Focused change begins with awareness. If you don't know where you came from, or your destination, you walk in circles, as so many people spend their lives- the circle of the day, the week, the month, the year. Once you have focus, you can set your direction, your intent, and move out on the path. You are the path, shaping itself. I am no more a dowser, that is redundant, I am whatever I am seeking, knowing what I seek is knowing myself, here. A dowsing hunter-gatherer is a fully alive, completely functioning human being, one with environment/surroundings, giving back as s/he takes, shaping and improving the environment.

Western babies are often isolated in cribs, in nurseries. Starved of the music of human interaction, they jump feet first into activities, and maintain this pattern.

They may even accelerate it with coffee, sugar, drugs, even loud pulsebeat music that shuts out analysis, and takes us back to feeling some of what our thinking covered up.

Western culture is ego, purely foveal vision, numbness desperately seeking... something- but what?, focus totally on the material particle, while ignoring the wave, the spirit. Western culture's essence is addiction, especially addiction to the ego, and disrespect and disregard of relationships.

Native children raised in undisturbed communities are carried by their mothers, for at least a year, and get regular stimulation, and perspective. They learn to pay attention, first, before acting, to understand context first, before the text.

They don't push immediately to the answer. They remain open, so the complete answer can download. Native peoples live Systems Theory in their lives. They tend to not have art, because everything they do is beautiful. They know to stay quiet, to speak only when necessary, that without the chattering of the inner monkey mind, intuition is just there, always available.

They do not overburden the frontal lobes with analysis, they don't limit themselves to the surface of consciousness. Instead, they spread out the work in the "cloud" of deeper mind, ancestral awareness, instinct, intuition, archetypes, and the larger mind, or extended selves, the circle of life. They grow up with stories of how everything fits together, of a life view that is based on

Systems interacting with each other[95], of relationships in interference patterns[96].

Western mind is like Crime Scene Analysis, paying careful attention to the physical clues, and reacting. Native mind, ideally, is training people in the right way, so they are part of their community, so they support themselves out of dowsing and intuition, with their needs met, so that they rarely if ever turn to crime[97]. They simply know the right way to behave, mostly.

When I fox-walk, in the woods, silently, at 1/3 or less the average person's pace, a whole new world opens up for me, in the same forest. To know something is to come into relationship with it. When I move through a forest, I become the forest, my hair as leaves, feeling a two-legged being walking on me, with squirrels climbing up my arm, birds sitting on my fingers. I walk slowly, with the rhythm of the forest, just as I marched in a marching band, in high school, to the rhythm of the drum.

---

95 Westerners see two stories, over and over- Cinderella, or rather the story of Medea, for women, and Jason, for men. Every Spanish telenovela soap opera is a variant on Cenicienta, I mean Cinderella. Every romance novel is a variant of the story of Medea- the tall, blonde handsome stranger comes from afar, to take her away from it all. All too often, he later dumps her, because she isn't interesting any more, because all he sees is the physical. Even the book of Proverbs, in the Bible, discusses this. Jason was a troublemaker, who went out to raise Cain in a vehicle, with his drinking buddies. Western relationships are shallow, sometimes nonexistent. Westerners live in fear, isolated from each other. At night, instead of campfires, Westerners gather around the electronic fire of the Television, which pumps out images of gross disrespect, violence, and hopelessness, and endless competitions where many lose, and few win. Westerners are obsessed with death- from Frankenstein, to zombies, to dead food that comes in its own convenient coffin. Will you have chemo with that? Westerners tend to be so toxic that many cannot breed, so expensive fertility treatments are necessary- which involve hormones that cause cancer, as the package inserts note. For Westerners, more is always better, that's just the way it is, and there is not enough for everyone. This is the song of the material. I live in this culture, and this is what I see, when I step out of it. Sure, it has its good points, also. Understand this, though, so you can also step out of it, into dowsing. Western culture creates problems. Dowsing solves them.

96 The world of healthy relationships, and the scientific mind, aren't very compatible. Here's a story. Let us imagine you're on your wedding night, with a hot partner. You just got to the honeymoon suite, and you are ready for a memorable evening. Your partner pulls out a large case of scientific instruments, and starts setting them up. Your partner says s/he has no confidence in you, as a spouse, and so is going to record what goes on, to see if you are any good. There is a video camera, numerous sensors to tape to your body, a pressure monitor under the sheets, a large dashboard of indicators. Your partner promises you a million dollars if you perform well, but you realize that your partner has some extreme standards of what they expect in a spouse, that you will not meet, and that s/he has 1 million reasons to ensure that you never meet them. You realize your partner will never let you meet those standards. This doesn't do much for the evening, does it? Yet the Amazing Randi, and company, feel quite justified in saying that the flow of communion in relationships, as dowsing, doesn't work. I'll take this analogy further. When I'm in dowsing consciousness, it approaches sexual communion. I couldn't care less what kind of illusions scientists have, I enjoy communion greatly. I don't need the presence of some cretin trying to prove whatever hare-brained theory they have, which is not based on direct experience.

97 So, you say, what is their idea of punishment, for criminals? Sometimes it was banishment. Prior to WW II, the then rare alcoholic wifebeaters among the Dakota people were simply shunned. If that's not possible, for example, in Haiti, they play on fear, to turn them into zombies, with hypnotic suggestion. Apache scouts could play mind games with criminals, shapeshifting into fearful images, till they confessed. This is actually common in traditional communities, the storyteller Donald Davis has a story of this, the Truth Chicken. Criminals generally operate best when they can be anonymous. In indigenous communities, no-one can be anonymous, and there is far less crime. Severely disturbed indigenous communities, those under stress from Western culture, are another story, of course.

I move without purpose, just to observe, connecting with the spirit of the woods. Somehow, I intuitively know something of what the forest knows, and see the streams of people, and animals, and plants, and the wind, that come through it, all at once. I get out of verbal space, of thinking, and just observe, and feel, without inner talk. All feelings have a reason, so they are part of it all. I flow with the flow. I am one with the waveform, as the question, crystallizing with the answers only when I need to. Each day is a fractal extension of the last day, and year, and century, and millenium.

I am one with the trees, the birds, and open to the new notes of the music, seeing 360 degrees, in 3 dimensions, or is it 4?

No reaction, no fear, no judgment, no filtering, I am one with the flow of the forest. It feels so natural. Only ego can separate me, and it is dormant now. I have only to become who I truly am, to enter the dowsing state.

All is music, sine waves, flowing, pulsebeat, rhythm, waves on the beach. As I enter the music, I become one with the forest, I shape-shift into it, I am hunter and hunted, Sun pouring out, leaf drinking in, full, empty, all and nothing. I can be a forest creature of 10 yards/meters in diameter, I can grow, I can contract. I am the Big Bang, exhaling, with a red shift, and then inhaling, with a blue shift. I am beyond what I can analyze, or even model in language. It is all patterns of light, and information, and modulation.

I notice the sine waves of the variations in the ground, the slow motion ocean of trees growing, falling, decaying, growing again, leaving pits and mounds. The forest is alive, the trees are cells in its body. I would like to try Native American blindfolded running, here, because I feel the trees without needing to see them.

The tracks are interesting. The space between the tracks is like the space between musical notes, this is the soul, the spirit, the quantum waveform[98].

---

98 Tom Brown, Jr. had us put our hands into a track, and to shoot our spirits back, on the track, to the animal's birth, to

This is music, as surely as the music the wind plays, when it strums the trees and grasses. The music is the soundtrack for a Powerpoint presentation, of images.

There is no need to fight for breath, as I did when I was born; it all just comes to me, in great abundance. I know there is no competition here, that there is only relating, we are all part of the dance, the concentric rings of creation. I know confusion, also, which is good, because this means I am learning. This is the path of fascination, and curiosity.

This is the world of dowsing[99]. When we awaken our indigenous selves, we get continuous intuitive downloads, course corrections to stay, and continue, on the path. We move forward, in trust, and our larger self guides us.

Interface areas are always interesting. We live at the interface of the earth and sky, for example. There are few people living 100 miles up, or 100 miles down. Wear of mechanical parts happens usually at the interface, that's also where you need the lubrication, and case hardening. In nature, some would call this edge areas- where forest meets field, for example.

Deer like to eat the plants of the field, with a nearby forest to escape to. Border areas are interfaces. The shore of the lake is interesting. A fish swimming over a flat bottom seeks out what stands out. The ships sunk on flat bottom ocean floors, near Guadalcanal, in WW II, have become coral reefs, of a sort, full of fish, for fish like that interface.

Dowsing occurs at an interface, also, the interface between conscious mind and deeper mind. Dowsing is truth. Insincere people don't grasp reality, because they don't live it.

---

its ancestors. Then we shot our spirits forth on the track. One student got to the end of a track, and looked into- a living room. Later, he visited someone's house, and the living room looked familiar. He adjusted his perspective, and realized a mounted deer head looked out with the same perspective as he saw before, of the living room.

99 At the 1984 ASD convention, I heard this joke, at a presentation. The wife of one of the dowsers there, Dwin Gordon I think, allegedly was asked how Dwin dealt with sex. The wife thought they'd asked about flying, on an airplane. She responded, "Well, he's only done it twice. The first time, he vomited, and the second time, he lost his hat". Spaniards call misunderstood communications like this Sea Bass Dialogues, los dialogos de los besugos. The funny thing is, they go on all the time, even in dowsing, and people still get good results.

The dowser who trusts his/her intuition, and senses, and speaks truth, can be trusted. As you use your senses, if you quiet your mind, your senses extend.

If you pay attention to the whole environment, using mainly peripheral vision, and hearing, and shut down the thinking mind, your senses start extending. You can sense things way beyond anything Westerners can imagine[100]. Geronimo could "hear" the cavalry, at 10 miles away[101].

The Gods must be Crazy compared footprints to a daily newspaper of what is going on. This is the song of the track. Tracking, to indigenous peoples, who know it as part of life, is a state of being, not an analysis. It is instant access to the information and perception of the deeper mind, with great clarity. Being specialized is like hoping for the big hit, in Vegas. A generalist, seeking small wins, is more likely to survive with money intact, at least, and to win consistently[102].

An animal is only the present manifestation, the particle, the current expression in flesh, of the spirit, or quantum probability wave, of the animal. Animal behavior flows from the template of all of that kind of animal, the animal morphic field, to the individual. Animals follow their instincts, or intuition, they listen to the song of the tracks in the morphic field.

Squirrels follow vertical trails, up trees. Birds follow sky tracks, that are as clear to them as highways are to us. One can track animals without visible tracks. This is sometimes called shadow, or spirit tracking. It is dowsing. See through the bird's eyes, feel yourself with wings, enjoy the air, and the bird's eye view, shapeshift into the bird, which is possible with creative imagination, and you know their trails.

---

100 My favorite visual image of this is the extendable ears, from *Harry Potter.*
101 Military people know that intel- knowing your target, or enemy- is the key to success. If Geronimo knew where the cavalry were, as he did by the age of 40, he couldn't be defeated. He wasn't defeated, he chose to come in, to help his people. The French lost the war of 1870, with Prussia, because the Prussians had fantastic intelligence, from Wilhelm Steiber. This led to WW I, which lead to WW II, where the Germans lost, because the allies could read their communications. Erwin Rommel was the Desert Fox, until he lost his intel section at El Alamein.
102 When you go into a casino, you notice they look really nice. And every dollar that went into building that casino was given by someone who was going to hit it big. I know a way to guarantee winning 100% of the time, in Las Vegas. I guarantee it. Stay out of the casinos, and go to the pawn shops. This is how trackers think.

Water is flow, a living metaphor. Become the water. Flow like the water, know yourself as joyous flow in the now, reflecting sunlight like an ever changing gem, finding the right path with gravity, flowing, your belly thumping on the rocks of the channel, your arms almost scraping the side of the bank.

Feel yourself as a raindrop, then a droplet of water, then a gurgling flow into a rivulet, then a small stream, then a river, and then you join into the ocean, then you go up into a cloud... perhaps you swim inside a fish, or a living being on land, cleaning it out, taking up its toxins, and dumping them when you can, with your friend the sand, perhaps.

A look at where an animal beds down, which is usually known as a lay, is instructive. You know the animal feels safe there. It is probably a warm microclimate, in winter.

Water, also, has its lays, doesn't it? Underground, some dowsers call them domes. Domes tend to be associated with upswellings in the earth's magnetic field[103]. You may find a grandfather tree above a dome. Ponds can be a lay, for water. Notice how water likes to be in flow, also. White-water rafting is a great way to understand the ebbs and flows of the spirit of water, I've found.

How do you change, when you carry salt? Pollutants? Bad feeling from humans? When you know the dance, the music, of the water, you know its spirit, and all the beings it travels in. Only your conscious mind separates you from all that is. If you step out of this, you are one with all that is. You can dance the dance of water, of beings, of minerals, because you are one with them. You can locate them easily, because it is like locating a part of yourself. Without all of what you are in relationship with, you do not exist. When you realize you aren't really you, you are only an expression of something larger, you can light up different parts of your larger self, to dowse, know, and incorporate them.

---

103 I have found upswellings in the earth's magnetic field in every college campus I've ever been to. When I come into the University of Michigan, it hits me about a mile out of central campus. I felt it strongly at the University of North Carolina, Chapel Hill. The books of Richard Leviton cover this in more detail. I first heard him at an ASD conference.

Going beyond merely following your standardized question chain, to dowsing intuitively, happens when you cross the border between self, and what you seek. You think, feel, move, and flow as what you seek does, shadowing it. You are in the same world, the same place.

Ego-focused individuals have self as the foundation of their experience, and models of the world. To them, phenomena are external, and alien. Native hunters know the dance of the animal they hunt, and so don't need to communicate. They know and assume their roles, in the hunt, just like wolves in a pack. They communicate with a glance, or twitch. They form a super-entity, a larger being with a body of say 5 wolves.

Navy SEAL teams communicate this way[104], and so do great sports teams, and other highly focused groups, such as the Rockettes in New York, or great martial arts or acrobatic teams. The better ballet companies are in this state.
A great football player knows the dance, the spirit of the game, and expresses it here and there, in perfect or near-perfect expression, as possible. People like this communicate with [metaphorical] Skype, with images, rather than the much slower, [metaphorical] Morse code of spoken language. Time doesn't really pass, in this state.

One becomes one with what one seeks, and the path becomes easy, almost effortless. When one moves naturally, with the flow, without thought, ancestral memory, and intuition, and perception, all start surfacing, like a ball held underwater in a pool, and then released. Intuition, and the landscape, give us a clear GPS map. Actually all wild animals dowse their environment. A kit fox can hear a ticking watch at 100 m/yards. Is that purely physical sense at work?

Symbols are part of life. Start seeking them out, in daily life. The deeper mind communicates at times with symbols, signs, dreams, hunches, intuitings, gut feelings, images, odd sounds, leaps in awareness, and many other ways.

---

104 The movie *Zero Dark Thirty* gives you some idea of a SEAL team in action, though of course it is Hollywoodized. I almost fell off my chair laughing, when the one SEAL said he was listening to Tony Robbins, on the helicopter going in.

The human mind imposes, sees, or intuits order, or pattern, to what could be seen, at first glance, as random.

The stars are a random bunch of lights in the sky- or are they? Stories of the stars are told in most cultures. Different cultures may use different constellations. Dowsing in time takes one into realizing the fractal resonance of all creation. The spirals of a galaxy, the beginning of a relationship, a birth, life, all follow the spiral form. Pay attention to detail, pattern, and process, for they all sing their song.

What if the solution to every problem was waiting inside the problem, waiting only for you to awaken it, with the attention that asking the right question brings?

E. Remembering your dreams- waking & otherwise

1. Keep a journal and pen, or .MP3 recorder, by your bed.
2. Write down a question before you go to bed. Obsess on it. You could put a glass of water by your bed, drink a little, and plant the idea that when you wake up, and drink it, you'll have the answer to your question, as José Silva recommends.
3. When you start to wake in the middle of the night, or in the morning, do not change your body's position, as this will erase the dream.
4. In a very delicious, sleepy state, go over the dream in your mind. You can use mnemonic pegs to store the images. Run them two or three times, to nail them down.
5. Moving your body as little as possible, grab your notebook or recorder, and write down keywords and high points of the dream. Then write the narrative. The less sense it makes, generally the more powerful the message is.
6. Then look at the question you asked the previous night. Let your mind free associate from the dream, in relation to the question. Dream books usually are not very useful, because most people have a dream symbology that is unique to them.
7. You can, of course, ask for more information the next night[105].
8. There is nothing stopping you from getting into a drowsy state, during the day, to ask questions, to dowse. Thomas Edison and Salvador Dali did this by holding a bottle or spoon in their hand, over a plate, as they sat in an easy chair, to keep themselves from going all the way to sleep. They dowsed creative solutions this way[106].

As you work with the deeper parts of your mind, with this book, you will find dreams more important.

---

105   P. 40, *Dr. Judith Orloff's Guide to Intuitive Healing*, Dr. Judith Orloff.
106   I mention this in one other place. Why twice? Because I really want you to "get this", that with the right questions, you can dowse solutions to any issue.

F. Quantum finesse

Each part of the universe is unique and interconnected to all that is. When sending waves and receiving waves meet, they change each other, and change occurs. Mind and matter are different phases of the same thing. They are unified by consciousness, which is everywhere[107]. If you observe particles and objects as being real, that is what your universe will consist of. If you observe the fluid, wavelike nature of reality, you can be aware of the in-between infinite place that holds universes of possibility[108]. In a multiverse of parallel universes, we choose what we consciously experience, through our choices and intent[109], which is a form of projective dowsing.

Objects come into existence, dropping out of the quantum waveform of the possibility, at the moment an observer pays attention[110].

If we let ourselves observe the observation of reality choices being selected, we open up many new possibilities, because we pay attention to the way we pay attention[111]. We exist as pure energy, and so does everything else.

-People concentrating on the material world vibrate ~250 Hz.
-People operating in the energy range vibrate 400-800 Hz.
-Mystical personalities can vibrate between 900 and 200,000 Hz [112].

That spiritual level of increased awareness of expanded consciousness, of being both alert and very relaxed, with a sense of connection to everything in the Universe[113] from the heart, begins in the Alpha EEG.

---

107   Pp. 36-7, *Reality Shifts: When Consciousness Changes the Physical World*, Cynthia Sue Larson.
108   Remember high school geometry? Between any two points is another point, repeated to infinity?
109   P. 50, *Reality Shifts: When Consciousness Changes the Physical World*, Cynthia Sue Larson.
110   I have a friend, who does research into obscure areas. I am always asking dowsing questions, for books that would help him. Over ten years, I have found more books than I ever dreamed possible, to help him. The same search subject on Amazon.com and other such sites pulls up different books a month later, a year later. It is as if my seeking is actually creating these books from the Void. Gary Douglas has noted the same process, with Art Deco antiques. Notice that, in your own life. I've seen people create jobs they really liked, using this method, for example.
111   P. 51, *Reality Shifts: When Consciousness Changes the Physical World*, Cynthia Sue Larson.
112   P. 54, *Reality Shifts: When Consciousness Changes the Physical World*, Cynthia Sue Larson, citing Valerie Hunt.
113   P. 56, *Reality Shifts: When Consciousness Changes the Physical World*, Cynthia Sue Larson.

The Lipan Apache name for the Alpha EEG Brainwave state, of about 7-11 Hz, is land of the spirit, or energy, that moves behind all things. Reality shifts tend to occur in this state. Generally, they are not perceivable by those who have their attention focused solely, and only, on the physical level.

Changing perception, as in dowsing, is an example of a reality shift. Reality shifts are part of our cooperative co-creation of reality, as we choose what will be real. Reality collapses, or is compressed, into existence, based on our intent[114] and attention. Of course, you can only notice reality shifts in what you remember, and have an interest in[115].

Reality is very fluid below the surface of what we think is real. Perhaps our consciousness travels from one multiverse to another. Or perhaps, what appears solid and real is actually appearing and disappearing, because reality is in flux, just as with electrons.

We could choose to create beliefs which allow us to trust the physical world to support and sustain us, as we become more and more aware of how effortlessly the physical world can change[116]. Most people do not pay much attention to the world around them, and so miss out on a lot.

If you pay attention to the world around you, with artists' eyes that notice details, it is easier to notice reality shifts[117]. People who experience the dreamlike nature of reality usually notice reality shifts better, while those focused on the purely physical don't[118].

One of the easiest reality shifts is to notice is how your mood and feelings affect search results on the Internet, or your experience of a game, and, of course, your dowsing.

---

114   P. 106, *Reality Shifts: When Consciousness Changes the Physical World*, Cynthia Sue Larson.
115   P. 107, *Reality Shifts: When Consciousness Changes the Physical World*, Cynthia Sue Larson.
116   P. 108, *Reality Shifts: When Consciousness Changes the Physical World*, Cynthia Sue Larson.
117   Developing artist's eyes is very useful, for noticing the world. I met a fellow who was a Marine, in Vietnam. He was and is an artist. They put him on point, because they knew he would see more than the average person. He survived that war.
118   P. 135, *Reality Shifts: When Consciousness Changes the Physical World*, Cynthia Sue Larson.

People with exceptional powers of perception are intelligent and open-minded, aware of their shortcomings, adaptive rather than controlling, and they tend to lack hard expectations[119].

Reality shifts and dowsing breakthroughs are more likely to occur at moments of emotional flow, in an ecstatic, energized, loving, open, relaxed state of mind, when life feels magical and wonderful, and one feels the flow of energy in and around a high rate of vibration[120]. This is beyond the Beta EEG state in which Western culture spends most of its waking time.

You don't need to believe in a higher power. Divine intervention occurs for people of all religions, and no religion. The only difference is that believers may regard surprising shifts as miraculous, while nonbelievers attribute them to luck[121].

Science and spirituality do mix. If you believe in something greater than yourself, you have a better chance of staying healthy longer, and healing more quickly, should you become sick[122]. Dowsing is much easier, also.

It is like being in a boat, noticing that it now sails into the waves, making life easier, and doesn't take them on the side any more. It's like playing monopoly with a stash of hidden $500 bills, or of having Lady Luck bless many of your endeavors, somehow. Somehow, time and opportunities just open up, especially around helping others. You may, in time, notice you enter co-creation, with the Creator, and that this can be a lot of fun. This is not easy to describe, it is better just to notice the experience, and enjoy it.

---

119   P. 146, *Reality Shifts: When Consciousness Changes the Physical World*, Cynthia Sue Larson.
120   P. 147, *Reality Shifts: When Consciousness Changes the Physical World*, Cynthia Sue Larson.
121   *Creating Miracles*, Caroline Miller, cited P. 113, *Reality Shifts: When Consciousness Changes the Physical World*, Cynthia Sue Larson.
122   P. 76, *Dr. Judith Orloff's Guide to Intuitive Healing*, Dr. Judith Orloff..

G. Energy is Spirit is nothingness where something is born of observation

We are changing from second to second, anyway. Time is a lake of ripples, of past, present, and future, started by the pebble[123] of each moment, not a river[124]. Each new pebble changes everything, past and future.[125]

All realities stream from the now. When we make changes in a more focused way, with new measurements and perceptions, we get enmeshed in a new way, in a new reality.

With sufficient charge, a structure pops out of the immanent, into manifestation. The Void of all possibilities, the zero point field[126], is the stage on which all this plays out[127]. The Hawaiian word for zero point energy is *Mana*. Mana is pure spirit[128], pure life force energy, flow. It has no shape, no texture, no color.

---

123 Small changes can amplify into completely unexpected results. Systems with feedback loops can amplify and grow these changes. In this nonlinear world, a tiny cause can have a massive effect. Paraphrased from P. 120-121, *Leadership and the New Science*, Margaret J. Wheatley. Some call this the Butterfly Effect, or the straw that breaks the camel's back. One man's actions in Tunisia led to the Arab spring.

124 The lake analogy comes from P. 72, *Parallel Universes of Self*, Frederick Dodson. Between this and parallel Universes, massive change is possible now, since the past, present, and future are only what you think and create them to be. A new perspective changes everything. Past and future lives may be coterminous with the present- p. 49+, *Beyond Reality*, by Shelley Kaehr.

125 There is a Buddhist concept, that every thought and feeling instantaneously reaches the limits of the Universe, as a ripple, and returns. Every good deed you do, every high grade thought you entertain, affects the morphic field of the whole, making it easier for others to do. Service is done even with thought and feeling. This is my understanding of p. 82, *Seven Experiments That Could Change the World*, Rupert Sheldrake.

126 Zero point energy is very much like the *Force* described in the *Star Wars* movies, *Chi*, the Life Force Energy used in Oriental martial arts, *Baraka*, for Sufis, *Wayrrull*, as noted at p. 205, *Dreamkeepers*, by Harvey Arden, and green energy, for Green Lantern fans. In Quechua, it is *Ushai*. In Shuar, it is *Arutum*. It is *LungTa*, or Windhorse, among Vajrayana Buddhists, and *Khiimori*, for Mongolians. It is *n/um* for the !Kung- P. 73, *Portals: Opening Doorways to Other Realities Through the Senses*, Lynne Hume. It is *Waa* for the Tiwa, *Diyi* for the Apache, *baaxpée* for Crow Indians. It is Goddess energy, Uli in particular, and the Holy Spirit, depending on your theology. It may be dark matter. Alvin Maker, in Orson Scott Card's series, runs in the green energy state, just as Native American, Celtic, and Tibetan runners did, for long distances. This may apply more generally than one might think. As one example, the Shedd Aquarium originally made up chemical seawater, based on analysis. The fish died in it. Then they started adding real seawater to their perfect chemical copy, and the fish stayed alive. People who eat fresh, raw live foods seem to be healthier than those who eat a lot of processed food. Chi Kung classes teach direct experience of the Chi, if you need a reference point. There's nothing quite like direct experience to personality debunk the debunkers.

127 Your success comes in direct proportion to your alignment with the Void, the field of all possibilities. You already know what you seek, at some level, there is no need to focus on it. Align yourself to the Void, in no-mind, and allow your heart's desires to come to you. The elephant boy does not lift the log. The elephant lifts the log. In the same way, you cocreate with the quantum field, the Void. The field already knows what you want, even before you ask. "Before ye ask, I have answered." Get out of your ego, your mind, and let the field bring you what you seek. Let go of the state of wanting, and enter the state of being what it is you seek. This isn't difficult, because you are already connected with everything you could ever want, through your heart. See yourself already present with what you seek, rather than wanting or craving it, You compress the mold, with intent, and the field pours itself into your mold.

128 This is a spirit so pure that the Christian system calls it holy, which is similar to whole, or holistic.

If you explore belief systems, not just as feelings[129], but as shapes, you notice that belief systems have boundaries. Mana has no boundaries. It is pure intent[130], pure potential.

How do you get it? One way is to breathe deeply. What if you focused this, as strongly as Carlos Castaneda says? Breathing is in the now. It is the waves of spirit[131] falling on the beach of the material, in and out. You can close your eyes, and hear the waves on the beach, I mean your breathing.

Breathe all the way down to your stomach. If you breathe from the place you have stress or tightness, it relaxes, it integrates into the flow, the resistance dissolves.

Pure spirit, or energy, is who you really are, under all the masks and identities. It's where you came from, and where you go back to. It is the Quantum waveform. If you get really stressed out, just breathe deeply, for a while, and your stress level drops. You structure quantum potential with conditions, habits, rules, beliefs, feelings, expectations, resentments, and thoughts[132].

An energetic schematic is a wave front which transforms a pattern. An example of an energetic schematic is focused intent. *Focused intent is the feeling of it already done.* **How would it feel, if it was real right now?** That is an example of an open-ended dowsing question which sends the subconscious mind on a search, which it will continue until it finds an answer.

Questions like this activate dowsing, through the Law of Resonant Attraction. They are also a form of weak quantum measurement, that allow for numerous new possibilities, instead of fixing one, and only one, possibility into form.

If you want to change your experience, *notice what you notice*, now. This is your baseline, or reference point[133].

---

129   Examine your feelings. Where do you notice them, in your body, or space? Where do they start? What is their vibration- fast, or slow? What is their depth, texture, quality? P. 23, *The Breathing Book*, Donna Farhi. How else could you describe them? This helps to break up blockages to emotional flow.
130   Pure intent is the ability to be in the heart, which generates, and does not analyze.
131   Pure spirit is unmanifest, and cannot be experienced or discerned through ordinary perception. It is the fundamental nature of everything. Anything you experience, know, or sense is an emanation of spirit. P. 227, *The Keys of Jeshua*, Glenda Green. Breath means spirit, in many languages. The word respiration is similar to spirit.
132   Which could be summed up as vibrational patterns.
133   <u>Reference points are simple nodes around which massive change can happen.</u> For example, one man

Use questions to find a new state that does not match your usual expected outcome, move into it, and be one with it. Notice what is different. For example, if you want to be wealthier, enter a state of feeling wealthier now, in the monopole of the heart, without the need for external reinforcement.

When you hold the new feeling state, or intent, and then let go, the old pattern recoheres into infinite possibility, and recrystallizes into something new.

Avoid judgment[134], because judgment ties up your parallel processor, your brain. An infinite number of possibilities and altered realities are available to you, at all times[135].

Example: Years ago, I set an intent that anyone or anything I saw, heard, felt, or was otherwise aware of, got healing energy, with no effort necessary by me, and no need for feedback. I have since changed it so that I do get feedback, so that I know what's going on. It works. That's all I need to know. I don't care how it works, why it works, or anything else beyond observable results. I don't share this with those who operate from the Newtonian model. Why bother? I do get results. That is enough for me..

---

was in charge of mobilizing troops for World War I, in the USA. This was an incredibly complex problem. Troops had to be mobilized fast enough to get them to Europe, but not so fast that they sat waiting for months in camps, doing nothing, because they didn't have equipment. This part of mobilization went well. That man was asked, after the war, how he did it. He said he calculated how fast each recruit could be issued a pair of pants, which he felt was the basic element of a uniform. That was how he guided the mobilization. Without a reference point, there would have been chaos. With the reference point, it went well. This is a very significant point, much of what you see in this book is reference points that allow for massive change for the better. The acetamide crystallization demonstration, where a crystal seed dropped in a supercooled acetamide solution crystallizes the whole mass, in high school chemistry classes, is another example of this. Don Juan told Carlos Casteneda to look at his hands, to maintain lucid dreaming. Pp. 6-9, *Lucid Dreaming*, Robert Waggoner. Discussed also p. 175, *You the Healer*, José Silva.
134   Judgment was the original sin. P. 173, *The Keys of Jeshua,* Glenda Green.
135   If you limit the desired outcome to what you think you want, you eliminate 99.9999999% of the wonderful possibilities that are better than the best you can imagine, many of which could happen right now, or even retrocausally, that is, in your past, shifting your past, from the present. Everything in our universe is oscillating possibilities, which have the potential to change at any time.

Solving Problems with Dowsing **171** A book for new dowsers ISBN-10: 1482688573

VI. Intent, energy, and transformation

A. Basic ideas about energy useful for transforming it
In working with shifting energy, or we could say transforming information, it will be helpful to know some basic principles. We can assume that these five things are real:

- **light**, which consists of photons, or flow
- **vibration**, and frequency
- **modulation**[1], or information[2], which is related to torsion physics
- **resonance** between states[3], and entrainment[4]
- the Universe has positive intent for you, and **intent shapes the Universe**

1. Everything that exists in the physical world started out as, and has a counterpart in, the nonphysical world. Example: When a martial artist breaks a board, s/he starts by exhaling. The practicioner sees his/her hand already through the board, before anything physical starts. The board is broken before s/he hits it, by the energy.

2. Energy follows thought and feeling. Energy is your most valuable asset. Clean up your energy, what's inside, and you clean up your life, outside. Energy is potential, the amount of good that can be done. The more energy we have, the more good we can do. Frequency is the speed which an element vibrates. Everything has its own unique vibration[5]. Everything moves in cycles. The sun has a cycle of 365.4 days.

---

1   Amplitude Modulation, A.M., and Frequency Modulation, F.M., of the carrier wave, are the information that is decoded by your radio into sound, for example. You choose the channel of information you want to pay attention to.
2   Information is the creative energy of the Universe. It is dynamic. Without information, life cannot birth anything new. It is essential for the emergency of new order, for creation, and for manifestation. All life uses information to organize itself into form. Any being is a process of organizing information, not a thing. Information has a longer lifespan than the material it is associated with. Have a look at the Roman imperial eagle, on the back of a quarter dollar coin minted before 1999, in the USA, for example. The information remains long after that empire disappeared. A cell is a memory that has built some matter around it, in a pattern. Consider the Nautilus shell, the embodiment of the Phi ratio. Paraphrased from P. 95, *Leadership and the New Science*, Margaret J. Wheatley.
3   The whole universe flows, based on resonant attraction, like seeking like. If you seek something, love it, and note that it loves you.
4   Another way to say this is that relationships are all there is. What exists only exists because it is in relationship to everything else. Nothing exists in isolation. P. 19, *Turning to One Another*, Margaret J. Wheatley.
5   One example of this was Royal Rife's microscope, which showed that microbes have unique vibrations, and that putting in a 180 degree out of phase wave, a phase conjugate, cancels out the microbes.

The moon has a cycle of about 28 days. The Earth has its Schumann resonance, which is, by way, increasing.

The more good you do, the wealthier you will be, unless you choose to block that. What we concentrate on grows, and energy flows where attention goes. Nature is the energy that moves in all things. There is a matrix[6], or cosmic blueprint, of everything, and every thought. The blueprint of creation is wired into this, immanent, waiting to be called into form, by intent.

3. Energy is everywhere, in everything, and it responds to human thought and feeling, especially expectation, and intent. Anything that can be imagined is possible, because energy follows thought, feeling, and expectation. Imaging is a form of intent that shapes the future. It is an information compression. So are belief systems about limitation, abundance, and dowsing.

Belief systems are a <u>symptom</u> of intent[7]. Your belief systems create your life, and they are dominant in all events in your life. Events, and trauma, occur, but that is not what causes problems. The <u>interpretations</u>, the **judgments** we put on things, are what causes problems, because they block flow.

Energy in space has intelligence that responds to human thought and feeling. Belief systems are <u>interpretations</u> of phenomena, not phenomena. The map is not the territory. Whatever you measure or perceive, you influence. We attract what we think about, whether we want it, or not.

The intelligent human mind can and does *shift energy, potential, and quantum waveforms,* with *intent.* Intent means *feeling the shift already complete,* or *being in the feeling state of it already being complete.*

Know that you can consciously create and influence change. Have clear intent, and use open ended questions- quantum power questions- to start the process. Possibilities open up[8].

---

6   P. 222, *Multidimensional Man*, by Jurgen Ziewe.
7   Kenny Brinson
8   *How could this get any better? What else could happen?* Try these on for size. I ask them every single day. Have you realized, yet, that with the right questions, you can solve problems, and discover or accomplish anything?

Distract your conscious mind, keep it busy, while the greater consciousness is working. Dowsing and self-healing are forms of self-empowerment. People helping people is self-empowerment. Use what works for you- if you get results, it works.

You don't need to know how electricity works, to turn a light on. If it works, you did it right. Everything has a frequency. You can change anything in the world, by changing the frequency, or creating an opposite frequency[9].

4. Know that *you create every single thing in your life*. It doesn't matter if that's true or not. As soon as you install this belief, the world conforms itself to your belief.[10] The Universe is your Yin manifesting partner, whatever thoughts and feelings you give to it are returned, as things and events, on the shift back to Yang polarity. Ask for what you want. You will probably not get what you don't ask for.

This is far easier than you may think. Given the Infinite Worlds hypothesis in Quantum Mechanics, you have a near infinite number of worlds to choose from.[11] Choose one that you like better.

Another way to say this is <u>your thoughts and feelings- your intent- create your world</u>. If you don't like what's in your world, change what is within. Flip the polarity, from negative to positive. Also, *the only time that ever existed is right now.* You are creating your past and your future, now. You can only change in the moment, right now. If it helps, you may notice that *you have a staggeringly powerful energy field available in the now.*

5. *The space between atoms has consciousness, and even choice.* The double slit experiment in Quantum Mechanics is one demonstration of this, and also of the power of human consciousness[12]. Human intent at work in the nonphysical world shapes future events, which, in time, become the present.

---

9   Dr. Ben Johnson, cited at Pp. 137, 138, *The Secret*, Rhonda Byrne.
10   If you installed the belief that you don't have control, then the Universe responds to that belief. If you install the belief that Quantum events only occur in the subatomic level, the Universe responds to that belief.   If you install the belief that you dowse extremely well, the Universe responds to that belief.
11   P. 63, *Ten Thousand Whispers*, notes this, as does Dr. Richard Bartlett.
12   This is worth reading about, on Wikipedia at least.

The future is raw, pure energy. Thought [which is what is "thought"] is expectation of future. When thought meets raw, pure energy, it becomes reality.

One can dowse, or scan future possibilities, and past memories, on one's timeline, find negative or undesirable energy formations, and remove, deactivate, or revision them, with intent.

Always be open, stay in the question, don't weld yourself to your answer. Change is the only constant. Be aware of what you intuit, what you know from outside sources, and the difference. Let your awareness lead you, even and especially when it doesn't make sense, and when you have no idea where it is taking you[13].

6. *Energy can be impressed upon, or entangled with matter.* This is a kind of Quantum Entanglement. We are affected by the energy of an area[14]. Thought-tracks, and feeling-tracks, of habitual thought and feeling, build up as morphic fields[15], the same way a path in the woods shows many footprints[16]. You can also affect the past, with intent. An anti-particle is the particle traveling backwards in time, in Feynman's interpretation[17]. If a particle can do that, so can intent.

Past directed channels of quantum information can be used, as well as future directed channels[18]. We are exchanging energy with everyone and everything, as part of the flow of creation, so everything is shifting, just like sand on a beach. Each wave of information transforms the beach, metaphorically.

---

13   Milton Erickson told a story, about when he was a boy. He found a horse. He had no idea whose horse it was, so he mounted the horse, and guided it in the direction it wanted to go. The horse led him straight back to its barn. Other people were amazed he could do this. Why? The horse knew where to go. All he did was ride the horse. -P. 205, *Therapeutic Metaphors*, David Gordon. Working with stuff that is outside your consciousness feels very much the same. You could ask, *"Where does it want to go?"* and let it go there.

14   If you don't believe thought affects an area, sleep the night first in a summer camp, then in a funeral home. Tell that to your skeptic friends, too. Avoid bars, hospitals, places that feel bad, slaughterhouses, and so on, any area that feels like bad medicine, for this reason. Seek out places and activities that make you feel good.

15   Morphic fields may be part of David Bohm's second enfolded order- a super information field of the whole universe, as described at p. 149, *The Hidden Domain*, Norman Friedman. Bohm further notes that there is a similarity between thought and matter. All matter, including ourselves, is determined by information. Information determines space and time. P. 327, *The Dancing Wu Li Masters*, Gary Zukav. You will see the word **information**, or **modulation**, again.

16   Skeptics build up a morphic field of there being no paranormal around them, which is fine, if that's the universe they want to live in. I like a universe with the paranormal, because it is so much more fun and interesting, so that is a quality in almost every universe I inhabit. I only enter a skeptic's universe if it's useful. They are so violently closed to any other perceptions. As Voltaire said, *I am very fond of truth, but not at all of martyrdom.*

17   P. 639, *The Road to Reality, a Complete Guide to the Laws of the Universe*, Roger Penrose.

18   P. 603, *The Road to Reality, a Complete Guide to the Laws of the Universe*, Roger Penrose.

Energy is intelligent, a form of consciousness. It already knows where to go, and what to do. When you add intent to the energy, the energy gains purpose, and directs energy to a specific goal.

Passion fuels it. We let the energy lead us, and we flow like a symphony with the energy as it moves, and seeks its destination[19]. Let your intent be for the greater good, better than the best you can imagine, for best effects.

7. *Positive thoughts are orders of magnitude more powerful than negative thoughts*[20]. You can clean up decades of negative thought in weeks, or even days, or hours, and at times even instantaneously, because of this.

8. *If you aren't looking at it right now, it exists only as energy, potential, or quantum waveforms.* From a Quantum Mechanics point of view, unless you are looking at it, or touching it, right now, it exists only in the Quantum Wave Field, the Void of all potential, as potential. Your expectations, which grow from your belief systems, collapse your world into existence out of potential from moment to moment, when you look at it. Be careful what you believe. The Universe conforms to fit your belief system. Quantum Wave Forms will collapse into what you believe is the truth. Many physicists do not believe quantum phenomena occur in the world of human scale. As a result, quantum phenomena do not exist- for them- in their perception.

The Amazing Randi collapses his skepticism into his results. Actually, he is correct. Since he limits himself to only those possibilities that exist in the Beta EEG brainwave state, and the physical world, paranormal phenomena do not exist for him, or anyone else who enters his universe.[21] Proof is not necessary in the realm of perception[22], i.e. direct experience.

---

19 Pp. 90-1, *Touching the Light*, Meg Blackburn Losey.
20 as noted in the book *Power vs. Force*, by Hawkins.
21 I have no problem with people who say Science, or Jesus, or the Qur'an, or the DSM V, or the Merck Manual, or the Jedi Code, or the New York Yankees, is the only truth <u>for me</u>. It's people who forget those last two words who cause problems. And, just for kicks, test the accuracy of the current Evolutionary model. It's under 50% accurate. Now test the creationist model. It's also under 50% accurate. So they're both wrong. Except they are right, in their individual universes, because that is what they believe, and their universes conform to their beliefs.
22 P. x, *The Elves of Lilly Hill Farm*, Penny Kelly.

9. The human mind is shaped by, and shapes, its environment. Suggestions work. If that wasn't true, advertising on prime time television wouldn't cost six figures per minute. Children spend their time in lower brainwave frequencies.

Sometimes they get negative programming. If they are told "You are going to catch cold", or "idiot!" they will follow directions. If they are told they will get a cold and keep it until spring, they will. Notice these patterns, and shift as necessary.

10. There are three parts to mind: *Conscious*, Yang, or rational mind; *Subconscious*/Yin, and *Superconscious*, or monopole, which, with the physical body, make a Medicine Wheel, with spirit at the center. Each plays its own role. Some psychologists only accept the conscious mind. Their world conforms to their belief. The three mind model has been around for several thousand years. It is more empowering, so I use it. If you ask a question that takes three minutes to state, you are fixated in your conscious mind. Simplicity is power. *Clarity is power*. The closer to oneness, the more powerful. Complicated things are disempowering. Seek the simple. The Superconscious is simple, it is all unity.

If you doubt this, read the fine print in any contract, or package insert for a drug. Recognize the fear and greed that put it in there. The conscious mind is analytical, it tends to over-analyze, and worry, complicate things unnecessarily, and see divisions.

The subconscious mind takes direction from the conscious mind. It holds belief systems[23], and trauma, and runs the autonomous nervous system. The Superconscious mind sees everything as one. Your subconscious mind does not know the difference between an actual happening, and imagined happening in a deep state of mind.

---

23 The subconscious mind processes around 60 million bits of information per second, that we know of. The conscious mind handles 6-8, which is why phone numbers are 7 digits long. The filter seems to be the Reticular Activating System, a cluster of brain cells activated by what we believe to be true. The RAS filters out anything we don't believe or accept as true, and possible. Randi's Amazinging Disempowering System does this, for example. The subconscious mind is the "Prover", which creates events to prove beliefs to be true, within this filtering system. You hear self talk like *I knew that was going to happen*, *That always happens to me*, and *It happened again*. The RAS and selftalk form your comfort zone, of limitations. Habits can be your chains, or your wings... as you open up your Comfort Zone, your life gets better and better. Richard Bach's book *Illusions* gives you an idea of what's possible, for someone with a very open RAS.

Only the conscious mind can make that distinction. That division may be an illusion[24], anyway. Our perception and scientific perception of reality does to reality what a meat grinder does to formerly living flesh.

What is real, which is far beyond what we can perceive, is processed by our senses, and mind. What we get is metaphorical sausages, processed perception, that only vaguely resemble what is real[25].

All problems, and all disease are the result of blockage. Remove the blockage, and the flow heals[26].

11. The best way to learn is stories, because the formula is in the story, and you remember stories. Humans crave and love stories[27]. Stories give and hold meaning to experience. People live their stories.

Have you noticed that when you change your stories, you change your life?

---

24   *Illusion is the first of all pleasures.* -Voltaire   You know, in dreams, that sometimes really odd stuff happens. If you want to play with illusion, start noticing the dream-like aspects of your waking life. If you remember the first *Matrix* movie, Neo notices a replay of a scene, as a slippage of the show. I notice these in my daily life. They are fascinating.
25   -paraphrased, Professor Durr, lecture at the Deutsches Museum,   from a series, Science for Everyone, in Munich, 1998, cited p. 61, *Cosmic Ordering for Beginners,* Barbel Mohr, Clemens Maria Mohr.
26   Remove an invisible barrier, and the desirable physical changes take place of their own accord. P. 181,   *Quantum Healing,* Deepak Chopra.
27   *The Key,* James N. Frey.

B. Brainwave states and other points

The brain flows in cycles per second. This is measurable on an EEG. They are as follows.

0-3 cps is: *Delta* [also the main brainwave state of a child, 0-3 years old]

4-7 cps is: *Theta* [also the main brainwave state of a child, 4-7 years old][28]

8-14 cps is: *Alpha*

10 cancels stress, and is the conduit to universal awareness. Breathe deeply in this state.

15-20+ cps is: *Beta*

The **Delta** frequency is the land of the shaman, in Lipan Apache terminology.

The **Theta** frequency is the land of the spirit.

The **Alpha** frequency is the land of the spirit that moves behind all things.

The **Beta** frequency is the land of the living dead. It is the land of the flesh, of the mass media, and of many scientists still in the Newtonian paradigm[29]. Raymon Grace notes that 20 is the frequency of death. Businesses on the frequency of death generally aren't doing well.

Alpha and Theta are where great things start to happen. This was not really discussed in *The Secret*, and this is a major and critical omission. The Alpha EEG state is a dreamlike state. The Theta EEG state, 4 to 7 Hz, puts us in the zone, in balance with nature's Schumann resonances, and our subconscious mind[30].

Ed Stillman notes that dowsers function at all the brainwave frequencies, including the universal energy of 10 cps.

---

28   The alpha and theta levels, specifically 10 Hz, are the "kingdom of heaven" within us- p. 226, *You the Healer*, José Silva. These levels roughly correlate with the Hawkins Scale, also.

29   Does your computer work, when the power is out? No? Are you sure? Don't you have to be in a state where you have power, for your computer to work? It is the same way with every sequence in this book. You need to be in at least the alpha brainwave state. If you stay in Beta, in RandiSpace, nothing will work. Period. How well does your vacuum cleaner work, when it's not plugged in? Without power, you are just going through the motions. Go to where you have power. Also, these sequences work better if you are properly hydrated, and breathe deeply. Eating a diet that energizes you also helps. These may seem mundane, but they are not, they are very important points, which are part of the context of peoples using these sequences. Learning to use pictures, and feelings, and intent, at the deep levels of mind, opens all doors for you. "*Change things in the world by merely envisioning them.. love change[s] the world each time it replace[s] unlove.*" - p. 18, *Power vs. Force*, David Hawkins. Not using the deeper levels of mind is like staying in the first grade. You can do it, but it makes for a boring life. Richard Dawkins is a fun read, but he is only one channel I like multiple channels. The History channel is fun, so is the Sci Fi channel, and the Cartoon channels offer intense learnings, sometimes.

30   P. 137, *The Human Hologram: Living your Life in Harmony with the Unified Field*, Dr. Robin Kelly.

Some brainwave researchers use the term Gamma brainwaves, for this, and Gamma can go as high as 100 cps.

The **Gamma** frequency moves through all levels, apparently[31].

1. The Universal vibration of about 10 cps is present in the ionosphere. It is the frequency of God, the Great Spirit, the Void of all possibilities, or the energy that moves in all things. José Silva always worked at this level, when solving problems[32].
2. If you look up at about a 30-45° angle, this lowers your brainwave frequency to 10 cps. This is the universal intelligence station on your radio dial, metaphorically. Note portrayals of religious figures in classical art, who are often portrayed looking up, at a 30-45° angle. If people don't have the answer to a question, often they will assume this pose unconsciously, to retrieve the answer. I did it in school, myself. It works.
3. The alpha frequency in hands removes pain. You can enter anesthesia in the right brain wave state, which is theta[33].
4. *The power of thought is in low brain wave frequencies-* a relaxed state of daydreaming. When you daydream, you create pictures in the mind- and you can create non-usual results. You are healthier if your brain waves vibrate at a lower frequency. The king's chamber of the great pyramid, Japanese gardens, vacation sites, and many restful spots put people in the alpha frequency. Stress speeds up brain waves. Stress enzymes weaken the immune system.
5. There is no time or space at the energy level. This domain is holographic, and fractally resonant. This means you can do energy work, energy transformation, or get information, from any distance, instantaneously. Time is not linear.

---

31   It is the level of the Coyote, Creic, Road Runner, Tao, the crack between the slices of light, til Eulenspiegel, Trickster, and all the other teachers like them. Dr. Richard Bartlett, and Meg Blackburn Losey, note they spend a lot of time in Gamma, and so do Tibetan Buddhist monks. It also seems to be where master dowsers work.
32   This is the origin of the advice "sleep on it", or "your best counselor is your pillow". You access this level in your sleep.
33   Steven LaVelle used to demonstrate this, by putting on glove anesthesia, putting his hand in a wolf trap, and springing it. That was a very convincing demonstration.

The past is created[34] continuously in your memories. In spin network theory, there is no specification of time. So quantum information can travel one way or the other, past or future, along a spin network line[35]. Wrap your mind around that!

6. The future is composed of thoughts not yet materialized. *You can time travel, energetically.* When someone says, "If I had known what I know now, I would have said..." Now, you know this, and you can go back to the memory, and say it. You can also move forward, or laterally to alternate dimensions, and get information you can use. Alternate realities are accessed from the present moment[36].

7. Since everything has consciousness, and choice, *you can talk to and interact with anything*[37]. In the dentist's office, for example, you could tell a tooth to turn loose, and have it removed without anesthesia[38]. You can put imaginary oil on a bolt that just won't turn[39]. You can talk to and communicate with the nonphysical, and the apparently inanimate[40], as well as you can with people. A loved car will work better. Talking to computers sometimes works[41]. Respect is a very useful part of effective communication.

8. *Healing tricks work for a time, then one must learn something new.* The energetic world is very hospitable to new people with clear intent, however, that world encourages growth. We don't need complete information. In fact, we cannot perceive all the information involved.

---

34   The past has no existence except as it is recorded in the present. Past, present, and future are completely interpenetrated. P. 145, *The Hidden Domain*, Norman Friedman.

35   P. 963, *The Road to Reality, a Complete Guide to the Laws of the Universe*, Roger Penrose.

36   P. 139, *Sound: Native Teachings and Visionary Art*, Joseph Rael.

37   The *Ruba'iyat* says this: *For I remember stopping by the way To watch a Potter thumping his wet Clay: And with its all-obliterated Tongue It murmur'd--"Gently, Brother, gently, pray!"* Clay is symbolic of the Ether, being formed by intent. Speak to the wind, rain, and the storm, to calm it down. -Pp. 65, 66, 67, 83, *The Elves of Lilly Hill Farm*, Penny Kelly.

38   You can talk to plants to help them grow, you can talk to your fishline and hooks to help them catch fish, your tools. P. 58, *The Magic of Believing*, Claude M. Bristol.

39   As I was writing this section, I needed to install a bolt on a metal door, with self-tapping metal screws. I knew the job would be difficult, and it was, my hand hurt. Then I thought, why am I making this difficult? How does it get better than this? So I imagined the metal, in the path of the screw only, as like butter. It took ¼ the time to get the rest of the screws in. I play a similar intent game with turbulence, when I'm flying, which never takes more than two minutes to end turbulence.

40   When I was in college, Dr. Aram Yengoyan noted that within a year after the introduction of South American medicinal plants, in the 1970's, in the Philippines, Filipino curanderos knew what they were good for. This puzzled the scientists. Oh, they read the literature. No, the curanderos were mostly illiterate, and couldn't have paid for the books, and the books weren't available anyway. Oh, they had labs with many lab rats. No, they didn't. At that point, the curanderos were asked how they found this out. They responded, simply, "*Oh, we asked the plants, and they told us.*" This is a form of dowsing.

41   P. 153, *Reinventing Medicine*, Larry Dossey.

9. All we need is the willingness or intent to do something. For example, you could test for the presence of non-beneficial frequencies, energies, or whatever, with a dowsing device, Y/N. If you get a yes, you could ask that they be removed, or transformed into something beneficial.

10. A lot of stuff happens to us because we put up with it, and don't shift. You could use dowsing devices such as a bobber, or pendulum, or pair of pliers, and mentally state the intent to raise the energy in a town, or your workplace, or your home.

11. You could ask to raise life force to 100%, then the energy level, then the love level, then the cooperation level. You could ask to raise the energy, in body and home, to the highest appropriate level for the best good of all involved. You could ask for the most appropriate energy to be placed around you, your coworkers, and your workplace, allowing all to work efficiently and cheerfully. You could ask that hormone levels be put in balance. This is not any kind of medicine, it's just playing with intent. It's better if someone inside the system asks for help, as in a school, but you can still effect change even without that.

12. Test the energy of a person at home and the workplace. There are always problems in the place with the lowest energy. Low energy could indicate problems. Why not shift the low grade energy? You don't have to feed a machine quarter dollar coins, when you do this, it's free.

Dowse: Y/N *Does your dowsing system understand all this?* If not, intend the download of that understanding. You do that by feeling it done, in a very relaxed state. Any information you could ever want is only a dowsing question, or the expression of focused intent, distant from you. Dowsing opens the portal to a whole new world, well, actually multiverses of universes of whole new worlds.

What does absolute truth feel like?

What does infinity feel like? Have you realized you are an infinite being, yet?

C. Focused Play

We don't focus on the process. We focus on the <u>outcome</u>, just as you would using a GPS. We focus on the emotions and sensations of how we feel, when <u>we have reached the outcome</u> of our intended reality. We imagine that outcome, with all of our senses and emotions. We release the intent of that reality, which is the feeling of it already real, into the universal process, and fuel it from heart space feeling.

We leave the details up to creation, which provides the new reality from the infinite possibilities that are available. The outcome will usually be even better than we could have imagined, if we allow for this. It comes about more quickly, because there are no limiting details to hold it back. We do follow up on intuitive urgings, and ideas.

We can merge with the consciousness of other creatures, persons, objects, morphic fields, or anything we seek information from, and dowse and download useful information. There is no limitation to consciousness. It can access any time and space, cross dimensional barriers, and go anywhere you intend[42].

What does the center of the Sun feel like? ... and you are there, in imagination. This is the basis of remote viewing.

---

42   Keith Varnum dowsed an archeological site in the Southwest, this way. Once a year, the hunters apparently met with the spirits of the animals they would kill, for meat, that year. The animals would report, on time, even in snowstorms, trembling a bit. Is that real? I don't know, I didn't live there, 1,000 years ago. But it could be. What if you were in business, and you met, in imagination, with the people who would buy from you in the upcoming year, and you set the energy connections, the sacred geometries, on optimum level... but that is advanced, please ignore this.

It is important to be respectful with remote viewing, privacy is relevant. You can offer healing imagery, at this point[43]. Offering healing imagery is simply compressing consciousness, to affect the arrangement of our information, or to influence change or transmutation of energy fields[44].

A soul lives in multidimensional levels of reality simultaneously. Usually all the parts work together in alignment. Trauma may take these parts out of alignment. These parts can be re-assimilated[45], with intent, and dowsing is very useful feedback.
Creation is in a constant state of motion. Energies are constantly flowing through each other, like water in the sea.
We are constantly exchanging energy with other people, and energy systems, in our environment. We are constantly in the flow of creation. When we are present in the now, we become more aware of the subtle signs, and follow signs to make good choices.

Energy is a living form of consciousness. It is intelligent[46], and it already knows where to go, and what to do. When we add an intent to that energy, the energy gains purpose, and focuses and aligns itself, like a laser beam. When we add passion to the intent, it powers the energy towards that goal. Energy wants to play with you, and it wants to come into form, as healing beauty. If you doubt this, please dowse it.

It is better to serve the larger Universe, which could be showing up as just one other person, rather than just our own selfish goals. It is best to let the energy lead us, if we are sensitive to the energy, and how it feels.

We recognize subtle shifts, in dowsing, and guide our actions accordingly. We follow what each body or situation tells us, to a useful result. Every situation and person is unique. So our actions will also be unique[47]. Dowsing is play. Play is life[48].

---

43   Pp. 38-62, *Touching the Light*, Meg Blackburn Losey..
44   P. 66, *Touching the Light*, Meg Blackburn Losey, and the entire book, *Dowsing and Self-Healing*.
45   Pp. 75-7, *Touching the Light*, Meg Blackburn Losey.
46   You might read about the double slit experiment, in Quantum Mechanics, even in Wikipedia. Dr. Richard Feynman said this was all of Quantum Mechanics.
47   Pp. 87-94 , *Touching the Light*, Meg Blackburn Losey.
48   Theater is life. Art is truth. Television is furniture. Television news is junk food for the mind.

D. Tips for Imaginal work and play

Whatever you are working with is not infinite. If it is finite, then it has boundaries. If it has boundaries, then it has shape and form. If it has shape and form, it is subject to change, especially by intent. Notice that the Universe wants to help you create- for it grows when you grow.

Notice that negentropy, the tendency to greater order, and life, is far more powerful than entropy, the tendency to decay, because it operates from infinity. Entropy is limited to the physical level. Negentropy is not. Images are Yang, intent, placed in Yin potential, or the quantum possibility field.

You can play with imaginal work in any position. Sitting in a straight-backed chair may be the most useful[49]. Deep rhythmic breathing, with an intent to be quiet and relaxed, is very helpful[50]. Begin your breathing with the out breath, which stimulates the parasympathetic nervous system. This helps you to relax.

The in breath is Yin, the out breath is Yang. Intent is yang, imagery is yin, however imagery work is yang, so start with the out breath[51]. Once you're comfortable, and ready to begin, breathe out and in, deeply, at least four times.

You use imagery every day. What did the house you lived in as a child look like? What color is the nose of the blue polar bear in the corner of your room? What color are the sheets on your bed? Describe the route you took getting from home to work, or school, last week?

Some people turn images into labels, names or categories. For this work, which to me is more like play, see things just as they are. This also means not having any desire or fixation on results. Live totally in the now, for this work, just like kids do when they play. Whatever else you do, do not compare yourself with anyone else[52].

---

49   P. 34, *Healing Visualizations: Creating Health through Imagery*, Gerald Epstein, MD.
50   P. 35, *Healing Visualizations: Creating Health through Imagery*, Gerald Epstein, MD.
51   Martial artists time strikes, which are very yang, to coincide with the outbreath, which is also yang.
52   Pp. 210-2, *Healing Visualizations*, Gerald Epstein, MD; and Dr. Richard Bartlett, José Silva, and others.

In particular, do not compare yourself, or any part of your life with Photoshopped fantasy in magazines, romance novels, adventure novels, or other kinds of fiction. See things just as they are, without judgment, and with only those comparisons that are useful. Here is one sequence for playing:

1. Notice what you notice.
2. Whatever images come up are correct for you. You cannot not do it right.
3. Trust the process, and play with whatever comes up.
4. It may be useful to use the opposite of whatever shows up, or at least to balance it. If you notice what appears to be an excess of water, you might want to use fire, or at least to drain out the water. Sometimes the stupidest approaches, and the ones that make no sense, are the most effective.
5. Use whatever shows up. Ask for help. Angels don't exist, until they do. Whatever you discover in the process, whatever answers you find, ground them into daily experience by using them physically. If you asked the question, *How can I serve?* you will get an answer. Follow-up on it, and you will get better and better input.
6. The answer to your latest dowsing question may pop up, or something else useful. Or you might be totally blissful in the moment.

With imaginal work, Less is More[53]. When you feel the sensation, the imagery has done its job[54], or been picked up by the subconscious. Think of imagining as a small seed or a match. Imagining could take between one second and five minutes[55], just as Mike Dooley says. Overdoing crowds the subconscious, and shuts down what you want to happen. Intent trumps technique. Imagine yourself being a successful dowser.

---

53 Some useful maxims: *less is more, simpler is better, implicit is more powerful than explicit, copy first- then be creative, have fun, pay careful attention to detail, pattern and process; vary your patterns; try new things; profile carefully- know your subject well- and then let inspiration download; raise more questions than answers, strike indirectly if possible, not always directly. Use anticipation.* As Bruce Lee put it, *no way is way.* Be like water- flow into and through the situation. Being totally unpredictable like this is also very useful for raising children. You can't keep up with them, but you can keep them off balance. And as you throw the creative stuff at them, their brains are laying down new neural pathways, and they are getting smarter. My older daughter was a rebellious teenager, but how easy is it to rebel against water? She told me at 20 that she had keen B.S. Meter, because of all the things I'd done. This is a useful thing for a 20 year old to have, don't you think? The above is also a good place to create art from.
54 P. 40, *Healing Visualizations: Creating Health through Imagery*, Gerald Epstein, MD.
55 P. 40, *Healing Visualizations: Creating Health through Imagery*, Gerald Epstein, MD.

E. Morphic fields

Morphic fields are structured with layered intent. To say "I am a doctor" is to invoke the morphic field of what it is to be a doctor, as an example. The Swastika has a morphic field, several thousand years old. However, it was greatly polluted between about 1926 and 1945. Archetypes live in morphic fields. Rupert Sheldrake discusses these at great length. Many dowsers work in morphic fields, without knowing it. This is the place of remanence, tmeplates, patterns, of object-oriented programming of the mind.

Morphic fields do not make rules. People make the rules. The rule of the morphic field is "Do as I do"[56], which is useful in some cases, but not useful in others. The morphic field stores the pattern of how it "should be", the ideal world, as well as a stored up accumulation of judgments, and fixed conclusions. There are hierarchies of morphic fields. Archetypes draw power from a morphic field, and sometimes several morphic fields.

Everything you have ever accepted, believed, experienced, felt, imaged, internalized, and thought, forms a vast matrix or grid, your personal morphic field, your personal energetic signature[57]. Comfort zones are morphic fields, in part. One way to envision the points of possibility is as a space-time periodic lattice[58], a grill, a matrix. The cover was chosen to show that everything exists on a lattice, like this. Look closely, and you'll see it.

Those who get out of morphic fields become either leaders, or renegades. Leaders know they can get out of the morphic fields, while renegades aren't entirely sure. The key is to leave the morphic field without struggle. Of course, the leaders set up new morphic fields[59]. Good dowsers have mostly gotten out of the morphic field of mass consciousness.

---

56   P. 22, *Reality Transurfing IV*, Vadim Zeland.
57   P. 67, *Matrix Energetics*, Dr. Richard Bartlett.
58   P. 959, *The Road to Reality, a Complete Guide to the Laws of the Universe*, Roger Penrose.
59   Pp. 31-2, *Reality Transurfing IV*, Vadim Zeland. The classic example of this is Einstein, who said, "For rebelling against every form of Authority, Fate has punished me by making me an authority."

People who think about the object of a habit emit energy, on the morphic field's resonance frequency[60]. Watching a TV show, as one example, means exchanging energy with a morphic field. Be aware of your intent, as you watch.

In the flow of information you will find something useful to you related to your goal[61], something that has helped me greatly in writing this book. Morphic fields will do everything to stabilize the structure[62].

Morphic fields, by themselves, are not systems. They are systems, however, when considered as part of living beings, in the world of form. A direct connection, and a feedback loop, exist between a morphic field and structural elements. They affect each other. Every dowser who has ever lived contributed to Dowsing's morphic field.

Morphic fields do not have intelligent control over a structure, because they have no conscious intention. The consciousness of a morphic field is more like an algorithm[63]. Bureaucracies and corporations promote people to key positions, because they conform to the system, not because of any special merit. This is because bureaucratic morphic fields are interested in stability, not in intelligence, or change, or even long-term survival.

In fact, all bureaucracies develop mechanisms to inhibit their own proper function[64]. This is why creativity and taking initiative are punished[65]. The structure teaches you to want what the structure needs, in a sort of enslavement of intent[66].

Low-grade morphic fields enslave human intention in a sort of matrix, very much like the matrix in the movie of that name. This is one reason why Void surfing is so very freeing. Energy information entities [Morphic fields] are created and sustained by the thought and feeling energy of living beings.

---

60   P. 52, *Reality Transurfing IV*, Vadim Zeland.
61   Pp. 56-59 , *Reality Transurfing IV*, Vadim Zeland.
62   P. 33, *Reality Transurfing IV*, Vadim Zeland.
63   P. 34, *Reality Transurfing IV*, Vadim Zeland.
64   *Systemantics*, John Gall.
65   The workers in corporations are peasants, supervised by bailiffs and seneschals. Since peasants are, by definition, stupid, there is no point in listening to them.
66   Pp. 42 to 45, *Reality Transurfing IV*, Vadim Zeland.

Solving Problems with Dowsing **188** A book for new dowsers ISBN-10: 1482688573

Pendulums [morphic fields] cannot realize conscious intention. However, the low grade ones gulp down conflict energy, and motivate people to behave in a way to generate even more conflict energy for them to eat. This is particularly true in [superentities such as] crowds[67].

If you find yourself trapped in morphic field malaise[68], you can ask, *"What am I doing here? How am I aware of what's going on, how is all this helping me? How could I be spending my time better? Is this thought mine? If not, can I simply return to sender, now?"*

Generally speaking, dreams and goals are realized with the help of Morphic fields, because Morphic fields amplify intent- as long as the intent is expressed in the present tense. Dowsing interacts with morphic fields. Walt Woods' dowsing ability is a morphic field of itself. There are hierarchies of morphic fields.

Since Morphic fields amplify intent, it is important to think only about what you want, pleasant thoughts. Ritual creates and sustains a morphic field. Everyone performing a ritual now is connected with everyone who ever performed it before[69], through the field, fractally. You may still be in a Newtonian universe paradigm, so I won't tell you that you also connect with those in the future, as well.

F. Observer effect

The observer is connected to, part of, and influences what is observed. *Perception is Reality.* Our world is a dream theater, and your intent is the script.

---

67   P. 14-15, *Reality Transurfing IV*, Vadim Zeland.   In military basic training, or boot camp, the super entity of the unit forms between the third and fourth week.   Workplace culture is an example of a morphic field   There is a morphic field about the idea of the United States.   Some of its archetypal manifestations include Uncle Sam, and its shamanic ally, the bald eagle.   Books have morphic fields around them, which get more defined as more people read the books.
68   Comfort zones are morphic fields, in part.   They can be suffocating, at times.   The American TV program *Candid Camera* used to show the power of morphic fields and expectation.   They might, for example have a group of people on an elevator, all facing an unusual direction. Whoever got on the elevator would face in the same direction.   In Russia, they play with this, a group of people who don't even know each other use the Internet to agree that at a specific time, in a specific place, they will perform an odd act such as, for example, one hundred people taking out umbrellas on a clear day. -P. 21, *Reality Transurfing IV*, Vadim Zeland.
69   -Rupert Sheldrake, cited p. 32, *Matrix Energetics*, Dr. Richard Bartlett, and many Native Americans.

Solving Problems with Dowsing **189** A book for new dowsers ISBN-10: 1482688573

As the Observer[70], you can change the script. Expand your senses. They perceive 0.00000000000000000001% of what's going on, at best. The more awareness you have, the more power and energy you have.

Use *Hakalau*, the Hawaiian word for splatter or peripheral vision, for example, to expand your perception. Listen with your heart. *Attention creates. What you concentrate on grows, Energy flows where attention goes.* Put your attention on what you want. Ask your quantum power questions, your dowsing questions, to open up your awareness in a particular area.

If you seek light, put attention on the light. It is important to know yourself, because you are a self-similarity of the Universe. Influence over the outside starts with influence of the inside. When surroundings and effects cease to shape us, we shape them. Shaping your own energy is the same as shaping universal energy. Respect, acceptance, humility, and so on, are all useful in this transition. You reinforce what you observe. Dowsing is a kind of observation.

G. Perception can create infinite universes

Changing the arrangement, filters, focus, foundational beliefs, input, organization, patterns, priority, representation[71], or sensory ability of the data, changes the Universe.[72] This is playing in morphic fields. Understanding the patterns gives influence. Awareness is power and finesse. What does not succeed simply lacks awareness, or power, or it may not be in the right context.

---

70   Dear Experiencer: I am your servant. I am required to give you everything you ask for, with your attention. I always give you everything you think about the most. I resonate to the vibration of your every thought. I feel what you really feel. I try to talk to you, but you lose confidence in yourself so quickly. You change your mind so quickly, which keeps me running, and tired. You criticize me for going against you, but I can only give you what you ask for. Do you really want what you ask for, with your attention? Why don't you keep your attention on what you want, long enough for me to give it to you? I am required to fulfill your every desire, but you have to trust me. If you change your mind, I can't give it to you. Doubt is a slap in the face for me. Your beliefs channel your attention, and your attention forms your beliefs. I am your reality.
Signed, You.
71   Think of these as vibrational patterns.
72   I remember reading about a consultant who was told by a client that he felt as if he had a gun pointing at his head, in a situation. Now that is serious. The consultant said, "So, what color is the squirtgun [water pistol]?" The client's frame of reference totally shifted, and he started laughing.

Consciousness- mind- is everything. The world conforms to your beliefs about it. Reality is determined by the observer. Each person's Universe is unique to them. If it works, of course, it is true, and of course, truth is entangled with belief. Obi-Wan told Luke that Truth depends on perspective[73]. You may notice that for some dowsing, instead of simply finding what's there, you create new possibilities with your questions, almost new mini-universes.

H. Planes and Hierarchies

Start from the highest, and work down. These hierarchies go up, apparently without end, fractally, into spirit and essence, and come down into the grossest matter, even to the subatomic level. Each plane is under the control of the plane above it.

Each plane is its own universe, with laws, rules, assumptions, morphic fields, processes, dowsing paths, and ways to change[74]. You work within those limitations, in that plane only. If you find an unfriendly, stuck, or uncooperative energy, condition, or state of being, go up a level or two.[75] A dowser seeking water is operating at one level. A dowser diverting a water vein is at a different level.

As you dowse, you may run across the group souls, the intelligences, of animals, trees, plants, and minerals[76], who work for the lords, or hearts, of each plane or level. Oh, wait, that"s advanced, please ignore that. Respect, and cooperation towards achieving goals that benefit all, are very useful, here.

---

73   Here's a fun demonstration of this. Stan Tenen has showed that the spiral of manifestation throws shadows, depending on where the light is coming from. Different angles produce different shadows, which correspond to the Hebrew, Arabic, and Greek alphabets.
74   An aumakua, or Deva, or angel, is only supreme in its own universe or domain. Others are supreme in their own domains.
75   Recall the Einstein quote: *The problems we have cannot be solved at the same level of thinking which which we created them.* When in the problem state, we simply create more problem. Go anywhere else, instead. Hilbert space allows for multiple dimensions   P. 76, *The Hidden Domain*, Norman Friedman. Space with more than four dimensions is **hyperspace.** I have seen theories allowing up to 12 dimensions, and perhaps more.
76   P. 32, *The Divining Heart: Dowsing and Spiritual Unfoldment*, Patricia and Richard Wright.

I. Phase conjugation/destructive interference

Gestures, names, procedures, sequences, symbols, words, &c. when done backwards, phase conjugate at 180° an effect into nothing, as with noise-canceling headphones. An example of this would be to speak a former spouse's name backwards. You can phase conjugate an energy apparently out of existence[77], or at least intend this. This is very useful for dowsers dealing with noxious energies. You don't even have to know what the energy is, to counter it. Since we know far less than 1% of what exists, this is, then, extremely useful.

J. Playing with energies

Get into a playful, energetic mood. Rub your hands together, vigorously. When you feel some heat, pull them apart, and form an imaginary energy ball[78]. If you'd care to, let it fill with blessing, and let it go to whoever most needs it now. Or, you can pull it like it was chewing gum, and stretch it out. You can shape it.

It's "just" your imagination anyway, right? Have a friend do this, with their hands apart, and put your hand through the energy line connecting their hands, at the palms. Notice the feeling. The first time I did this, I could feel it immediately. There is no score, you don't need any result, just play. The comic book character Plastic Man springs to mind.

Make a lightsaber out of it, duel with your friend. Turn it into a blue Frank Sinatra sword, like at the end of the movie *Who Framed Roger Rabbit?*

Feel your own energy field. The feedback you get is perfect. Feel the energy field of a plant. You're just playing. Notice that your energy flows together, in confluence, with what you think about[79]. Let the energy form into a nice imaginary card for your significant other, or a rose, or a fountain of rainbow light.

---

77   Dr. Royal Rife used this to kill disease organisms- p. 3, *Touching the Light*, Meg Blackburn Losey.
78   I taught my nephew this when he was 8 years old. He and his friends would throw energy balls at each other, and they could always tell what color they were. Also discussed at p. 73, *Instant Intuition*, by Anne Jirsch, and p. 40, *Healing with Quantum Energy*, Ryu Takahashi.
79   Pp.176-195, *The Reconnection*, Eric Pearl, has a more elaborate version of this, if you want more. The above is adequate, though.

Solving Problems with Dowsing **192** A book for new dowsers ISBN-10: 1482688573

Let it become an ethereal fan, blowing nice energy to you, notice how that feels. It is infinitely plastic, this stuff. And it's just your imagination. Imagination, now, that's a fun place to play.

Remember the story of *Aladdin and the Lamp*. When you get a picture of the lamp, pull it out of the screen of your mind, and have it in your hands. Rub it some. See if a genie comes out. Does it matter what happens? No, you're just playing. What does the lamp want to do? What does the genie want to do?

What does the energy want to do? Could you wave an imaginary magic wand, and let Santa appear? What gifts does Santa have for you, right now? Is it the red-suited Santa, or the Santa from *The Lion, The Witch, and the Wardrobe*? Or some other kind of Santa?

Or perhaps you'd just like to feel better. How would you feel, if you felt better? Where do you notice that? What is the texture, the temperature, the weight or lightness, of that? What if you could shift your energies, effortlessly, just by being aware of them, and letting them become their optimal form?

What if you simply let the energies at work, or your home, simply go to their optimal level, right now? You don't need to know how. Most energy systems seek this state, now, and with your concentration, you let them recohere into the Void, and collapse back into being, in their optimal form.

And what would it feel like if your home was at the best possible energy level for you and your family? What about your workplace? Community? Perhaps they all could just fall right into their ideal energy state, just like water seeking out its channel, right now? What other parts of your life could fall into perfect alignment, right now?

VII. Intent creates everything in our lives

Our belief systems, and world, flow out of our intent, so that is a good place to start. My mother learned from an old China missionary that you could simply intend that you have a parking place. Her word for what she did was prayer. Correctly done, intent and prayer are same thing. **You feel it done, in your heart.** It worked for her every time[1]. Neither of them ever studied anything like what is here. They just did it. And it worked[2]. Every time[3].

Intent is interesting. One can take a practiced, detailed intent sequence, or dowsing sequence, and run it, with a single trigger. With practice in this, in time just bringing a situation to mind will mean it's taken care of, without any specific request[4]. Before beginning anything significant, it is useful to have a simple ceremony, which includes stating your intent[5]. Examples include weddings, oaths of office, initiations, and dowsing.

A. Enter the intuitive state, to get useful information

1. Say:
I am a clear channel to my higher self/fountain of light[6]/Source...
From my higher self...
There are many other more complicated sequences. Try them. This statement of intent is at least simple, and easy to remember.

2. The mind has two basic activities, or modes. It can only do one or the other. The first is *mind talk*, which runs on the batteries of memory. This is the default. Mind talk has feelings, images, sensations, and thoughts, and is usually focused in memories of the past, or fears about the future The second is *mindfulness*, which runs on the power of Source, in the now.

---

1   Cited also p. 72, *The Magic of Believing*, Claude M. Bristol. I have known people who could intend that money shows up, in the same way. I have done this myself, though I don't understand the process to the extent I would like to.
2   Manifesting parking places is a good place to start. Pp. 28, 29 , *Manifesting your Heart's Desire*, Fred Fengler and Todd Varnum.
3   Also used by David Schirmer, cited at P. 65, *The Secret*, Rhonda Byrne.
4   P. 97, *The Divining Heart: Dowsing and Spiritual Unfoldment*, Patricia and Richard Wright.
5   P. 33, *The Divining Heart: Dowsing and Spiritual Unfoldment*, Patricia and Richard Wright.
6   P. 56, *I Turn to the Light*, Connie Bowen.

This is the portal that opens up to <u>intuitive guidance</u>. Entering this state requires conscious choice to do so, at first.

Mindfulness moves through *attention, concentration* and *meditation*[7], into what Tom Brown, Jr., calls the Sacred Silence. The monkey mind activities of analyzing, annoyance, commenting, conceptualizing, evaluating, frustration, judging, labeling, ranking, reviewing, and worrying are a process of storing the present moment into memory[8], as interpretation. Mindfulness exists only in the now, outside of time, as flow[9]. This is the dowsing state. It feels spacious. At some level, it is infinite.

Attention is the continuous experience of a chosen point of focus. It happens when we observe our experiences, rather than sleepwalking through them. Attention and observation allow us to experience life directly in the now, without interpretation, judgments, and distortions. Concentration is deeper attention, which takes you below the surface characteristics, to a more comprehensive understanding of essential nature[10].

When talk, and noise, and distraction move out of awareness, the empty mind remaining enters meditation, the Sacred Silence, which can include feelings of clarity, peace, and tranquility[11]. The deeper level of this is no-mind, "mushin", in Japanese.

Learning mindfulness starts with the decision to do so. It continues with solitude and silence. The stillness leads to insight, mental clarity, physiological healing, relaxation[12], and better dowsing.

Patience, as focused persistence, is also helpful. A good place to start is to pay attention to breathing. Simply observe it. Take a deep breath, into your belly, and as you exhale, make a *haaaaaa* sound.

---

7   P. 31, *Intentional Healing*, Elliot Dacher, MD.
8   P. 34, *Intentional Healing*, Elliot Dacher, MD.
9   Thich Nhat Hanh has some great books on mindfulness, if you want more. What is here is sufficient.
10   P. 35, *Intentional Healing*, Elliot Dacher, MD.
11   P. 36, *Intentional Healing*, Elliot Dacher, MD.
12   P. 39, *Intentional Healing*, Elliot Dacher, MD.

That means you are breathing from your *dan-tien*, the hara point, your energy center or core. You take in life energy here, also.

When you breathe shallowly, in your chest only, you are cutting off your life energy, and stuck in your head. This is the place of worry, stress, and anxiety. Just breathing deeply for a while is very relaxing. Mindfulness is noticing the feelings, sensations, and thoughts that arise from breath to breath. It is doing things one at a time, with full attention. We open to life, not how we imagine it should have been, or should be. It is accepting things just as they are, in the moment[13]. This is the dowsing state. Dowsers go fishing at the shore of the Void of all possibility, with questions.

As soon as you notice an image, analyzing, annoyance, boredom, commenting, feeling, frustration, judging, labeling, sensation, thought, worrying, or distraction, simply observe this. Allow it to move through you, and quiet down. Gently put your attention back on breathing. Notice your breathing. Where do you feel your breath move? Is it in your mouth, or abdomen? Notice the movement. Do you breathe into your chest, or all the way down to your abdomen[14]?

After some minutes of this, you could ask yourself a question, "*What is the primary issue I could work or play with?*" Notice the answers and thoughts that come up, and especially the insights. This is a very good place in which to ask all quantum, that is, dowsing, questions. Meditation is simply being present when mind-talk, exterior attention, and concentration stop. This is the natural mind, the dowsing mind.

Note that you get short periods of emptiness, and pure awareness, the gap between thoughts. This is no- mind. Even the span of time of the beat of a mosquito's wing is enough. One mindfulness exercise is to sit in a chair comfortably, and to count your breaths. If you forget the number, start over again at one. You can count on your fingers. Do this for three cycles of ten[15].

---

13   Pp. 182-3, *The Breathing Book*, Donna Farhi.
14   P. 48, *Intentional Healing*, Elliot Dacher, MD.
15   P. 51, *Intentional Healing*, Elliot Dacher, MD.

Mindful eating means starting in no-mind. One then perceives the food with all of its characteristics. Take a spoon, and with total attention, place the food in your mouth. Notice everything about it. Chew as slowly and thoroughly as you can. Notice everything. Taste it. Note the movement of your jaw. Swallow it with total attention. Pause. Do the same thing with the next spoonful.

You can notice that eating is a gift. The sky gave rain, the Earth gave nutrients and soil support, the plant gave fruit or seed. You gave money and time. Notice that everything associated with the plant is now connected to you, as you are connected to it. When you finish, spend a few minutes in silence, and give thanks for all the gifts that came together to feed you[16], from the ultimate source of all that is, Ultimate Generosity[17].

Conscious living means installing useful habits, which crowd out time wasters. It lowers energy consumption by increasing harmony, and is a training in mindfulness. The most important part of this is daily practice, which is best scheduled, and done regularly. In time, it becomes a habit.

Daily practice needs to include relaxation, which could be a progressive relaxation. It could include Yoga, Tai Chi, Chi Kung, or other mindful activity. It could be breathing. See also the Practice section towards the end of this book.

A progressive relaxation[18] could start with your head. Tense all of the muscles in your head. Hold for about 3 seconds, and then relax. Notice the incredible feeling of relaxation in your head. Do the same thing, slowly, with your shoulders, arms, chest, abdomen, hips, thighs, legs, and feet.

Pay particular attention to the incredibly blissful feeling of relaxation, and allow it to go a little deeper[19]. This is a good prelude to entering the imaginary workshop, for higher level dowsing, if that's of interest.

---

16   P. 55, *Intentional Healing*, Elliot Dacher, MD.
17   P. 146, *The Universe is a Green Dragon*, Brian Swimme.
18   *The Relaxation Response*, by Herbert Benson, M.D., talks about this at some length.
19   I think this was started by a guy named Jacobs. My first experience was in a Psi seminar. I went really deep, and felt great! We then entered our imaginary workshops.

Breathing deeply is another kind of relaxation, which greatly helps dowsing. I was taught to breathe by Robert Winn and Lois Grasso, who were students of Judith Kravitz[20]. When I was born, my uncle delivered me. It seems I was coming out too quickly. So they injected my mother with a drug to slow down the birth. I've had a feeling ever since of other people holding me back, well, until I cleared it.

The placenta was cut immediately. I had to start breathing immediately, or die. I felt like I was suffocating. I resisted breathing because of the feeling that it hurt. As the breath opens, more life force energy flows in[21]. The breath is the movement of spirit in the body[22].

Regular breathing raises your energy levels. Love, power, and joy are accessed far more easily through full breathing. Every time we breathe, we take in power. Full breathing gives us a natural high, which makes it easier to let go of addictive behaviors[23].

Limiting beliefs can be cleared by changing one's breathing patterns[24]. Belly breathing cleans out limitations, develops the will, and grounds one in the body, improving the will to live[25]. Lack of breath in the solar plexus shows a separation between heart and will, which may result in fear and worry, and lack of integration[26]. Lack of breathing in the sternum shows a closed heart center, and the repression of love. This was usually done to protect oneself emotionally[27], especially as a child.

The chest area, above the heart, and throat, are where the higher will expresses. Problems in this area indicate limitations in expressing one's true mission in life, a lack of empowerment and direction, and perhaps lack of clarity about mission and purpose in life[28].

---

20 _Breathe deep, laugh loudly: The Joy of Transformational Breathing is her book._
21 P. 33, _Breathe Deep Laugh Loudly_, Judith Kravitz.
22 Andrew Weil, cited at p. 73, _Breathe Deep Laugh Loudly_, Judith Kravitz.
23 P. 117, _Breathe Deep Laugh Loudly_, Judith Kravitz
24 P. 31, _Breathe Deep Laugh Loudly_, Judith Kravitz.
25 P. 32, _Breathe Deep Laugh Loudly_, Judith Kravitz.
26 P. 34, _Breathe Deep Laugh Loudly_, Judith Kravitz.
27 P. 34, _Breathe Deep Laugh Loudly_, Judith Kravitz.
28 P. 34, _Breathe Deep Laugh Loudly_, Judith Kravitz.

If a breath starts in the middle area, this indicates someone who has trouble delegating, and must do it all by him or herself[29]. Robert Winn notes that the people who have trouble breathing in, have trouble _receiving_, and nourishing themselves. Those who have trouble breathing out have trouble _giving_, and releasing no longer useful energy.

I cannot begin to describe all the benefits of breathing deeply. I was taught to take in a deep breath, all the way down to the bottom of my stomach, in a relaxed way. I then let it out naturally, without forcing it, with no breaks in between, as "circular breathing". There are many other kinds of breaths. However, this is a good start. They recommended doing this for approximately 5 minutes per day. This is useful.

Robert Winn told me that how we breathe is how we live, that someone breathing at 30% capacity is living their life at 30% capacity. Ask the question: _"What do I want more of in life?"_ during a breathing session[30], as your breath tends to energize what you are running through your mind.

Breathing through the mouth is the best place to start, because it clears out blockages in the lower body, especially those associated with manifesting. If you notice unpleasant feelings, keep breathing circularly, until you get through them. They will become pleasant[31]. It can be useful to tone a sound during breathing, to break up resistance[32].

At some point, breathing suddenly becomes very easy, because you have entered natural breathing[33]. At this point, you may get an informational download[34]. Laughing heartily is a great way to move the breath through us. Laugh uncontrollably at least once per day[35]. Downloading is noticing information becoming part of your being[36].

---

29 P. 35, _Breathe Deep Laugh Loudly_, Judith Kravitz.
30 P. 24, _Breathe Deep Laugh Loudly_, Judith Kravitz.
31 P. 28, _Breathe Deep Laugh Loudly_, Judith Kravitz.
32 P. 26, _Breathe Deep Laugh Loudly_, Judith Kravitz. If you have musical experience, Laurel Elizabeth Keyes' book _Toning_ notes that the musical note C is very useful for this. She recommends using a pitchpipe.
33 P. 27, _Breathe Deep Laugh Loudly_, Judith Kravitz.
34 P. 30, _Breathe Deep Laugh Loudly_, Judith Kravitz.
35 Dr. Richard Schulze, who also says to learn 1,000 jokes.
36 P. xxix, _Touching the Light_, Meg Blackburn Losey.

3. Walt Woods offers a free .pdf download of his book *Letter to Robin*, which is a basic dowsing guide[37]. So,

3.

Dowse: *Can I, May I, Should I energetically download[38] Walt Woods' complete dowsing system?* Y/N, which is to say, you test[39] to see if you get a yes or no. If you get a yes, and in almost all cases readers will,

Dowse: *Are you [the dowsing system] willing and able to be downloaded to me, now?* Y/N

If yes, and for almost all readers it will be,

Dowse: *Is there any reason not to?* Y/N For almost all, the answer will be no.

Dowse: *Has it already downloaded?* Y/N Sometimes, it will already have done so, just by asking these questions. If you get a no, intend that it downloads now, energetically, to your consciousness, and notice what is different. That fixes it in place, with observation. If you'd like to, you can also download the .pdf, to your computer.

For the very few readers who did not get permission to download, examine your motives. Generally, service[40] to humanity will remove blocks. If your sole intent is self-gratification, without the intent to serve, you have given away 95% of your power, and a lot of the fascinating stuff in the Universe is not available to you. Set an intent that you serve humanity[41], if you want to increase your power, and dowsing.

Note the download sequence introduced here. You might Dowse:

Can I/May I/Should I download the complete set of knowledge from which this book was selected? Y/N

Is there any reason not to? Y/N [If you get a yes, respect that]

---

37   How do you determine percentages? Well, you can download Raymon Grace's circular dowsing chart at his website, you could use Walt Woods' circular dowsing chart, in *Letter to Robin*, free for download off the Internet, and you could even use a **protractor**, which is easy to get. Ask your question, with your pendulum swinging, centered at the center of your chart or protractor, and notice where the forward swing goes. Percent feedback is extremely useful. I use a pendulum mainly for percentages, as it is very quick for that.

38   This means you download Walt Woods' system as a template, as an energy pattern, not the computer file. What other templates, or energy patterns, could be useful to you, if you downloaded them, I wonder?

39   Basically, ask the question, and see if you feel at ease, or constricted. At ease means **Yes**, and constricted means **no**. Feedback makes you far more effective, in any field. Notice that truth feels spacious, and flowing. Notice that lies feel constricted.

40   People who have selfish motives have far less energy than people with noble motives, that include service to others. P. 63, *The Greatest Manifestation Principle in the World*, Carnelian Sage.

41   Evil persons would not be reading this book. If one is, I strongly recommend re-assessing your intent. Evil, which is to say causing intentional harm to innocents, comes at a very high price, much of which is deferred, with a high interest rate. You can get what you want in life, without intentionally causing harm to others, and it feels better.

If you get a No, intend the download. You will understand this book better.

For any kind of intuitive work, <u>shape your questions carefully</u>. You will get answers[42]. Your subconscious passes this data from your higher self, and it is very literal. This is why forming the right question is the most important part of dowsing.
<u>Dowse:</u> *What percentage am I influencing or biasing my answers?* If you get anything over 0%, calibrate, that is, intend that the percentage drops to zero.
<u>Dowse:</u> *Dowsing System, are you able and willing to drop my bias against getting answers through intuition to 0%?* Y/N When you get the Yes, <u>Dowse:</u>
Is there any reason not to? Y/N When you get the No,
Say, "*Thank you for doing it now, and giving me a clear feeling when it is done*". This can happen in under one second of clock time. Test and calibrate till this goes to 0%.

Entering wholeness, in your heart, is plugging into power

The small self is an ego construct of layers of identity, conclusions, judgments, opinions, and other crystallizations. The higher self[43] is one with everything, so it doesn't exist, except that it is all that exists. We go from small to large. Breathe deeply four times or more. 100 times would be great. Release the need to do anything to connect with your heart. Imagine an elevator in your head that goes down to your heart level, and use it now.

---

42   You've heard this before- If you ask if your car needs gas, you'll get two hits- it operates on gasoline, and it also uses oxygen, which is a gas. How can you get very specific- like, asking the percentage full, of the gas tank, for example? This is more useful. You can dowse for the number of miles/km your car would go, with its current gasoline, and the existence of the cheapest gas stations, on the route, as well. I knew people in the Army who would dowse clubs, for highest probability of meeting up with a certain kind of person. You can fill in the details. They seemed very successful, to me, also. One guy maintained three girlfriends, at any given time, I have no idea how, other than by dowsing. I find that dealing with one is quite enough for me, so I haven't explored this much. A woman seeking an ideal soulmate might want to ask how tall he is, say, where he lives, what kind of car he drives, perhaps his telephone number and address, what his fascinations are, where he hangs out, what kind of clothes he likes on a woman most, hhmm, that could be a very interesting dowsing question chain. I would do "The List" of all the qualities one wanted, first, before going to that level. Health, for example, is good. Having a heart is useful. Being unattached, and seeking a partner, is useful. The major blockage here is accepting that such a thing can happen. Also, be aware that with intent, one might actually be manifesting a soulmate out of the Void, oh wait, that is so advanced, no, forget this whole section.
43   If you enter the Void, you can ask your higher self for a message. You'll get it, no more than a sentence, either right away, or later. P. 177, *Freeing the Captives*, Louise Ireland-Frey. You can also give a message to your higher self to transmit to someone else's higher self, especially if you can't deal with them physically, as Max Freedom Long notes.

Watch your awareness go down through your throat, into your heart. Then the doors open, and you step out. The field of heart is everywhere. You might notice quiet, peace, and a feeling of calm. Have nothing in your heart. Be blank. Clear thoughts and emotions out of it. It is good to keep thoughts above the heart, and emotions in the subconscious mind, below the heart. Keep your heart empty. This gives you instant meditation[44], and openness to dowsing.

B. Plug into Universal Intelligence

- Look up at a 30°-45° angle. This lowers your brainwave frequency to 10, which is the universal intelligence. This is heartspace, a good place for planting intent. Joseph Murphy would access this state, and say *"I am being made aware of the Divine Solution now. God knows the answer, and I and my father are one. God reveals it to me this instant."*[45] Be alert to the download. This is powerful dowsing.

You can also drop intent in this space, like a seed put in soil.

Examples: Go to a lower brainwave state, close your eyes, and take a deep breath and relax. Here are three ways to use this:

- Say, in this state: *"I am totally healthy now and forever!"* Feel this to be true.
- Or say: *I now attract the ability, knowledge, and information needed to improve the world.*
- You could face in the direction of a given person when they're asleep. Fill your lungs with breath, and imagine them well. Breathe out.

---

44   You could see heaven as being the shamanic upper world, and also the chakras above the heart. You could see the lower three chakras as the earth, and the shamanic lower world. The heart is the shamanic middle world, and also the sky, in the Chinese system. The pelvis is the cup of Ceridwen, the predecessor of the Grail. It is a creative area, which digests food, pulls in energy, and is involved in digesting food, and making babies. Moving from head to heart means moving out of fear into love, out of worry into trust, out of thought into knowing.

45   Thomas Edison- you remember him as the guy who dowsed for technology solutions- spent a lot of time in this state. He would hold a bottle in his hands, so if he went to sleep, the bottle would fall and wake him. Salvador Dali held a spoon over a plate, for the same reason. This sequence by itself opens up the infinite Internet of all possibilities. If you phrase your open-ended question well, you will always get an answer, to any issue. There is no limit. This is also cited at p. 257, *Parallel Universes of Self*, Frederick Dodson. Salvador Dali and Edison were accessing the theta brain wave state. Yet a child a accesses this at will, by daydreaming. P. 53, *Shapeshifting into Higher Consciousness*, Llyn Roberts. Daydreaming is a great source of ideas. P. 81, *The Art of Humorous Illustration*, Nick Meglin. Dr. Elmer Gates improved over 2000 patents, by doing what he called Sitting for Ideas, in a state that was clearly at least alpha. Cited in *Think and Grow Rich*, by Napoleon Hill.

<u>Example:</u>   The survival mechanism is excited by trauma, especially if you see blood, and especially your own blood.
- Immediately drop your brainwaves, especially if you notice shock.
- Tell your body to stop bleeding, and heal itself![46] Better yet, tell it the accident never happened, wipe it off your timeline.[47]

C. Getting your Power back, in wholeness

These are force multipliers, though you probably wouldn't need to do them repeatedly.

1. You are far more effective when you are on the **cause** side of the cause/effect equation, to change your life. This is inside you. So shift to that side. This is a good start. Start feeling that you are infinitely abundant, knowing, powerful, wise- and whole. Put yourself in the state of being, of abundance, for example. You already create your Universe, whether you choose to acknowledge that, or not. These questions may help you get into the state of being of having already recovered your personal power:

How would I feel, if I had infinite abundance, awareness, power, and wisdom, now?
How would it feel to have absolute peace, love, joy, satisfaction, contentment, abundance, health, and everything that makes life worth living, now?
How would it feel, if I could effortlessly and instantly create anything I wanted, now?

You could state the following:
I am the Creator of my Universe.
<u>Dowse:</u> *% you believe this true.*
If under 100%, calibrate- intend it higher. Hint: you are this, even when you are pretending you are not[48].

---

46   The Three Fingers technique of the Silva Method, described at p. 111, *You the Healer*, by José Silva, is good to master, also, if this sort of thing interests you. My space is limited, and some people always want more. See also p. 115, How to Halt Profuse Bleeding, ibid.
47   Richard Bartlett sprained his knee in a seminar. He chose a Universe where that hadn't occurred, and his knee quit bothering him. P. 210, 233, *Parallel Universes of Self*, Frederick Dodson, notes similar incidents.
48   Hint: YOU are the observer, so you create your universe, by observing it into existence.

*I am not real. None of this is real. I am making it all up, right
now. This is only a point of view.*[49]
*I create everything, and everything that happens, I have
recovered all my power.*
I exist in a sea of Infinite Abundance, right here and now.
*There is no miracle too big for the Universe to create, through
me.*
*I have infinite power to create everything I want, and infinite
contentment, gratitude, joy, knowledge, peace, satisfaction,
unconditional love, wealth and wisdom.*
Test (by dowsing): *% you believe each statement true.* If under
100%, you may want to raise them, with intent. Or, you could install
these beliefs in your being via direct download. How do you do that?
Feel it already done, in a deeply relaxed state. This needn't take more
than 3 seconds of clock time, once you've practiced. What other
statements would be useful?

Perhaps you still believe something outside yourself is powerful.
You could reclaim your power from that, with a CCW spin, from
your perspective, using a pendulum, or bobber, or even your
hands, or mind. Appreciate how real it all felt, how amazingly
real it was, and how well it served you, in the game you were
playing, of not being powerful. Feel the power you gave to that
coming back to you, with high volume, feel it surging into you, in
a CCW spin. Hit the Turbo button, so it goes really fast. As that
power comes back, feel yourself expanding more and more, into
who you truly are, your True Self.[50]

**Put this process on automatic, and assign it a one word
code, so you can invoke it any time you feel less than
powerful**. I suggest *"recover"*. Any time you feel less than
peace, love, joy, satisfaction, contentment, and so on, run this
immediately, and let it happen in under one second of clock
time.[51]

---

49   It's all quantum waveforms, so yes, you really are making it all up. This is literally true. In fact you created this
book out of Quantum probability waves, with your intent. I was only part of the manifesting path.
50   This is similar to Native American, Chi Kung, Tom Brown, Jr., and Robert Scheinfeld's work. Bob says that as
you recover your power, manifesting gets easier and easier. For Scheinfeld fans, there is no Phase 1 or Phase 2.
There's only what you're becoming now. How do you know when you create your reality? Well, you're doing it right
now. Feel your feelings. Now say, *these sensations are my unlimited power for me to experience. I'm so glad I can
play with these.* Now say out loud, *If I can manifest the moment, now, I can manifest anything. I know and feel this is
true, right now.*
51   I have heard Native Americans say the white man has given his soul to the preacher, his health to the doctors, his
money to the bank, his decisions to politicians, and his kids to school, then he wonders why he feels weak; and that
White Man culture means working in jobs you hate, spending money you don't have, to buy things you don't need,
feeling bad so you can look good, to impress people who couldn't care less. There is wisdom in this. Start recovering

Any time a negative thought comes up, run this immediately. Run this on anything that makes you feel bad. **Now intend that it happens automatically, without your need to consciously run it, as when you are asleep.**

D. Clearing limitations to wholeness

1. Determine an area of life that is less than perfect. This could be body/health/well-being, career, creativity, emotional expression, family, finances, fun, lifestyle, relationships, service[52], spiritual, and so on.

Dowse: *presence of **vibrational patterns** adversely affecting that specific area of life,* Y/N.

Note that with this sequence, it is not necessary to know what they are, unless you just feel really drawn to that. I personally don't feel the need to examine my garbage, before it is thrown out. Your subconscious mind holds all trauma, and garbage, and limiting belief systems. Like a four year old child, it comes to you, with bad feelings, and trauma, asking "Daddy, is it ok to throw out the garbage now?" If you don't respond with a yes[53], it keeps holding on to them. Pay attention to how you feel. If you feel bad, this could be your subconscious mind, with a load of garbage for you to take out.

Dowse: ***how many*** *vibrational patterns? 1, 2, 3, 4?* Keep going till you hit on a number. Don't obsess about the number, or if it's correct, what you are doing is precisely defining something for your attention to shift.

Dowse: *% inherited.* Could be 100%.[54]

Dowse: *% adverse effect on you.* You could check for effects like addictions, anger, bad habits, bad relationships, fear, guilt, heart problems, kidney stones, low self-esteem, and so on. Or not.

---

your power, from wherever you have given it away, today.

52   The Universe helps people who help others. Pour love and kindness into other people, because the Universe will bring it back to you magnified. In manifesting, this is more important than focusing on what you think you want. Also, it's a lot of fun! There is a certain moment of perfect beauty, when I feed someone's interests well, and they realize I do not expect anything in return from them.

53   Breathe into all negative and stuck feelings. Keep breathing until they are gone.

54   The method above is quick. It will also pull out beliefs and blocks that are not expressible in language. If you like a somewhat slower, more detailed process, another way to do this is to list all of one's negative attitudes about, for example, money, as on p. 105, Ten *Thousand Whispers*, by Lynda Madden Dahl, or *Money is my Friend*, by Phil Laut, and to shift polarity so they are positive and serve you. This takes longer, so I don't use it much.

Solving Problems with Dowsing **205** A book for new dowsers ISBN-10: 1482688573

Ask your dowsing system to <u>remove the emotions</u> from all the vibrational patterns adversely affecting that specific area of life. Your pendulum, bobber, or energy sense may show a CCW spin until done. Or you can just imagine this. You could say *"Is my dowsing system willing and able to remove the emotions from all vibrational patterns adversely affecting that area of life?"* Y/N. When you get the Yes,

<u>Dowse:</u> *Is there any reason not to request this? Y/N* When you get the No, intend that this has already happened. That means *feel it done.* If you didn't get a yes, and then a no, rephrase your questions, or redefine what you are working on.

You could also *ask that the energy be transformed, to whatever would be to the highest good of the person, and you.* You may notice a CW spin, till done.

<u>Dowse:</u> *% issue is affecting you/person.* If over 0%, repeat process until done.

It may be necessary to repeat, over time, as you clear out different layers. It's worth it.

2. Here's another way to do this, at an identity level:

Choose a reality, or chain of events, you have experienced a lot, and perhaps don't find useful. Become the observer. Observe it, without passion, until you no longer react to it, till your polarities on it, including analysis, belief, judgment, labels, memory, opinions, and thought about it[55], lose charge. It naturally dissolves and returns to the Void.

3. Pick an experience. Run the *drop down into heart, plant intent, let go* sequence, to reprogram the belief that generates it. If that's too simple, ask yourself this Quantum Question: *What beliefs would generate this experience? What am I trying to make others wrong, and myself right, about?* Write the answers down. Then ask how you can prove that belief true- which takes you to the core belief. Ask about the secondary gain, that is, what you can be right about, if it continues.

Now rewrite each of them as the belief you want, instead. Feel the new beliefs real, as a memory. You could spiral them, clockwise, into you. Fill them with emotion.

---

55   The NLP folks might say to change the submodalities, and you can do that, too. I have not found that necessary.

<u>Attention</u> creates the new belief, <u>emotion</u> charges it, and <u>action</u> embodies and grounds it. Feel this true in your body. All this can happen in one second of clock time.

Act as the new reality, doing what you would do, knowing with absolute certainty it is real. Maintain for 21 days, if necessary, and it is totally real[56]. You may want to calibrate the belief. If, for example, you got a great job, but there is some aspect not good, you would want to adjust the belief.

You may have already noticed that installing a new belief can happen, even if you don't discharge the older belief. The new one may overwrite the old one. Lag time between intent, and showing up in the flesh, is also directly related to your beliefs about what is possible.

It would be useful to install the following key program:
My heart and soul are in command of my total being in all aspects, dimensions, moments, places, times, and ways. My heart aligns with and aligns my total being for effective, satisfactory installation and operation of all affirmations, which are installed for the highest good of all, doing only good for myself and others. They remain in effect until revised or canceled by me. All requests I make of my intuition go through my heart. All replies given are truth, based on information obtained from all possible reliable sources. If information is not available, or cannot be given, this will be communicated clearly.

The following principles may be useful, in understanding intent, energy, dowsing, and manifestation. You may wish to test the % that you believe them[57]. If you are at 100% on all of them, you have a marvelous foundation. You are never given a wish without also getting the power to make it come true[58]. What other statements would be useful to install?

---

56   Maybe you have a friend who seeks more money, or a better job. Do you run the celebration party, or does he? Who is there? In your imagination, raise your goblet, and shout: "Here's to your fabulous new job/salary increase!" Don't think of the friend's boss, because that is a how, and limits the possible outcomes. Neville would say build an event structure that implies your desire is already real, and enter its form with strong feeling. Don't worry about others. They can't create it, your imaginal act does, by opening the door to it. Run the movie regularly, to compress this into experience.
57   It is best if we make intentions to serve the highest and best good of all concerned, including the Universe, and to intend this or something better, to open up more pathways of possibilities
58   You cannot desire what is not already yours, slightly out of phase with you. A parallel self has already experienced it. If not, you couldn't feel, imagine, or even be aware of it.

- *Humans are the otters of the Universe. It is more fun to manifest dreams than dramas*
- *I am connected to all that is by thought and feelings. There is no separation*
- *I am happy to be who I am*
- *I am not circumstance, effect, outcome, or thing; I am the Creator of these*
- *I can be, create, do, dowse, experience, have, manifest, and resonate with anything I can imagine*
- *I deserve the best life has to offer*
- *Intuition responds to intent, and guides me on the path to my goal*
- *My world is my reflection*
- *Since I am my own Source, nothing is done to me. I choose whatever enters my Universe*
- *Since I create everything, everything is perfect, just as it is*
- *The Universe is my creation partner, and it joyfully creates whatever I think, feel, and believe*
- *Thoughts, feelings, and beliefs become things, they create my world*
- *We are on this planet to grow to live fully, we are here to thrive, not just survive*
- *What is true for me is my truth, it feels good because I am aligned with it*
-

Knowing the above, or your equivalent, you could make a statement of intent like: *I commit to act on, believe, embody, listen to, and speak my truth, so I have clarity in choosing what I create. I create this, knowing it comes without fail, in divine order and timing. I align my beliefs, feelings, thoughts, words, and all vibrational patterns with my truth, knowing I don't have to see it immediately, since the real work is in the unseen. Knowing this, I know that everything unfolds perfectly towards my goal, or something better. I monitor my thoughts and feelings, and flip the polarity of what does not serve me, to what does serve me.*

<u>Dowse:</u> *% you believe this to be true.* If under 100%, you may wish to adjust this.

Simple intent is feeling it real, now.[59] People who live in the Newtonian[60] and Cartesian world, which is limited to physical things and the flesh, miss out on over 90% of life. There is a Wampanoag story about how the heart tells us what to do, and the head tells us how to do it. When we mix those up, life becomes unpleasant. The rational mind or the head analyzes. It sees opposition, enemies, difficulties, and problems. It worries. The heart knows everything is one. Manifesting is done through the heart[61].

What was the most beautiful experience you ever had? How would something even better than that feel? Now?

---

59 Neville Goddard recalled a woman noting that she and her husband owned a house on Long Island, for summers, and leased an apartment in New York City, in winter. They sublet the apartment in summer, which paid for opening their home on Long Island. She was nervous because it hadn't yet been rented. Neville asked her where she would sleep that night, if the apartment was sublet. She said Long Island. He told her to imagine sleeping there, thinking about the apartment being sublet. Two days later, she told Neville someone qualified showed up, and wanted immediate occupancy. He got it. She was happy, and slept in Long Island that night.

60 There is no action at a distance, except gravity, in the Newtonian universe, right? Current medicinal approaches force doctors to be local. This is a false identity, for it disregards that we are nonlocal beings in space and time. Pp. 53-4, *Recovering the Soul*, Larry Dossey. Test this idea. Stare at the back of someone's neck, intently. If they aren't drunk, high, or totally engaged in something, they will turn around. If you keep staring, they will meet your eyes. Military snipers are taught this, and they never hard focus on a target, until they are ready to pull the trigger. This is not possible in the Newtonian model, but it occurs. Animals also feel hard focus, as well, even through telescopic sights, if they are not distracted. Which is more important, the model, or the experience? A positive use of this is blessing someone, with total attention, seeing them in their magnificence, as they truly are. They will react to you far differently than if you only see them in their flesh and limitations.

61 One simple manifesting exercise: Relax, Breathe deeply, Enter heart space. Imagine the majesty and beauty of the whole natural world, and become it. Feel the sunlight on your leaves, feel your veins flowing as streams, feel your backbone as a ridge line. Notice your heart opening in total thanksgiving and appreciation. Imagine that you have all that you seek, and that everyone else does also, in harmony, living at peace, in happy communities, sustainably, respectfully. What would it be like if people lived harmoniously in the universe now, I wonder? Feel that, and let it crest. Just before the crest, breathe that feeling out into the entire world with a *HAAAA* sound, on the outbreath, at least four times. Feel it real. Do this for about five minutes, daily, if you like.

Solving Problems with Dowsing **209** A book for new dowsers ISBN-10: 1482688573

E. Quantum Questings- powerful states of being

The most powerful tool we have is questions, because they focus attention. Look up at about a 30 degree angle. Ask yourself a carefully worded question. Forget about it, and in a few days the answer comes. If it doesn't, keep asking yourself the same question. It will eventually come[62].

You always get answers to your questions[63]. Questions invoke a questing by the subconscious mind. If you ask a question, your subconscious mind will seek out the answer, until it either finds that answer, or you stop it[64].

Certain kinds of questions invoke major searches. Questions create your reality. You create your questions, and your questions create you; you make your decisions, and your decisions make you. You know people whose major question is how they can get by, or survive, doing as little as possible. Their lives are not interesting, unless they have a very spiritual focus.

Then there are people asking how they can have adventure, fun, and excitement in their lives. They are more interesting. Some questions are so powerful they can shift your entire being[65], and lifepath. Why questions tend to create mythologies, though. Why questions are for philosophers, and people who need to create stories[66]. Ask "How...?" and "What...?" questions, they are a lot more practical. If you must ask why questions, at least ask positive why questions, like *"Why am I always in the right place, at the right time?"*

---

62   P. 96, *Reality Transurfing V. Apples Fall to the Sky*, Vadim Zeland.
63   *Judge a man by his questions rather than his answers.* -Voltaire
64   A very common question, asked or unasked, is "Why doesn't anybody care about my problems?"   What a worthless question! What would you do with the answer to that question, even if you got it? Feel the following worthless questions: How come nobody cares about my problems? Why am I always broke? Why am I fat? Why am I so dumb? Why is this always happening to me? What's wrong with me? Why do I not seem to get anything I want? Why do others get the good stuff, and I don't? What am I doing wrong? *Questions like these are based on the lie that you have some major flaws, and need to be fixed or repaired.* Those questions feel sick- because they are sick. You'll get answers, too, and they will be depressing. Say *cancel, cancel, cancel, cancel,* you don't want that negative energy around. Why questions generate stories, and mythologies. These could be useful to back up a positive belief. Why not ask, instead, *How does it get better than this? What are the infinite possibilities for something better than the best I can imagine coming into existence?* I want my subconscious mind working creatively, with questions like that, not reinforcing negative judgments.
65   The Abraham-Hicks Quantum Questing Question was "How can I more effectively help more people achieve their desires?" P. xx, *The Amazing Power of Deliberate Intent*, Abraham-Hicks.
66   Change your story, by way, and you change your life. Questions can do that. Living in your dream is at least more fun than living in drama.

That is a much better question to be asking. Would you like to refocus the questions that have crystallized your life as it is, to something better? We could call these questions Quantum Questing Questions, or Ecstatic questions, because they change your state, just in the asking.

Dowse: Ask yourself *"How could this be different?"* Enter the difference[67].

Wouldn't it be more fun to focus your attention on more exciting questions? Like: *What can I do to make sure this never happens again? How can I have fun losing weight?* Or better yet *How can I have a blast losing weight, improving my health in dynamic ways, while really having fun?* (Now doesn't that feel better?)

How can I learn lots of new, fun, exciting things, now? How can I learn many new things that will increase my delight in life, joy, vitality, and happiness? What would I really enjoy doing, that would dramatically increase my income?

Think of your mind as a genie- which always answers your questions. Somebody always says, "Well, that may work for you, but my situation is difficult. OK, fine. It would be pretty bad to be in jail, right? Tortured?

Colonel Rowe, U.S. Army, thought so. As a POW in Vietnam, he was really depressed by it, and was ready to die. Then he noticed a mouse, in his cell. Having nothing else to do, he watched her. She was feeding her children. There wasn't a lot of food, but she was going out and finding it. He noticed that she was missing a leg- that she was getting around on 3 legs. Well, that's pretty bad, he thought.

He studied how she moved, and realized that she was also blind. Here was a blind, 3-legged mouse, in an area with not much food, continuing her mission. He decided that if she could do it, so could he[68]. He started climbing out of his depression.

---

67 An example of the use of this question is the basis of the career of the master chef Ferran Adria, cited at p. 25, *Ferran: The Inside Story of El Bulli and the Man who Reinvented Food*, who knew what food and cooking were, and then asked what else they could be.

68 As a quantum question- *so, if this mouse can continue on, so can I, right?*

It's all in the "frame" you put around events[69], as Viktor Frankl, who survived Nazi concentration camps, said[70]. Your situation is probably not that bad. So, it is a lot easier for you to ask this question: *"What's fantastic about my situation?" "What's good about this, that I am not seeing?"*

Hey, ASK THE QUESTION, with deliberate, genuine intent. You will get an answer, that's just how your brain works. Ask questions that cover the entire process. "How can I be sure my Christmas cards are out on time?" is not the same as *"How can I be sure my Christmas cards are received on time?".*

Here are a few more questions: *What would you do if you knew you couldn't fail? How would you act? What would you see, hear, and feel if that were true? What would it feel like to create your life's work, far ahead of any schedule you'd have dreamed possible, even with grossly inadequate resources, like others have done?*

Life is short, my friend. How would you live your life, if you knew you only had 24 hours to live? Because, you know, you really don't know how much time you have. All the "things" people say they want are only a means to an end, a feeling. What use is a car if you can't drive it, for example? People want "things" to help them achieve peak experiences, especially joy.

So. *How can you make your life a succession of peak experiences, as you have fun improving your community, yourself, and your family? How could you make your goals- like realizing your life's mission- so alluring, attractive, energizing, enticing, exciting, and seductive that you just spent all your available time going after them, doing everything you possibly could to attain them?*

The Universe always answers your questions. *What about asking questions that shape your Universe in more useful ways?*

---

69   Before I got married, I set the thermostat in my room at 40 deg. F., about 4 deg. C., in the winter, and used one thin blanket, to increase my resistance to cold. I shivered all night, which meant I slept and exercised at the same time. I like that. For some readers, that would be agony. Agony for me is the high temperature my wife now requires.

70   It's all in what comparable you choose, as my father, who was an appraiser for a time, used to say. If you compare yourself to movie stars, you may not come off very well. If you compare yourself to a homeless person, you may come off better. Choose your comparables carefully. Notice that the mass media wants to make you feel bad, with unattainable comparables that are actually not realistic.

How about asking questions that change awareness in such a way that our world also changes? Following is a list[71]. <u>Don't read it.</u> Just let your eyes dance on it, and skim the list. Notice what you notice.
Form your own questions, based on where you'd like to go in consciousness, and in your life. Ask yourself five paradigm expanding power questions, like these, every day[72].

The ability to ask a good question is priceless, because <u>good questions invoke power, possibilities, and abilities beyond your regular boundaries</u>. Sometimes, answers appear even before the question is out. It is as if the answers are immanent, waiting for you to call them into form, by a focused question. Try these Quantum Questings, to see how they alter your space:

Have I chosen success, or not yet success?
How can I always be aware there is always more than enough for everyone?
How can I be aware of the best new options, now?
How can I be in a space where all are in abundance, of everything we seek?
How can I joyfully fill other people's lives with joy?
How can I learn to let go of it all, effortlessly, each time I feel stressed?
How can I make the right and perfect financial decisions now, from the heart?
How can I notice what I have not yet noticed, that helps me and others?
How can I find myself in pure intent, and let it effortlessly guide me all day?
How can I make peace with, and align, that part of me?
How can I notice events that are in beautiful alignment with my higher self?
How can I pour love into this situation?
How can I support myself lavishly and abundantly, creating fantastic value, doing what I most love to do, easily and effortlessly?
How can I trust, feel, and play in the abundance of the Universe, now?
How can I trust, let go, and let the Universe take me to the perfect place, now?
How can we get back to love now?[73]

---

71   As I write this section, new Quantum Questings leap out at me, from books, media, and experience. This is a tiny few, to give you an idea of what they are.
72   -Tony Robbins
73   Marshall Sylver, *Passion, Profit, and Power.*

How could my dowsing get fantastically better, easily and effortlessly?
How could my dowsing heal some situations even before I start scanning them?
How is this helping me to grow into a better person?
How well is that working for you? Maybe it's time to ask better questions?
How would having a great answer to your biggest question totally change your life for the better, now?
How would having extremely useful answers improve your abilities, business, career, energy level, energy levels, family, health, joy, love life, prosperity, and skills?
How would your life change if you could realize your biggest problems are already solved, you just haven't quite realized it yet?
If you have an insoluble problem, why not tell yourself you have another problem, instead, which can be solved[74]?
In transcending this, and getting to the next level, how can I help myself and others in a wonderful way?
Since it's already real, how can I notice it fully, now?
Since you're making it all up anyway, why not make it up so it's more useful, joyful, and fun[75]?
So you want to doubt that you always create your reality? Which part did you want to doubt first?[76]
So, situation, what would you like to say to me?[77]
There are two positions in the Void. In one, you have already reached your goal. In the other you haven't yet done so. Which position are you in, right now? Which would you rather be in?
What can I do to have fun, adding to other people's well-being[78]?
What can I give?
What could you do now, that you are not currently doing, to have fun?
What else can I do, to serve?
What if you could awaken healing and manifesting powers in others, effortlessly?
What if you could manifest instantly with your thoughts and feelings?
What if you already had an enormous flood of money, and you could use it as you please?

---

74   Pp. 198-9, *Quantum Healing*, Deepak Chopra.
75   P. 23, *Beyond Human: Claiming the Power and Magic of your Limitless Self*, Jaden Phoenix.
76   At p. 103, *Holding a Butterfly*, Lynn Woodland notes that almost all of her female clients who had been raped had also been sexually or physically abused as children. They learned, at some level, to expect to be harmed. Peace Pilgrim once hopped into a car with a rough man, to sleep. He later told her that he had intended to harm her, but that the totally trusting way she went to sleep meant he couldn't. I remember an apartment manager, who must have weighed all of 90 lbs, soaking wet, in a very bad area, who would face down larger drug dealers who had automatic weapons. She just didn't care, she had pure intent, and she made them back down, without having weapons herself. She was unharmed, and retired in good health, after more than twenty years of living that way. Thanks for that lesson, Cassandra.
77   P. 246, *Lucid Dreaming*, Robert Waggoner.
78   I read a book written by a Navy SEAL. One of the Master Chiefs in charge of his training told the troops they should always leave a woman feeling better about herself, than before. That is a good rule to apply generally, don't you think?

What is beautiful, helpful, and magnificent about this?
What is the lesson for me in this problem, or growth opportunity?
What service could I provide, that people would gladly pay for?
What would I be experiencing, if I had just obtained my desire[79]?
What's the gift for me in this problem or situation? How can I put it to use right now?
What am I really appreciative of – right now?
Why do I feel abundant, blessed, contented, guarded, guided, on vacation, protected, and relaxed?
Why do I notice everything is perfect, just as it is, now?
Why do I play with creating in a new way?
Why is it getting easier and easier for me?
Why not imagine yourself successful?[80]
Would you rather be right, or joyful?

Many years back Virginia Satir worked with some welfare recipients. She knew everyone can be be self-sufficient. She saw them once a week, and got a little petty cash.

After meeting everyone, she asked, *What are your dreams?* They thought she was nuts, and said, *We don't have dreams.* She asked about when they were children. One woman said, *I have a major rat problem. Gosh*, said Virginia. *What would it take to fix that?*

Well, she said, *I need a new screen door.* Virginia asked, *How could her door be fixed?* A man said he used to do work like that. Virginia gave him some petty cash to get supplies. Next week, the door was fixed. Virginia asked that man how he felt. He said, *Funny thing, I'm feeling a lot better.*

Virginia got them started dreaming, with that, and other small successes. One woman wanted to be a secretary. Virginia asked, *What's stopping you?* She said she had no child care. Virginia asked if there was anybody in the group who could take care of her kids. Another woman volunteered.

---

79   P. 50, *Manifesting your Heart's Desire*, Fred Fengler and Todd Varnum.
80   P. 31, *Psycho-Cybernetics*, Maxwell Maltz.

Everyone in that group found employment. The man who fixed the screen door got a handyman job. The woman who took care of the children got licensed to do foster care. In three months, they were all self-supporting, and off welfare.

Virginia did that many times. Most of what she did was asking questions.[81] Raymon Grace did exactly the same thing[82], with a similar group.

What role(s) would you like to play, in life's movie theater?
How would it feel, if you were already that role[83]?
What props could you add, to reinforce that?

---

81 Most goals in the USA are "negative", like how can we reduce crime, say. What is the positive alternative? What is the exciting goal so compelling that violence just isn't interesting any more? Ask questions- the universe always answers them. If you don't like your life, ask new questions. Questions structure awareness, and action, and in time everything else. I'd like to ask some new questions:

* How can we inspire people to go inside themselves, for the great reserves of strength, character, and energy there, so that they abandon their illusions of powerlessness, and heal society, by using the power of cooperation, fascination, and feeding interest? How could we so inspire people, that they just abandoned all the negative things they do, because they just weren't interesting any more? How could we create an economic system so compelling, so fascinating, so inspiring, that the negatives in our present system just vanished for lack of attention?

* How can we serve more people in a better way that is more fun? More effortlessly? How can we help change society's "channel selector" to the joy, happiness, and love channel, instead of the nightmare channel it seems to be on now? How can we help wake up the entire planet, to the Eden that our planet once was, and can be again?

*How can we find great fascination in learning to use our attention, and respect, to bring a new world into being?

*How can we have fun creating sparkling, harmonious, joyful, healing beauty in everything we do? More than enough resources exist to solve all problems. That is true here. How can we reconnect the healthy systems of the earth, then, so that every nightmare people live now becomes a forgotten memory, preserved only in dusty archives? Everything necessary to create this is already in existence, now. How could we have more fun growing into awareness of this?

*How can we have more fun, healing our communities, through our work? How can we so fascinate people with community improvement efforts, how can we help them have so much fun, that they forget about TV and the other time wasters they engage in, and just pitch in and create their local communities as a paradise?

*How could I have fun, using my gifts, strengths, abilities, and attitude shifts helping the world and humanity, too, making good money, in ways right and true?

*How could that societal system be so powerful, so enticing, that violent and immature people recognized that it was just a lot more fun to mature, and work with others? So powerful that people just enjoyed and learned from each other, in fun ways, and grew to spiritual levels that we cannot dream of at this time?

*How could we create that same economic system, in the next 5 years, so that everyone has a job, housing, good food, is incorporated into a healthy community where their needs are met, and interests fed, with the opportunity to pursue happiness?

*Since beauty is food for the soul, how can we add more beauty in our lives? In Bali there is no art, they just try to do everything well, in a beautiful way. How could we do everything we do in a beautiful way?

*Who doesn't fit into our community? How can we bring them in, so they can have fun expressing their unique gifts? What you put your attention on grows. How can we use our attention to create ideal communities?

*How could we help every living being realize their heart-felt dreams, effortlessly, joyfully, and lovingly, as we realize our own?

There are always 2 choices in life, in everything. fear, and love. I regret most of the choices I made out of fear. I don't regret any choice I made out of love- not one. Will you choose to give energy to what you love? If so, you'll GET MORE OF IT! Now that is cool. Let's keep in mind that the national news media have one interest: money. They get it from advertisers. Advertisers get money by people buying stuff. People buy stuff... because they feel like crap, because of all the fear in the world. A community organizer I heard once said they put all that negative stuff on the news to keep us fearful, and afraid of each other, so we won't unite, and drive out the bad guys. Well, I don't know if that's true, or not. If ideas like the above spread, though, we might actually get a critical mass together, maybe we might even heal the world. It has to start somewhere. Maybe it could start by sharing useful ideas.

82 He treated a similar group with respect. He asked some questions: *How many of you are exactly where you want to be in life? How many of you have children? How many of you want your kids to be just like you? If I could show you some ways to improve your kids' lives, would you be willing to listen?* He got some strong interest, and shared some of José Silva's ideas. They got off welfare. Very few people on welfare want to be there. I wonder what it would take, to get empowering ideas into their heads and hearts?

83 Some people question the value of fictional roles. It's all fictional. The Jack Sparrow character of the *Pirates of the Caribbean* movie series is more interesting than Johnny Depp's "real" personality, and this is true of so many actors. So you actually recover your power by entering a fictional role. This is useful.

Could you alternate, back and forth, in your old and new roles, to see how they are a polarity? Could you take your new identity, and enter a Medicine Place "holodeck" that supports it, and interact with it?

Could you pick up a real object, feel it, and then feel it in your imagination, alternating until there is no difference?

Could you do this with the role?

When you are totally in your new identity, in that state of being, could you notice that you don't need techniques any more?

And that there are no limiting beliefs, because the new reality never had them?

F. Power Questions get intuitive information quickly

The right question summons the answer, as it is asked. The right question speed dials the answer. It is best to ask these questions in a very relaxed state.

Relax, breathe deeply, enter heartspace[84].

Obsess on your question.   [Why didn't I get that promotion?]

Notice your immediate impressions. [Picture of past, getting out of bad job, into much better job.]

Interpret impressions, based on question. [I need to seek something better.]

Questions are useful. You can ask angels, elementals[85], devas, God, any helpful being you can conceive of- even the Stay Puft Marshmallow Man, Gumby, the Muppets, Noddy, the Lone Ranger, Jesus, George Jetson, the Smurfs, Maxwell's "demon", Ho Tai, or your dowsing team, to help you with any area of your life. They are simply CGI's- Consciousness Generated Images[86].

---

84 *Practical Intuition for Success*, by Laura Day, has over 200 pages of sequences like this one, far more than I can add to this book.

85 You can easily contact them in imaginary workshop, or nature. To contact the air spirit for the first time, a windy day, especially on a hill, is good. Just say something like "Hi, Spirit of Wind, I'd like to speak with you, and work with you to help heal the Earth." You'll get a response, probably of feeling. Any change at all is a response. Contact the water spirit, for the first time, near a body of water, especially when it's raining. To contact fire, sit in the Sun, or in front of a fire, even a candle. To contact the earth, it's helpful to be sitting on earth, especially a hill, near a large rock, or in a cave. It helps a lot to have a real need, question, or a decision that you need to make. Ask for help and give thanks and trust that the response will come. Franz Bardon has a very ornate way to contact them. The Findhorn people do this also. I saw this most recently in Pp. 215, 216, 221, *The Elves of Lilly Hill Farm*, Penny Kelly.

86 Religious images are mostly generated, right? Were cameras available, in the time of Jesus, the Buddha, etc.? So why not generate your own?

Presences seem to precipitate from another dimension when you have questions. They aren't real until they are. They might be experienced as a being of light, an Angel, or something impossible to describe[87].

There two parts to this: <u>Asking</u> for help, and <u>Noticing</u> the help that's been received. Trust and follow the answers that come from love, abundance, and lightness, rather than fear, heaviness, and worry[88]. Ask your higher self or anything else, <u>What do you want to tell me</u>?

If you need guidance, ask God, the Angels or whoever, about it. Hold the intent that you've given that question to heaven, or the Void, or deep mind, and trust that you'll get an answer, and you will. It may be very subtle, and easy to overlook at first. If you get a live answer, ask the "caller" to identify themselves[89]. You can ask them to turn up the volume.

God's voice is casual, direct, friendly, funny, and sometimes slangy.
Archangels tend to be very direct, formal, and mission oriented.
Angels tend to use archaic informal speech patterns. They may also express only in things happening, in a very peaceful way, as if they would have happened that way anyway.
Devas, or angels of plan, or group souls, are very peaceful. To me, they are something like talking to a very peaceful person, living in a paradise, unless they are upset about something.
Nature spirits, angels of place, tend to be very task-oriented.
Avaiku, aka Therapeuti, are very direct, like Hawaiians and Native Americans.
Mr. Magoo sounds like Mr. Magoo.
The higher self sounds like an ideal version of you.
The ego is the monkey mind of worry or fear, and depression.
Homer Simpson sounds like Homer Simpson[90].

---

87   P. 207, *Reinventing Medicine*, Larry Dossey.
88   P. 101, *The Angel Therapy Handbook*, Doreen Virtue.
89   Pp. 102, 113, 116, *The Angel Therapy Handbook*, Doreen Virtue.
90   Don't laugh. Homer is pure id. This is a useful spiritual lesson. Ok, now laugh.

The subconscious does not use language, usually, and will communicate in symbols, signs, dreams, hunches, images, knowings, and awareness capsules.

All questions are answered[91] even before they are asked. The level of awareness causes any lag time, in the answer showing up.

G. Dowsing Question Chain examples

If you want to hear an example of question chains, go to the emergency room, with a pain. They will ask you where it is, what drugs you are allergic to, when the last time you had the pain was, are you nauseous, are you on medications, and so on. They are going from the general to the specific, they are "chunking down". They aren't dowsing, obviously, but the process is similar.

Let us recall the spirit of dowsing. In reflective dowsing, it is finding obstacles to the flow. In projective dowsing, it may be initiating a chain of action to remove the obstacles. This is the heart of any question chain: identify the obstacle, first.

I hesitate to include examples of question chains, because they are so very much in the moment, yet people can treat them like holy writ. These are only one track, of a particular question chain, based on my being in a very specific place, with a specific awareness in time. Your chains will be different. If I followed the same path again, I would have a different question chain myself. These are examples of tracks, only. You could follow them to learn from them, however, understand that every track is different.

---

91 To help someone else, breathe deeply, enter heartspace, and have the intent of conversing with their team. Then ask them *What do you want me to know about this person?* Notice what you notice. Then ask *What would you like me to tell this person, from you?* Notice what you notice, and pass this on as appropriate. Then ask, *Is there anything else that would be useful for me to know?* Take appropriate action on what you get.   -Pp. 128-129, *The Angel Therapy Handbook*, Doreen Virtue, and the Psi IV seminar, of Thomas Willhite, probably copying José Silva methodology.

Mine tend to be projective dowsing, in these examples, because I enjoy that greatly. All of my projective dowsing is done with the intent that whatever happens is for the highest good of all, by way, and that is very important[92].

Question Chain 1:

I was aware of a street drug market, in a city. I knew a reformed drug dealer, who knew the area well. This is useful, for feedback. I set intent that I would be totally effective, and entered a relaxed state of mind. I went to the area [this is not necessary, however it helps.]
I felt the morphic field, of the drug dealing. A street level drug market is a living super-entity. It forms itself up at a certain time, in the day or night, it ingests money, and excretes drugs, then it falls apart to go dormant at a certain time. It has its teeth and claws- the weapons of the dealers. It is a parasite on the area. It also has its weak underbelly- the consumers, who come in afraid, and skittish[93].

Once I grokked the morphic field, and the physical area, I set an intention to clear out all the tracks in the field, related to the drug trafficking. I opened up a firehose of brilliant light, metaphorically, and washed it all out. I set up some thoughtforms to maintain this cleansing. I set up some thoughtform walls, and traffic barriers, and traffic signs, so that customers would feel the need to go elsewhere. I could have put bright imaginary searchlights on the dealers, with cop glue, so that any cop that saw them would be very attracted to them.

---

92 This is important. Some years ago, without really thinking, I set up an intent to find a woman. I did, and it was fiery. The problem was that my intent wasn't clean, or for the highest good of all. She was an alcoholic, a bad one. After two alcoholic spouses, well, pain had finally taught me wisdom, and it had to be broken off. I did not act for her highest good, or mine. I have made many stupid mistakes in my life, and they have taught me wisdom. Pain is the most patient of teachers, I've found. Yes, you can dowse for partners, however, you want to have very clean intent around this. Clean your subconscious out first, and prepare your physical environment. Some people put more time into getting and caring for pets than they do for spouses. This is not useful. Dowse in a focused context, for something this important. Do as I say, not as I did. You'll be happier.
93 If all I had was rational consciousness, I would know to scare them, first, perhaps a block away. They are easy to spot- they are the kids from the suburbs, driving their parents' BMW's, Mercedes, and so on. The book *Freakonomics* goes into great detail on these drug markets, which are run very similarly to McDonald's. Anyway, in dealing with customers, one could make friends with the sheriff's department, and send a postcard to the vehicle owner, saying something like "Thank you for visiting our community, which many criticize as being full of drug dealers, murderers, and prostitutes, at 3 AM, Saturday morning. We welcome your confidence in the safety of our area, and look forward to more visits." One could take a video camera, even without a chip, and conspicuously film the cars, or take pictures of license plates. I've seen where some people would put bricks through the windshields of these cars, but that is force, not finesse. I am interested in finesse. Dowsing offers finesse.

I could have put twice lifesize laughing clowns, pointing out the dealers with oversize pointers, saying, "Over here, officers! He ha!" I worked for about twenty minutes.

Than I left. I did a little more work remotely, another five minutes. I went back there, three months later, with the reformed drug dealer. He had seen this area much of his life. He said it was improved beyond anything he'd ever seen, he was utterly astonished. Five years later, the area was even better. You can do this work as a dowsing question chain, also, if you wish:

1. Setting of intent- *"What would have to happen so this area is cleaned of all low grade energy, with the help of this area, and any and all beings able and willing to help."* These are important.
2. I relaxed, breathed deeply, and entered heartstate.
3. I asked: *Are there tracks in the morphic field, of drug dealing? Y/N?* I get a Yes.
4. I asked, *Dowsing system, are you able and willing to erase these tracks, in the morphic field, and to replace them with the expression of the highest and best purpose of this area?* I get a Yes, Y. *Is there any reason not to?* No, N.
5. I said, *Please do so now, and give me a clear physical feeling when this is done.* I waited a minute, or so, and got the feeling.
6. I asked, *Dowsing system, are you able and willing to erase the memory of the drug market, from all of its customers' minds?* Y *Is there any reason not to?* N
7. I said, *"Please do so now, and give me clear feedback when it's done".* I waited a minute, and got the feeling.
8. I asked, *"Dowsing system, are you able and willing to guide the drug dealers into newer and better ways to make money, and do whatever else is necessary, so they just don't come back here?* Y *Is there any reason not to?* N
9. I said, *"Please do so now, and give me feedback when this is done."* I waited, and the feeling came.

10. I asked, *"Dowsing system, are you able and willing to put the spirit of confusion into this place, so that anyone who wants to buy or sell drugs just forgets what they are doing, and is guided to do something else?"* Y *Is there any reason not to? N*

11. I said, *"Please do so now, and let me know when you are done."* I waited, and got the feeling.

12. I asked, *"Dowsing system, are you able and willing to do any other work, that would erase this drug market as an entity, and replace it with the highest and best expression of this area?"* Y *Is there any reason not to? N*

13. I said, *"Please do so now, and signal me when done."* I waited, and got that feeling.

14. I like to play with archetypes, so I also put 20 foot tall angels in the area, warrior angels, with a war face. I also put up thoughtform signs, that said, *"Sorry, drug market out of business."*

15. Now, you can do this, one by one, as laid out here. You can also run this as an intuitive download, in less than a minute of clock time. You can also open a portal to do all this, in two seconds, but that is advanced. Learn it in sequence, first, then start running it on automatic[94].

Question Chain 2:

Many years ago, I walked to work on a specific route. There wasn't much nice to see. So, I started a chain.

1. Dowsing system: *are you able and willing to make this place look nicer?* Y[95] *Is there any reason not to? N*

2. I said, *"Please take whatever action is necessary, to accomplish that goal".*

3. Just for kicks, I put in four thoughtforms, of fountains of healing energy, working 24/7, about 10m/yards high, along the path. It's cheap fun, for me.

4. Within a few months, the city decided to beautify the area. The newspapers made comments about why on

---

94 A business owner would want to know how to reverse this process, of course, for a business that actually serves the community. Claude Bristol's book *The Magic of Believing* describes just this. It was written in 1948. I cannot imagine running a business without ideas like that, myself. It may be possible to download this book free from the Internet, now. 95 I know someone is going to ask, why hasn't it worked for me yet? Ah. Now ask yourself the power question- are you in the question, or in the conclusion? If you want results, is it better to be the question, or the conclusion that shuts off possibilities?

earth the city chose that area, when other areas needed it more. I like to see confirmation in the news media, that is useful feedback.

Question Chain 3:

Raymon Grace teaches a course on projective dowsing. I also like the *Theta Healing* approach to this, when I feel like I need structure. I really like Raymon's idea, of seeking out criminals, in the Bardo, and clearing them of whatever is causing them to commit crimes. He waits till he sees their acts mentioned in the newspaper. I don't. I like to go hunting in the Bardo, and I don't need feedback beyond what my dowsing system gives me.

1. I ask, *Dowsing System, is there a rapist/serial killer within 50 miles/80 km of where I am now?* Y
2. I say, *"If there is more than one, can we focus on the worst one, first?"* Y *Are you able and willing to clear them?* Y *Is there any reason not to?* N
3. I say, *"Please clear them of whatever is causing them to do this, sending that on to its proper place, and put these people on the path of their mission and purpose in life. Please signal me when this is complete."*
4. I continue, until I get nos, to that first question.

Question Chain 4:

Who among us doesn't lose keys, or something? I used to find them by quartering the house, using an L-rod, and so on, but now I just use Switchwords, from James Langan's book.

1. I say *Divine reach keys.* This activates dowsing for them.
2. I empty my mind, relax, breathe deeply, and enter heartspace.
3. I walk through all the places they could be, with my mind relaxed, and close to blank. When I get close, I get a clear feeling of where they are, reach out, and get them[96].

---

96 There is a powerful morphic field you can also use St. Anthony, St. Anthony, please come round, something is lost and needs to be found. Please show me X. Generally, one pledges to give money after the item is found. In Catholic countries, there are boxes for St. Anthony convenient in larger churches.

Question Chain 5

I happen to like old churches, however, there will often be concentrations of less than useful energy, in churches. When I feel this, I do the following, sometimes on automatic:

1. *Dowsing System, are you able and willing to clean out whatever energies don't belong here, sending them to their proper place, and to open up the channels for the highest level of energy consistent with the highest and best good of all, here, now?*   Y
2. I say, *Please do so now, and let me know when you are done.*
3. I love playing with archetypes in churches. Generally, I like a bright white searchlight beam right on the podium, angels around, and amplification of all high level thoughts and feelings.
4. I like setting up Turbo thoughtforms for speakers in the church, such that deep spiritual truth comes through in whatever they say, and that services are cathartic, feel great, and slingshot people to spiritual awareness, always for the highest good of all. Of course you could also do this in other public places, even movie theaters. If you lay in positive thoughts on paths many people walk, this has interesting effects, also.

Solving Problems with Dowsing **224** A book for new dowsers ISBN-10: 1482688573

I wonder how much fun a person could have, playing with energies, and healing beauty?

What would it feel like, to be a child again, living in a Universe full of Wonder, Excitement, lots of fun stuff to explore, lots of new ways to play?

What if you could do that, right now, with all the awareness you have, as an adult, so the play is even more fun than ever before?

VIII. Playing with intent

A. Setting Intentions

The core of all essence in manifestation is **joy.** Whatever you choose to intend, be sure it is joyful to you, and others. Get rid of all words that describe states below 200 on the Hawkins scale, or words that make you feel bad, as they are double plus ungood[1]. Instead of saying someone feels bad, you'd say they don't feel good. This accesses good[2]. All language is hypnotic. Be sure your hypnosis has only positive suggestions.

1. Be totally aligned with with the intent.

- Focus on the **good**, not on the lack. If you are work-ing on a good relationship, focus mostly on what's good. For a job, focus on what's going right in the job. Energy follows thought and attention. See what you truly desire. Focus your attention at all times on your desire, despite any appearances to the contrary. Put lots of energy on metaphorical fruits and outcomes. Don't focus much on where you aren't manifesting your good yet. If you do, you will manifest not mani-festing your good, by observing this into existence.
- Delete counter-intention immediately, all the way to its roots, or incorporate it as a strength, as an integrated "synthesis" of the polarity.
- Record all the abundance that comes to you, and put a value on everything that comes to you, material and otherwise. Give noisy, heartfelt thanks.
- Abundance isn't about money, necessarily. It's about knowing, with absolute certainty that all your needs are met, effortlessly, and everything you desire is here now, or manifesting right now, for the highest good of all.

---

1   These include any words related to addiction, aggression, anger, apathy, blame, craving, despair, despondency, disease, doubt, envy, fear, grief, guilt, hate, hopelessness, humiliation, misery, obsession, panic, pride, problem, profanity, regret, revenge, sadness, scorn, separation, shame, withdrawal, and judgments including bad, broke, cheap, crummy, dark, difficult, down, expensive, failure, forget, idiot, ill, lazy, losing, mean, nasty, old, poor, rule, sick, small, stupid, trying, unfulfilled, weak, and worse. Any time thoughts using these words or feelings come up, flip polarity immediately, before they come out of your mouth.

2   I went through a small dictionary, and used a magic marker to mark out negative words. This takes too much time, however it's a good idea.

- Enough why overcomes any how limitations.[3]
- Know what feeling that getting it will give you, as you will be in that feeling, as the path to getting there.[4] It could be useful to know how much you want, when, and who you are with, when you have it. Don't obsess on this. Leave the door open for something beyond the best you can imagine. What makes it exciting?
- Ask Quantum Questions: *What is my next right and perfect step? How could I get started today, however small the way? How does it get much better than this?*

What would it feel like to have absolute power over your entire universe, to be able to do whatever you wanted, whatever gave you joy?

What would it feel like, to forget that, so when you remembered it again, you would appreciate it all the more?

Have you already realized that is exactly what you did, yet?

---

3   Brian Tracey said something like this.
4   *There is no path to peace; peace is the path* -Buddha, and a clear indication of the power of states of being.

2. "Chunk up" to Essence.

Focus on what you truly desire, on the desire of your heart, the ESSENCE, the energy, the cause; not on the result, outcome, effect, or "how", despite any appearances to the contrary. Go to the highest level chunk- the highest level of order, and focus on the ESSENCE, the state of being, and how you feel, not on results, and form. If you seek some thing- why? Is it for the feeling of liberty, or joy?

If so, intend and create the feeling of liberty. You might find, after creating whatever the physical thing is, that the payments are high, that the value drops too quickly... essence expresses in a better way than you may know at this time. Results always show the true intent[5].

What people may say they desire could cover up the fear about it. What will $1 million give to you, that you don't currently have? *How do you truly see yourself?* That is your baseline. *How do you want to see yourself?* That is your goal, the feeling state to be in, now. You can set intent for others. For example: *I see _____ in the right and perfect business, in the right and perfect location, for the highest good of all.* The highest good tag line is your insurance policy, that you aren't interfering unduly.

3. Abandon judgment and opinions

This impedes your own system, the way a sea anchor slows down a boat. Set an intent that you see other people in a great place, at peace, having already realized their true hearts desire. They are only reflections of you anyway, what you do to and for them affects you. Don't diagnose, don't analyze, see things instead just as they are. If you can do this- if you can notice that everything is just an interesting point of view, and see without judgment, you will open up your dowsing in ways you cannot imagine.

---

5   There are two ways to use intent. Once is to project a specific intent into the situation. This is useful, but limiting. One can also be open-ended: the other is to ask the situation to create appropriate imagery, or to notice what you notice and let whatever needs to happen, happen. P. 165, *Lucid Dreaming*, Robert Waggoner. Use both. I find the second one more fun.

4. See, hear, and feel things as they are

Feel your feelings just as they are, right now, without overlays of censoring, denial, or judging. The intentions below are in words, however intent is always a _feeling_, of whatever it is, already done.

Just saying words doesn't have that much effect[6]. _Feel the feelings of the good stuff being already real, now._ Stop playing the "what if" game, tell no negative tales.

Rewrite negative "stories" immediately as positive ones, perhaps with a one word trigger, and let negative emotions fully express, and then drain out. Take nothing personally. Spiritual masters never saw anything as other than perfection[7]. They saw everything in its perfection.

5. Simple intent statement examples

Set intentions based on what you truly want. Get out of the way, leave details to God, the Universe, Divine Order. See yourself in Divine Order. Take inspired action, based on intuition. Intention statements could begin: _I allow... I am... I decide... I feel so happy and grateful, now that.... I have... I intend.... What are the infinite possibilities for ... to happen, I wonder? What would have to happen for .... to occur, I wonder?_ Move towards being more open ended in your intent, as this opens more possibilities.

I allow myself to express my full potential now, in fun ways!
I feel so happy and grateful, that I am always in the right place, at the right time!
I intend everyone loves and benefits greatly from my energy, and is fully supportive of my mission now!
I intend great confidence, accurate intuition and guidance, and success, in everything I do!

---

6   Portions of what follows came out of fascinating classes in intent, taught by Paula Langguth Ryan and Tony Burroughs. This is only my understanding of what they taught. I missed a lot, I know.
7   Neville notes he once meditated on what he would be if he couldn't see fault, if all things were pure, and he didn't judge anyone or anything. He had a vision of himself as a being of fire, dwelling in a body of air. Heavenly voices sang "He is risen". There is no way to bring about perfection, without transforming ourselves. When that happens, the world melts magically before our eyes, into a reflection of our new self. He said we make the world through our imagination and feeling. He said we illuminate or darken our lives with our ideas. Those that help or hinder us are simply actors in a play we wrote the script for. Our ideas of ourselves free or confine us, through material phenomena.

I intend I am as I truly am, at my default state of peace, love, joy, being centered, and contented!

I intend I am focused on, and aware of, the next right and perfect step, and I take it now!

I intend I am full of awareness, confidence, relaxation, and every state I need! What are the infinite possibilities for this happening now?

I intend I am making a completely peaceful, joyful, smooth transition to my new ....!

I intend I am now open and receptive to clarity for launching my new, successful ....!

I intend I am whole, healed, and healthy, free of all blots on my ideal plan!

I intend I create a win-win result about [situation]!

I intend I have a fulfilling, fun, happy vacation, with an abundance of fun, and loving moments with my beloved!

I intend I hear negative chatter as birdsong, knowing others see only good in me and my abilities!

I intend I know all is unfolding in perfect order, for the highest good of all! What are the infinite possibilities for this happening now?

I intend I know and take the next right and perfect step, to realize my mission in life, now!

I intend I know everyone and everything is fully supportive of me and my mission now!

I intend I know that all my expenses are already taken care of!

I intend I know that everything helps me, in some way!

I intend I know that everything works for good, no matter the appearance!

I intend I now have all the qualifications to do whatever I'm guided to do!

I intend I now have my dream life, in a wonderful way!

I intend I release denial and judgment, seeing things just as they are!

I intend I wholly embody my true self, and my mission in life!

I intend my attitudes, behaviors, feelings, and thoughts are aligned perfectly with my highest desires!

I intend that everything that needs to be known is known, now!

I intend that I am blessed, guided, guarded, protected, and uplifted at all times!

I intend that I am one with my highest good, now!

I intend that I know that everyone involved acts out of love for the highest good of all!

I intend the perfect result manifests now, for the highest good of all!

You already know the next step. Dowse these, on a scale of 0-100, 100 being ideal, and intend any energy level below that up to 100.

Solving Problems with Dowsing **230** A book for new dowsers ISBN-10: 1482688573

6. Other thoughts

- In a quiet heartstate, ask questions, such as "*Is there anything I could do now to help this come into form...*" or "*What would have to happen for ... to occur...*" Act on the answers you get.
- Paper is magic, by itself. You can write down your intent.
- Speak <u>out loud</u> what you want to happen in your life, if you want to affect the physical world[8], as it being already real. Affirmations that create the feeling, and being state, work. Use your affirmation to focus the <u>feeling of it already real</u>. This will train your nervous system in success.
- Abbreviations of statements of intent can be useful if you have skeptics in your household. They are close to being sigils, such that no-one else understands what you've written.
- You can look at your intent statements, on the wall, at a 45 degree angle, to drive them deep. They are effective to the extent that you feel them true. Test % of this, and take it to 100%.
- You can record in a journal everything you are thankful for, especially hits, or results, from your intention.
- You may want to tithe in advance, giving thanks to the Source, God, or whatever you call it, for the good you have already recognized at the energy level, and are about to receive at the physical level.

What other ideas could empower your dowsing, and intent work? Go fishing in your deep mind, for a while, with that quantum question.

What would Jesus do?
What would Bugs Bunny do?
What would a clown do?
What would Masaki Hatsumi do?
How would a 12th level master handle this?
What if the problem had already solved itself?

---

8   -Franz Bardon.

B. Letting go of negativity

1. Relax, breathe deeply, and enter heartspace.
2. Be aware of a wetsuit, or robe, of all your negativity. It is not you, it is only what you chose to wear. Let your heartstar, your blazing star, send out a small column of light to each leg, and arm, and up into your head.
3. Let this stick figure of light expand, like a balloon, until it pushes all the negativity and low grade energy in your body out into the suit. Really feel this. As I write this, I am feeling it strongly. Let the robe come off, or let the wetsuit fall off you. You may notice that you are a fountain of light, sparkling light, lighting up everything.
4. This is your true self. You may notice an incredible feeling of joy. You might feel great gratitude, and ask, "*How can I serve?*[9]" and notice how good you feel.
5. An answer comes. Follow up on it.

A Native American elder I know says the purpose of life is to gather in all the learnings and such that you can, and then to pass them out freely, to all who will receive. As you go your way, with this attitude, you may notice that your needs are met, effortlessly, and that you maybe didn't need that one thing, after all.

A powerful quantum question for clearing any problem is "*What do I need to learn from this? Please show me the lesson, so this can be resolved forever.*" The shift to *what can I give?* is very helpful. Only our minds, thoughts, and feelings separate us from source, from God, from truth, and all that we seek.

There are other ways to clear blocks, if you need to. Entering the Sacred Silence helps a lot. You can engage in creative activity: art, dance, drumming, painting, playing music, sports, and so on. You can also express your gratitude, for say at least 30 things you are thankful for, and laugh a lot. Putting joy into other people's lives helps. Pouring love into the animal also helps.

---

9   P. 80, *Psychic Energy: How to Change Desires into Realities*, Joseph Weed.

Useful quantum questions for this include:

How can I see that the present moment is crystal clear, full of possibilities, now?

How could I notice that I am completely free in the present moment, with a future that is free to change?

How do I feel, being totally present, now?

How long ago did I release the negative patterns that caused me pain, since I learned their lessons?

How much fun could I have, playing with these methods, now?

How much fun is it, to awaken to my unlimited potential, now?

Isn't it wonderful that the present moment has only silence, light, and love?

When did all the disappointments, doubts, failures, and so on, cease to exist, in my past?

When did I first realize I can exceed my best, from before?

When did I realize that there is no failure, there is only experience?

Why are the answers to everything I seek within, and immanent, for me, now?

Ideomotor response- communicating with the subconscious- sometimes known as dowsing- is much more accurate than relying solely on mind. Dr. John Diamond, a pioneer in the field of Applied Kinesiology[10], entitled his book *Your Body Doesn't Lie*, because it doesn't, well, not without a lot of coaching[11], as with actors.

It helps to start off a test with statements like *From my higher self...* or *I am a clear channel to my higher self...* to set an intent of pure response, beyond the polarized mind. It is better to test statements, rather than to test questions.

---

10   Kinesiology, which is yes/no muscle testing, was promoted by Dr. George Goodheart. Books on it include *Touch for Health*, Dr. John Thie, *Your Body Doesn't Lie*, John Diamond, M.D., and of course *Power vs.Force*, Dr. David Hawkins. The American Society of Dowsers also teaches this.

11   You now know you can test activities, drugs, feelings, food, liquids, places, thoughts, water, and anything else, to see if they make you go strong, or weak. Your body is always in the moment, so it isn't distracted, like the mind is. Always test to be sure you are hydrated. Responses may be inconclusive if you are dehydrated, or your energy is blocked or out of balance. Test your medications to see if they distort responses. Artificial sweeteners: Aspartame, Nutrasweet; Monosodium Glutamate, Genetically Modified foods, hormones in meat, and sometimes electromagnetic fields can distort answers. Test for distortions, and clear them, before you start.

You would <u>Test</u> by stating *From my higher self... I have resistance to knowing I deserve love*, Y/N, and then maybe a percentage, rather than ~~Do I deserve love?~~

The subconscious is only and totally in the now. If you test the energy level of a belief, it might be very out of kilter- right now. Ask for the average energy level over the last week, or month. Because it is in the now, a question like "Should I invest in this stock?" makes no sense to it.

This is why you have a pendulum direction for wrong question/cannot answer. It is better to test the results of investing in a stock, and several other tests. A solid knowledge of markets and products would help. Test the fundamentals, and other aspects. Then see how you feel. If the answers don't feel right, quit, and go back to it later.

C. Energy boosters

Of course in doing this kind of play, you always pull universal energy, and you never use your own energy. However it may be useful to have ways to increase your energy. Stimulating the kidney meridian is particularly useful. Always stay hydrated with this kind of play. Cayenne pepper and water can be very stimulating. Start with very small amounts, of course.

Breaking your pattern by going out, and taking a walk, can help.

Energy saturation also helps. Imagine all the energy in the Universe, in all directions coming into you from infinitely far out, to pack itself into you. Feel your energy system totally saturated. Then let the energy powerfully explode out in all directions, taking with it anything that is not perfect, clear, and pure in your hologram[12].

---

12 Gary Douglas would suggest something like getting into a high state, of having already realized your dream, and filling up an energy ball in front of you with this energy. Fill this even more. Let it send out energy filaments to everyone and everything that could help. Start sucking energy from the Universe through them, and the filaments, into the ball. Let a trickle flow back to everyone/thing. When they show up, let the energy exchange equalize. Maintain this, and reinforce the ball every three days. Gary's books are filled with quantum questions, too.

Imagine yourself cutting the knots holding you back from doing what it is you seek to do.[13] You may find what seemed to be implants, which may be pure energy, holographic, or sometimes even physical. Who cares where they came from?

Notice what you notice with these. Usually these are not useful to a person. Just phase conjugate them[14] at 180°. The imagery in our minds does affect other people.

It is important to maintain positive imagery, in one's own mind. The higher your energy level is, the less other people's negative energy can affect you.

What would it feel like, to be, do, and have energy patterns that are better than the best you can imagine?

How much bliss and ecstasy could a person have, in life?

How would you feel, if you were happier than ever before, in your life?

---

13   P. 154, *Dream Healer 2: Guide to Self Empowerment*, Adam.
14   P. 187, *Touching the Light*, Meg Blackburn Losey.

IX. Checklists to play with

When you work with people, it is useful to get a listing of all of their problems, with rating of 1-10, 10 being horrible, and 0 being not present, or ideal state. Scan for all of these, don't limit yourself to merely physical issues. I recommend asking about at least:

1. Accident-proneness[1]
2. Conditions of spouse, children, relatives
3. Dreams – in sleep, and what the dream of having/doing/being
4. Economic conditions [i.e. relationship with money]
5. Emotional
6. Family/Relationships
7. Luck
8. Mental
9. Mission and purpose in life
10. Occupational
11. Physical
12. Remanence of trauma
13. Spiritual
14. Success/failure
15. What irritates them
16. What kind of excuses they make
17. What they are proud of
18. Who they want to impress, and why

Don't spend a lot of time in their story, if you can help it. Story is a tapestry woven by why questions. As with any list you can run your fingers down the above, and let your finger "stick" on areas that need to be cleared, or most need to be cleared.

---

1 P. 394, *Intuition Technology*, John Living, Professional Engineer..

A. Positive Belief Optimization sequence

Example: I deserve love, and am lovable.

Dowse: *% you believe this is true.* If under 100%, adjust.

Sample: I deserve to succeed. I deserve to make more than my parents did.

Dowse: *% you believe this is true.* If under 100%, adjust.

You can use this sequence after any intent is set. If under 100%, you might want to adjust, and also to adust your intent sequence so you get 100% the first time.

B. Having fun scrambling nonuseful/out of place energy

Dowse: % of pain, harmful bacteria and protozoa, miasms, virus, cancer, and other such problems that occur in a body with acidic pH, in this person's body/group/ organization/place[2]. If over 0%

1. **banish the spirit** of disease, or the non-useful energy, from all levels of the person/group/place's existence.
2. **deactivate the life force** of the non-useful energy from all levels.
3. **scramble the frequency** of the out of place energy.
4. *adjust the energy frequency to the person's ideal body frequency, fifth dimensional energy,* OR
5. *adjust the frequency to the frequency of pure water.*

6. *adjust the person/group/place's frequency to the ideal frequency.*

If working with something physical, do all this, then remove the physical evidence in your imagination.

Dowse: % negative effects of organizations, electromagnetic pollution including TV, microwaves, computers, cell phones, other devices, nuclear energy, &c. in your home. If over 0%,

---

2   You don't have to use lists that make sense, when you are measuring information. You could use a list of Kevin Bacon's movies, or episodes of Friends, a set of cookie cutters, baseball cards, or chapters in a romance novel. Run your fingers down it to see what sticks, and clear what seems to have stuck energy on it. This is a very good way to get specific about energies you don't understand, but would like to influence.

1. banish the spirit[3] of the negative effect from all levels of the person's existence
2. deactivate the life force of the negative effect from all levels
3. scramble the frequency of the negative effect
4. adjust the negative effect to the person's ideal body frequency OR
5. adjust the negative effect to the frequency of fifth dimensional energy

C. Balancing energies checklist sequence

As with any other list of processes, run through it once[4], and then you can put it on automatic. Of course you can add to this list, if you wish. I recommend tailoring such lists to your needs, always.

Run through it, item by item, only if you need to troubleshoot some persistent problem, and that will be rare.[5] You could add this to your dowsing intent statement, earlier, simply by intent.

Measurement mixes two systems, so that each has a record of the other[6].

Dowse: *% of ideal body frequency*, in MHz. If less than 100% ideal, intend it is at 100%.
Dowse: *% of ideal home frequency*. If less than 100%, intend it is at 100%.
Dowse: *% out of balance w/Earth Energy*. If under 100%, ask dowsing system to bring you, your animals, business, family, and home, back into total balance with the Earth energies. If you want feedback, you'll notice a CW spin.

---

3   Charles Lindbergh crossed the Atlantic in *The Spirit of St. Louis,* so don't laugh. All problems have a non-material component, which you could call energy, or in older terminology, a spirit.
4   This is described also at p. 147, *Parallel Universes of Self,* Frederick Dodson.
5   Walt Woods may have started this. Raymon Grace goes to town with this sequence, he is unbelievably good. By way, Raymon offers seminars in the USA, which are very good. How do I know? I dowse the before and after energy levels of Raymon's classes. You can, also. Also, they are actually cheaper than most seminars, because his support staff consist of whoever invites him, and him. He has a website, I think it is raymongrace.us, and videos and books available there also. This guy is a teacher you want to catch, he stuffs more usable ideas into less time than any other teacher I've had, though Richard Bartlett comes close.
6   P. 166, *Fire in the Mind: Science, Faith, and the Search for Order,* George Johnson.

Dowse: *% out of balance with creative force/higher intelligence, Great Spirit, God, etc.* Intend balance if necessary.

Dowse: *% out of balance with local energy.* Intend balance if necessary.

Dowse: *Energy level,* of the person, building, or situation. If under 200, or low, entities may be present[7]. Ask your dowsing team to take them to their proper place, never to return.

Dowse: *% out of balance with mission and purpose in life.* Intend balance if necessary.

Dowse: *% out of balance with Earth element.* Intend balance if necessary.

Dowse: *% out of balance with Water element.* Intend balance if necessary.

Dowse: *% out of balance with Air/Wood element.* Intend balance if necessary.

Dowse: *% out of balance with Fire Element.* Intend balance if necessary.

Dowse: *% out of balance with Metal/Aether element[8].* Intend balance if necessary.

If under 100%, ask your counselors to bring you, your business, family, and home, back into 100% balance with the energies/elements. If you need feedback, you will notice a CW spin, with a duration usually under one minute.

Dowse: *% adverse effects from electromagnetic fields, AC current, Sonar, cell phones, ionizing radiation, radionic pollution, and anything else in this range*

Dowse: *% adverse effects from geopathic stress lines, water veins, Curry lines, etc.*

Dowse: *% adverse effects from culture, heritage, religion of ancestors*

Dowse: *% adverse effects from negative karmic influence*

Dowse: *% adverse effects from negative thought forms and morphic robots*

Dowse: *% adverse effects from non-beneficial counselors or team members*

Dowse: *% adverse effects from noxious energy rays*

---

7   Eugene Maurey wrote an entire book just on this subject, and you'll find others, as well. The books this book you are reading came from discusses this at some length. If you have these present, just ask your team to take them to the light, where they get proper treatment, and cannot return to harm anyone. Don't obsess about them, don't be fearful, just ask for help. You'll get it. I got such help, long before I knew what I was doing, just by asking for it. I have no idea how that works, I just know it does work. These are usually the chief energy drainers, so it is worth learning how to deal with them.

8   Play with the aether element. You can invoke the Void, and sense surroundings, and act without thinking, without using physical senses.

Dowse: *% adverse effects from spirits of diseases or negative emotions, anger, fear, greed, etc.*

Dowse: *% adverse effects from spirits of co-dependency, strong emotional attachment as from past trauma, persecution, victimization, etc.*

Dowse: *% adverse effects of bad medicine, corporate propaganda, curses, hexes, ill wishes, manipulative efforts, spells, and so on*[9].

Dowse: *% affected by negative energetic patterns.*

Dowse: *% degree of feeling wanted at birth.*[10]

Dowse: *% of original soul present at birth.*

Dowse: *% of original soul present now, or percent fragmentation*[11].

Dowse: *Number of genes and switches to activate/deactivate.* Intend [de]activation as necessary.

Dowse: *Is soul present in this dimension?* Y/N. If no, bring it back with intent and love.

Dowse: *% of ideal of at least the following states:*

Contentment
Forgiveness
Freedom
Gratitude
Joy
Love
Peace
Peace
Prosperity
Satisfaction

Dowse: *% adverse effects from cellular and emotional memory, memory of the water in the body now, and and trauma of this and past lives.*

Dowse: *% adverse effects of vibrational patterns,* inherited, self-imposed, or by association.

Dowse: *% aura balance*   [ideal is 100% in balance]

Dowse: *% balance of right and left hemispheres of the brain.*[12]

---

9   People who say "Well, kick me", If it wasn't for bad luck they'd have no luck at all, "Well I'll be damned", or otherwise punish or judge themselves, are effectively putting a curse on themselves. Stop this now! Unless that's what you want.

10   If under 100%, adjust with intent.

11   100% whole is the desired state.

12   Heartspace puts these 100% in balance.

Dowse: *% compatibility of counselors,* yours and others. THIS IS IMPORTANT.

Dowse: *% fear of success, and % fear of failure*

Dowse: *% imbalance of blood flow to the brain,* you, or other, or group of people.

Dowse: *% of ideal, strength of nature spirits in body, and in land.*[13]

Dowse: *% out of balance with mass consciousness.*

Dowse: *% Compatibility of body cells, and spin of the cells*

Dowse: *% Desire for improvement* [ideally 100%]

Dowse: *Presence of any limiting agreements, contracts, oaths, promises, vows, &c.,* to include at least anything disempowering, chastity, loyalty, obedience, poverty, subservience, self-sacrifice, suffering, vengeance[14], any other flow limiting agreements, &c.

Dowse: *Presence of holes in energy field*[15], Y/N.

Dowse: *Presence of implants, microchips, other thought form technology, Y/N.*[16]

Dowse: *Presence of non-beneficial cords,* usually attached to chakras, Y/N. Follow that sequence to cut.

Dowse: *Presence of non-beneficial archetypes, Y/N.* Remove with intent.

Dowse: *Presence of other limiting programs, including brainwashing and other manipulation, Y/N*

Dowse: *Presence of polluted thoughts, Y/N*

Dowse: *Presence of self destruct, self hate, self punishment, self sabotage programs, Y/N*

Dowse: *Resistance to help* [-100% is total magnetism to help, here]

Dowse: *Resistance to improvement* [ideally 0% or less; -100% is total interest]

Dowse: *Presence, Y/N, of limiting beliefs*[17], *including at least:*

Anger

Apathy/Hopelessness

Blame

Craving

Despair

Doubt

---

13   Invite them in; thank them daily. Each organ and system in your body has such a spirit, as John Living notes. Mark this to add to your daily checklist.

14   P. 151, *The Angel Therapy Handbook,* Doreen Virtue.

15   Play with the Harry Potter morphic field, and say *Reparo!* when you see these.

16   CCW spin will take these out. I have no idea what they are, but I have felt them, and removed them.

17   You could also ask for any vibrational patterns under 200 on the Hawkins scale.

Fear
Grief
Guilt
Hate
Humiliation
Pride
Regret
Scorn
Shame
Unworthiness
Dowse: *Presence of repressed positive emotions*, Y/N
Dowse: *% balance, or ideal, of*:
Acupuncture points, and meridians
Acidic pH issues, fungus[18], yeast, and so forth
Amino Acids
Assemblage Point
Balance, inter-dimensional
Body and brain chemistry [% ideal]
Brain and Nervous System
Buddhic body
Chakras [all of them, not just the seven or fourteen main ones]
Command Center
Desire to live, in organs and body parts. Check energy of lowest part.
Disease conditions [you want 0]
Electrons
Elimination System [This is critical to health]
Emotional body
Glandular System
Gonads and Reproductive System
Hara Line
Heart and Circulatory System
Holographic double
Human Growth Hormone
Islets of Langerhorn
Lithium and other trace elements
Lungs and Respiratory System
Lymph blockages

---

18   Walt Woods has a similar list. Lists are always metaphors, it doesn't matter if they are complete- since you'll always ask "what other...?". **You can also simply run your fingers down a list, and find items that stick. This is faster.**

Solving Problems with Dowsing **242** A book for new dowsers ISBN-10: 1482688573

Mental body
Message Center
Miasms[19]- disease, or even experience by ancestor
Parasites [usually related to acidic body pH]
Pineal
Pituitary
Seratonin
Silver cords
Skeletal system
Skin
Solar Plexus
Spleen
Stomach and Digestive System
Thyroid
Triple Heater
Any other blockage
Any other quality you feel led to test
Obviously you would want these at 100% of ideal, or so. Thank your counselor team for their help.

How did you feel, when you were totally in the moment, as a kid, playing?

---

19   P. 177, *God Helps Those Who Help Themselves*, Hannah Kroeger.

A book for new dowsers ISBN-10: 1482688573

Wouldn't it be great to live in that space, now?

Wouldn't it be great if this was your natural state, your default state, and that the only person who can keep you out of it is you, yourself?

How would our world change, if people realized this?

As you realize this, did you know you are making it easier for others to realize this?

D. Energy transmutation

Create a belief system, or primary intention, or engine of consciousness, or thought form, that all energy entering your field is transformed into something very good for you. Note that hate mail, curses, and similar things, will be transformed into a very nice energy. You can pull fear out of the mass consciousness, transform it to prosperity, and have it sent to you. This is a win-win. You can pull any negative energy out of a situation with a CCW spin. Let it pile up. Let the negative intent evaporate into the Void. You can then reprogram the now neutral energy, with anything you like, such as prosperity, or fifth dimensional energy.

Example: Paying the bills sequence
Dowse: *I have to work very hard for my money*   Y/N
If yes, Dowse: % you believe it's true   Get a number
Intend the percent is now zero
Dowse: *Money flows to me in floods, no matter what I do* Y/N
If no, Dowse: % you believe it's true   Get a number
Intend this percentage to 100%
Put your bills in a pile. Feel deeply that all the envelopes hold checks for you. Nail this down, by writing *I am so happy and grateful, now that all this money has come to me!* at the top of a piece of paper. Now list each dollar amount, and add a couple of zeros. Get enthusiastically happy about all the money you've gotten! Then and only then, in that great state, pay the bills[20]. Note that you may need to clear related beliefs, or even onion-skin them down, i.e. remove them as you remove an onion-skin, layer by layer.

E. Making decisions with alternatives

Intuition is only ONE channel of information. Don't make major decisions based on one channel of information. Intuition is a useful supplement, not a replacement, for good choices.
Dowse: *What is the effect on me* in % of ideal, of
attending a specific educational course
going out socially with someone
medicines
nutrients

---

20   P. 105, *The Secret*, Rhonda Byrne, also Paula Langguth Ryan, and Raymon Grace.

specific diets
starting a specific exercise regiment
other choices
In choosing between alternatives, choose the best of several alternatives, being sure to include "something else I don't yet know of" as an option.[21] Choose the best product for you, of a range of products. This could vary, among people. You can do all this with portals, however that is advanced, learn it the slow way, first.

For making a decision, <u>Test</u> at least:
Overall health of situation. If low, reconsider doing anything with it.
<u>Dowse:</u> *% advisable to simply abandon sunk costs*, and get out if necessary.

Take each alternative, and
<u>Dowse:</u> *probability of successful outcome %.*
Take specific events, test probability of alternatives occurring, %.

You can do all of the above quickly, with portals, also. In time, you will find that you are led to the best choice, or to an alternative you didn't know existed.

<u>Dowse:</u> *%, result of a choice*, result of the second choice, third choice, etc.
If the first choice is 20%, and the second is 100%, you would obviously take the second one. The first one in this case would have a problem. You can also test each choice as a portal, in the same way. This is faster.[22]

As an example, on a trip, you could dowse:
Which proposed route of these choices would be the most harmonious? [Check list[23]]
Is the water safe to drink where we will be staying? Y/N
Do I need to buy bottled water, for health reasons? Y/N

---

21   This is described at pp. 2-4, *Every Word has Power*, Yvonne Oswald, in a similar format, and at p. 86, *Beyond Human: Claiming the Power and Magic of your Limitless Self*, Jaden Phoenix. I wonder why mapquest.com doesn't have this as an option yet.
22   P. 68, *Beyond Reality*, Shelley Kaehr. One of Dr. Richard Bartlett's friends was told a restaurant was out of something on the menu. He tested, with portals, and said it wasn't. The waiter was confused. He tested, and said it was on a shelf, behind something else. It was.
23   I do so love my GPS, but sometimes, if the GPS route doesn't feel good, I disregard it.

Of the five brands of bottled water available, which is the best for my family? [Check list]

Are there any issues in the car?	Y/N, [pretend you get a yes]
Is the issue in the motor?	N
Is the issue in the radiator?	Y
Is the radiator fluid low?	Y
Is that the only problem?	Y

With more radiator fluid added, is the car now safe to drive? Y
[Note the question chain here- you will be setting them up yourself, in dowsing anything complex.]

I need a particular kind of jacket. Of my choices of businesses, which one has it at the best price? [One could run one's finger down the list in the phone book]
Of the list of plants I have available, which one would be most appropriate for that corner of the yard[24]? [Check your list, perhaps by running your finger down it.[25]]
It may be useful to keep a dowsing journal, to see how you worded your questions, and how information comes up for you.

F. Optimization- making everything better
Dowse: *% of optimized energy state.* If less than 100%,
Dowse: *Am I able to run an optimization on my systems, invoking all useful sequences available?* Y/N If yes, which you'll get 99.99% of the time, intend that you are now optimized, with everything you and your counselors know how to do. This means that all non-beneficial programming is changed to be totally positive. It may even pick up some walled-off parts. You could set this up as a contingent process, to occur say every morning at 5 AM[26].
Test *% of optimized energy state*, for feedback.

You can run all of the above, as a portal, in seconds.

---

24 Pp. 38-9, *The Divining Heart: Dowsing and Spiritual Unfoldment*, Patricia and Richard Wright.
25 Machaelle Small Wright does this extensively, in her garden. Linda Runyon seems to have also done this. Feng Shui in the garden seems to he a sort of garden dowsing.
26 P. 156, *You the Healer*, José Silva. He suggests programming that every time you do one thing, or one thing happens, something else happens.

What if the Creator put you here to create beauty, healing beauty, for everyone, including the Creator, to enjoy?

What is the one question you could ask, where if you asked it, the answers to all of your problems would show up, easily and effortlessly?

If money was not a factor, what would you do with your life?

Have you realized yet that dowsing can take you there, here, now?

X. When it "didn't work"

Firstly, there is no failure. There is only experience- and quitting. All successful people persevere to completion. Counter-intention exists[1]. Or is it counter-intention to say this? The following is not a complete discussion, however it will handle most counter-intention. You may not need it, at all. If you do, here it is.

Robert Winn, Lois Grasso, Keith Varnum, and Deepak Chopra address counter-intention and resistance by breathing into it[2]. Notice any heaviness, or stiffness, and so on in your body. Breathe deeply, as you put your concentration on it. Allow it to be, flow, open up, pass through unchanged, or integrate.

Jack Schwartz states you can use controlled breath to get into specific EEG states. For Theta, one inhales for 4 counts, holds the breath for 8 counts, exhales for 16 counts, and rests for 4 counts. For Delta, one inhales for 4, holds for 8, exhales for 32 and rests for 4[3]. In a relaxed state, you could also
open a window/portal in that area
go to the heart of it, and allow it to dissolve
welcome it, and all other beliefs, evidence that it exists, feelings, memories, sensations, surges, and thoughts that come up with it
just feel it
relax with it
let go of wanting to change it
let go of the resistance
You were born with few fears: darkness, and loud noises. The rest were learned. As you look over the lists, see what resonates, stands out, or flashes on for you. Also:

* Break your habitual patterns of thinking and action. Question everything, ask Quantum Questions, suspend judgment, and test what you believe limits you. If you keep doing it the way you have always done it, you'll get the same results you always got, or worse. Be the question, not the conclusion.

---

1   Or is it counter-intention to say or believe this? Would it be better to belief that counter-intention does not exist, or at least does not exist in my world? At some energy level, it does cease to exist.
2   P. 78, *The Way of the Wizard*, Deepak Chopra. The others don't document as much. Shallow, rapid panting, the fire breath, as Winn calls it, can be used for a short time, if regular breathing isn't pulling the junk up fast enough. It is described as Kapalabhati, at pp. 158-9, *The Breathing Book*, Donna Farhi.
3   P. 55, *Intuition Technology*, John Living, Professional Engineer.

* Erase your conclusions, and what you are certain is true. What you think you know to be certain is far more flexible than you thought.   Even fixed prices for appliances and cars are negotiable, if you know the game[4]. Soften up what you believe to be true, fixed, flexible, and [im]possible.

* Fail magnificently. Do it badly, just for the experience. The first time I spoke in public, I was not good. So what? Did someone cut my head off? Did I even get yelled at? Did anyone care? No. I examined my mistakes, improved, got out of my small self, spoke from my heart, from passion, and within two months, was getting standing ovations for my public speaking. People told me I was more energetic than Zig Ziglar. I am by nature extremely introverted, so that was a surprise.

* Note that most self-limitations are excuses. Unless you have no vocal cords, you could speak in public. You might not <u>want</u> to. That is different from not being <u>able</u> to.   Never say you can't, admit that you don't want to, truth clears blockages. If someone offered you $10 million to speak in public, would you find a way? What about only $100,000?

* Stop identifying with the belief. If you say, "But that's true!" you know you are attached to it. You are not your limitations. You are the Creator of your life.

Are there really limits to how much ecstasy a person could experience?

I wonder how one would test that?

---

4 Know the products beforehand. Go in 2 days before the end of the month, when the salespeople are wondering how they will meet their quotas. Ask lots of questions, to get the salespeople involved. Note that you really need this one model, but you can't do it just now, you may have to go 2 models down, but that doesn't really meet your needs... and let the salespeople fill in the blank with a lower price. In hotels, this is called "price resistance", and they have a graded level of prices they can quote, to be sure they keep the business. Remember, hotels sell space in increments of time. If no-one is there in that time increment, they have no income. Always be friendly, of course. Haggling as most people do it involves insulting product quality. You can also shift polarity, and praise product quality, but note it is beyond you...

You can run the following on automatic, after you've said it once, though I like to say it out loud, myself.

"Dear folks, spirit, superconscious, thank you for taking me to the original intent of my feeling/thought of feeling negative or blocked about (Insert what you want gone or different below)

_____

_____.

on the most important timeline where it exists. Thank you for centering my core, and each and every area, alternate existence, aspect, layer, level, of my being on this original intent, above it. Thank you for taking it back to the light, and recrystallizing it as an intent for my highest good. Thank you for coming forward on my timeline, noting the disappearance of every intent and incident that grew out of this, in accordance with divine will, to the present moment, and then to all future and alternate timelines, so that I am filled with light, love, peace, truth, forgiveness for myself, and forgiveness of every circumstance, energy, event, person, place, and everything else which contributed to this feeling/thought. With unconditional love and forgiveness, I dissolve this intent and its outgrowths from my atoms, being, body, DNA, energy fields, heart, memory, mind, photons, and tissues. I release it, and let it go now, back to the Void!
I choose being

_____

I feel (note how you want to feel here)

_____

I am

_____

I enthusiastically allow every physical, mental, emotional and spiritual problem, and all their effects, and inappropriate behavior, that grew out of this intent, to quickly vanish back to the Void, until I am in the now, filled with light and truth of God/the Universe/etc. It is done and healed now. Thank you, Spirit, for helping me to recover my true magnificence. Thank you, thank you, thank you! I love you and praise God/the Universe/etc from whom all blessings flow.[5]"

_____

5   Adapted from a similar statement in Karol Truman's book *Feelings Buried Alive Never Die*, which is very good.

If you don't believe this, or feel it is effective, commence your use of this *on that belief*. For example, put "*Help me release my doubt about the power of this*," in the first blank, above. That's where you insert the belief or feeling you want to let go. In the second blank, put in your desired state, which could be, "*I now understand that the intent of any situation or condition in my life can be transformed in a moment*."

Use the above on any and all blockages. Once your blockages are clear, you have flow, and you can create what you wish. This is a lot more fun than wallowing in negativity. Pain is a patient teacher, however this method removes the need for pain. Now, run it on automatic. There are many other clearing methods, also, and you have the tools to go into the deep mind, and download them, now.

When you did something nice for someone, with no expectation of getting anything back, do you remember the light in their eyes, when they realized this? That is the moment of healing beauty.

What would it feel like, if even just 10% of the population created healing beauty, in this way? Have you realized yet that every time you create healing beauty, you beat a path down for others to follow, in this?

Thanks Karol! This book started as my own notes, my understanding of what I was learning. I change wording on stuff like this to what I like.

XI. Regular practice

Many authors of great books have great ideas- and then never assemble them into a framework for regular practice. This is particularly important for new dowsers! I offer the following, because it is easier to edit, than to write. Change it to what you like. If you feel any resistance to this, welcome it! It reflects a limiting belief.

Your attitude to the practice is precisely your attitude to what you seek. If you resist the practice, you are resisting what you seek. Everybody who does a practice regularly reports great results. The practice feeds your soul, and waters and fertilizes your goals[1].

As Mike Dooley would say, if you miss one, just do it next time. Never punish yourself. Your daily practice[2] will be fun, and it will inspire, nurture, relax, uplift, and otherwise benefit you. Stay flexible.

Some days, maybe you can't seem to do everything in your routine. Do what you can, now. The perfect is the enemy of the good, things will never calm down. Do it now, today, and take very small steps towards a better practice.

The conscious mind lives in fear due to separation, fear of losing control, which causes all of the pain in our lives. Oneness is in the heart. The mind asks how to get more, the heart knows it's already complete, and is thankful.

All resistance, and all problems, are due to limiting oneself to mind, to fused states, to intent crystallized during emotional experiences, beneath the pain. Love clears them, and helps you stay in the now. Ask yourself: *Can I let myself step back, and step out of my need for [what I think I absolutely have to have]?*

---

1   Repetition and emotion feed the subconscious mind. How is the constant hypnotic suggestion that you are no good unless you buy new products helping you? Why not instead tell your subconscious exactly what you like? Why not tell it that there's no need to grow old? Faith and inspired action can take you anywhere you want to go, and will take you far faster on the least energy path. Pp. 88-93, *The Magic of Believing*, Claude M. Bristol.
2   Chapter 18, *The Art of Spiritual Healing*, Keith Sherwood, recommends a daily regimen, as does *The Art of Chi Kung*, Wong Kiew Kit, and many other books.

If you need to get the flow going, play with new ideas, activities, something you've never done before. Play. Your subconscious is a four year old child, that loves to play. We tend to fear what would be most helpful to us. Get out of how you think it should be, and enter heartspace. Only the polarized mind is separate from what you seek.

When your intent is creation for the sake of beauty, joy, kindness, love, Oneness, peace, play, satisfaction, service, support for humanity, and all life, then you have the manifesting plugged into the power source.

The simplest entry into pure intent of heartstate is meditation. If you want mechanical help, to enter this state, I really like the Clear-Mind CD from Paul Bauer, which I think is still available at http://www.dreamsalive.com/Clear-Mind.htm. I don't get anything for saying it, I just happen to like it.

Note your two options:
-operate on the battery power of memories, in mental chatter, and doubt
-operate on the full power of Source, by living in the moment, in certainty

If you slip out of your magnificence, breathe deeply, and enter heartspace. Imagine how you'd feel if your intent is now real. *How would you feel if it is already real? Now?*

Each time you do this, you drive the nail deeper. At some point, your goal and reality join[3].

If you use the following list, just cross out what doesn't interest you.

---

3   It is so amusing to hear people say, "Oh yeah, I tried that visualization [or meditation, or dowsing, or ...] stuff once, and it didn't work". That is something like saying, "Oh yeah, I showed up to the first day of class in engineering school , but they wanted me to like buy these books, and show up regularly, and even do some stuff outside of class."

A. Daily suggestion
1. 3 times per day:
-Become the Observer. I intend I am in the moment, feeling my feelings, in full awareness. I am aware of my feelings, reactions, thoughts, and energy shifts. You may not yet have noticed that as the Observer, you are one with your higher Self. I notice this.

2. Morning:
a. on rising:
(1) I **write down the good ideas** that came in the night[4], which may include dowsing solutions
(2) I **give thanks** before my feet hit the floor
(3) I ask one Quantum Question Question, which could be as simple as
If [my main goal] were real, right now, how would I feel?
I spend about five minutes in that state, or as much as I can.
(4) I say: *I request a most benevolent outcome for today[5], with an outcome better than the best I can imagine.*
(6) I intend that the energies of my day are optimized[6], with a one word macro.
(7) I talk to myself in the mirror[7], saying at least "*You have a millionaire mind!*", and also noting my primary intent for the day. I use clear package tape to laminate slogans such as "*How many am I going to sell today?*" , "*How does it feel, already real, now?*", or "*How does it get better than this?*" which I put on the mirror. I look into my eyes, and calmly state what is real. I do this anytime I see a mirror in the bathroom. *What grand and glorious adventure will come my way, today, I wonder?*

3. During the day
a. This is basically my own intent process:

1. I relax, breathe deeply, enter heartspace.
2. I notice how I feel, as a baseline
3. I set an intent, such as *I am now a clear channel to my higher Self*

---

4   P. 85, *The Magic of Believing*, Claude M. Bristol.
5   Tom T. Moore goes into great detail on ways to use this, in *The Gentle Way*, if you want more.
6   I watch the hyperspace rotations of the geometric forms of the energy of my day, as it assembles itself into its optimal form. I feel this.
7   Pp. 101-5, *The Magic of Believing*, Claude M. Bristol. Billy Sunday, Winston Churchill, Woodrow Wilson, and many others used this. If his salesmen could triple and quadruple their incomes, during the Great Depression, using this technique, I think it will work for me.

4. I breathe 10 slow, deep, full breaths, all the way to my lower abdomen. I look up at a 30 degree angle.
5. I notice how I feel. If I feel any resistance, constriction, tightness, and so on, I run limiting belief clearing sequences, and test to see it is gone.
6. I set my intent again, in the present moment, until it goes through without resistance.
7. I relax even more deeply, through alpha, into theta.
8. I ask: *How would I feel, if [my intent] is already real, right now, in this moment?*
9. I inhale this feeling, for Mike Dooley's five minutes. I feel the living essence of my creation already real. I might touch my chest, at my heart. Remaining in state, I notice what makes my intent real- a specific feeling, an image, a sound, perhaps even a smell. The KEY is feeling it already done, in the Alpha/Theta EEG state.
10. When I feel done, in that peaceful, blissful feeling, I breathe deeply, and use three fingers on my right hand to tap my third eye- an inch, 2.5 cm, up from between my eyebrows. This is tapping in the nail, or tentpeg, of my intent, to nail it down, metaphorically.
11. I give thanks. I start my day with a high voltage visualization workout, even if only a minute per day. When I get up in the morning, I give thanks, put my fists high in the air, start jumping up and down, and say, YESSSSS!!!!
I say YES to everything in the flow, to the experiences I am bringing from inner to outer, the food in my refrigerator, the shower, where I am today, who I am, my car, clothes, family, channels of income, life's conditions, people and situations in my life, my past just as it is right now, and everything and everyone else! I ask for a most benevolent outcome for my day. I imagine anything, and overlay it with an energetic YESSSSSSS!!!!!

I get so charged up, energized, excited, jazzed, juiced, wired, and up about this day, better than the best I can imagine, full of wonderful surprises that I love to experience, that I can't contain all the energy! YESSSS!!!! is the vibration of joyful, radiant success, of bliss in the now! I run a tidal wave of YESSSSSSSSSSS!!! to everything and everyone in my Universe. If I feel constriction, I flow more YESSSSS!!! to it!

How good can a person feel? Sending all this out, I get even more excited, because I know it's coming back, even bigger and better! I FEEL this in my body.

Feelings are the power bringing my creations into form. I give them even more juice, now! Just one word shifts me into energy overdrive, I say it again, I give it up to YESSSSSSS!!!!! I feel my entire body with an electric shock, running thousands of volts of YESSS!!!! to my ideal self, to a huge wave of peace, love, joy, contentment, bliss, ecstasy, and everything that makes life worthwhile! As I do this, I help others on their path, so I amp it up, and get to YESSSS!!!!! I say YESSSS!!! even to the resistance, and watch it washed away, effortlessly! I say YESSS!! to all my dreams, knowing that as I get mine, others find it easier to get theirs!

I dowse whatever shows up. Daily practice is very helpful for developing ability. I dowse whatever interests me that day.

12. During the day, if I slip out of my magnificence, especially into doubt or frustration that it hasn't manifested yet, I go mindful, in the now. I breathe deeply, and feel my intent real. I live in the question.

Pick what you like, from this list:
I bring more **quiet time** into my life[8]
I check my **breathing,** and take a number of deep, relaxed breaths
I do one kind thing- a random kindness, for someone
I do something creative and fun, even if it is only goofy postcards for a child
I drink more pure water, at least a quart/liter per day
I exercise. Walking is good. So is a simple yoga or Chi Kung[9] exercise. Riding a bicycle, or swimming, is good. Dancing to music at home is good. Dr. Richard Schulze recommends an hour per day, and that you buy and enjoy whatever fun toys would support you in this

---

8   If you can do a weekend or a one-day retreat, or time in the woods, alone, do so. When I started doing this, I got so much intuitive awareness that I didn't have to work nearly as hard, and got better results.
9   Wong Kiew Kit's book *The Art of Chi Kung,* or one of Steven Chang's books, is a start. I like the Tai Chi of Cheng Man-Ching, myself.

I have unstructured time to play. I was told in a stress management workshop that spending the first half hour of the workday doing fun stuff would increase my productivity as if I had an extra hour and half of worktime. This was correct

I journal during the day. This may only be listing goals. That is powerful by itself

I look at the Sun, at dawn or dusk, and also during the day through hooded eyelids. On the inbreath, I imagine bringing in sunlight, to my entire body. I eat light, just like the Essenes, Hawaiians, and Apache did. On the outbreath, I release old tired energy

I look for opportunities to **help others**, to cheer them up, and follow through

I notice something really beautiful, and get totally into the here and now of noticing it.

I really appreciate some good quality in someone else, specifically, out loud.

I see people in their highest light, before dealing with them

I seek out **food that energizes.**

I set intent for something I'd like to get[10]

4. Evening

a. I take any change I found, and change from my pocket, and put it in the jar entitled "Financial Freedom Account", with total attention, imagining a jar full of gold coins.

b. I enter no-mind.

c. I say YESSSSS! I give thanks.

d. I ask one Quantum Question.

e. I tone. Breathe deeply 5 minutes.

f. If I have time, I do exercises from Wong Kiew Kit, Steven Chang's books, or Tai Chi.

g. I ask, *How do I feel?* I note the response, test for limiting belief systems, and clear.

h. I review to make sure I kept my promises. I don't make a promise unless I know I can keep it.

i. I listen to music and media that feeds my soul.

I dowse for unbalanced energies, and I balance them.

---

10   Claude Bristol said he knew a clergyman, who simply put out the thought that he'd like flowers in the church, to the congregation. Someone always showed up with flowers. He got memorial windows in the same way. P. 131, *The Magic of Believing*, Claude M. Bristol.

Solving Problems with Dowsing **259** A book for new dowsers ISBN-10: 1482688573

5. Before going to sleep:

If you are a student, wouldn't you like to study and sleep at the same time? You can. Do your studying just before bedtime. I used to do this for language classes, and it added hours to my studying. This is a very fertile time for any kind of intent play[11]. Ask a quantum question, like *What would the solution look like?* It is better to avoid watching violent movies. I don't watch them at all, because my dreams were full of violence when I did, and I didn't sleep well, or get much rest.

a. I revision my day to its ideal form, as Neville Goddard suggests, and also run a desired state.
(1) I breath deeply, relax, and enter heartspace. Heartspace, aka Alpha or Theta EEG, is the key to power.
(2) I pick something that didn't go as well as I'd have liked, or my desired outcome.
(3) I run it as a new movie, of the ideal outcome, looking out through my own eyes, hearing with my own ears, feeling the feelings in my own body. I notice some detail in it, which convinces me it is real. If you saw the movie *Inception,* notice that they checked detail to see if something was not real. This is the same idea. If I am living in a desired state not yet real, I notice a new detail each time I enter that.
(4) I really pay attention to how I feel, in the moment. I let that increase. I feel this surgingly real. I give it a lot of YESSSSSSS!!!! YES, I AM IN MY DREAM JOB, IT FEELS GREAT! I AM LOADED WITH ENERGY, I RUN THROUGH THE FRONT DOOR! IT FEELS MAGNIFICENT! I LOVE IT! YESSSSSSSSS!!!!!!

6. Waking up in the middle of the night

a. I always enter the feeling of my primary goal, already real, so I get an additional boost. Or I ask a quantum question.

---

11   Some Muslims believe that on the nights around the Ramadan fast, prayers are 100 times as effective. Some Christians believe the night of Michaelmass, September 29, is similar. I don't know if that's true. However, whatever you think about at night, just before sleep, will be chewed on all night long, by your subconscious mind.

B. Weekly suggestion

1. Saturday

a. I do some period circular breathing, Robert Winn's 100 Breaths, without counting

b. I pick or review three things that I'd like to happen. I write them down.

c. I clean out one limiting belief.

d. I give thanks.

e. I do a hobby or other fascination. Lately that has been this book.

2. Sunday

a. I meet with my intention group.

b. I seal off the space where I live, and intend that all low grade energy is transformed. I start by drawing a white circle around it[12].

3. Any day during the week

a. I do one random kindness[13]. Lately I've been picking up bread, from a church, and taking it to a homeless shelter.

b. I raucously celebrate any success, however small.

c. I do one "Deaf Frog" exercise. Where someone treats me badly, I "revision" my model of what happened, immediately, and thank them profusely, or otherwise react, as if they had done something really nice.

d. I review my daily exercises around my most significant intent.

e. I optimize the upcoming week, with intent.

f. I express sincere appreciation, or encouragement, preferably in writing, to one person[14].

g. I do a fast, taking only fresh, raw fruit juice, though lately that's been challenging.

h. I pick something I want to change, and flip its polarity. I concentrate on this for as long as one month.

---

12   P. 120, *The Magic of Believing*, Claude M. Bristol.

13   As noted in the book, *Random Acts of Kindness*, fwd by Daphne Rose Kingma, and p. 76, *The Keys of Jeshua*, Glenda Green.

14   My model for this is the story *All the Good Things*, by Helen Mrosla, cited at p. 125, *Chicken Soup for the Soul: 101 Stories to Open the Heart and Rekindle the Spirit*, Jack Canfield and Mark Victor Hanson.

Exercises to recover my energy

1. I ask about how each activity, friend, hobby, item, pastime, think, and work activity helps me, or lowers my energy. I get rid of one that lowers my energy.

2. Be aware of my boundaries. If I don't have them, and many children of alcoholic families like me don't, I set them up.

3. I go to the animal inside, and growl, for the pleasure of it[15].

4. I notice other people and situations just as they are, noticing they are unique, not wrong.

5. I notice that the people I judge, or react to strongly, reflect something inside me. Maybe I want to clear that.

6. I pay attention to what I buy. I ask, "Do I really need this? Does this make my life simpler, or more complex? Does this help me make money, or otherwise improve my life?" If I get a no, I re-evaluate my need to get it.

7. I pick one simple activity- closing a door, walking, brushing my teeth, listening to someone talk- and do it with total attention.

8. I stand back from my mind, and become the Observer. I just observe[16].

9. When I feel negative emotions, I accept them, and let them flow in some socially acceptable way.

10. Whenever I slip out of my magnificence, I step back, observe, and notice how the past is polluting the present. I laugh, and get back into my magnificence.

C. Monthly suggestion

1. I optimize my month, with intent.

2. I run a Ho'oponopono forgiveness exercise[17].

3. I spend half a day in nature.

4. I do something I would do, if I had already gotten the million dollar annuity. For example, I donate books to libraries that helped me.

---

15   Tom Brown, Jr., teaches this, because that is the part that keeps you alive in severe situations.
16   Tom Brown, Jr., recalled that his Apache teacher did this all the time.
17   Ihaleakala Hew Len's books go into this in some detail. You can basically say *"I love you, I'm sorry",* to whatever seems out of balance, for a time, until it re-enters balance.

5. I tithe my income to sources of spiritual teaching that feed my soul. If you can't start at 10%, start at 1%. This opens up the flow, and is well worth doing[18].

6. I pick someone in a restaurant, or store, or business, who was really cheerful and helpful. I write a letter to their boss, praising them, noting I'll buy their products till doomsday due to this fantastic service, etc.

D. Quarterly suggestion

1. I come up with a new Quantum Question around my goals.

2. I read a book just for fun, such as science fiction, which I enjoy.

3. I pick the most negative, nastiest person I know. I spend time zapping them with white light and love, talking things over with them in my imagination, revisioning[19] them as a spiritual master, and so on. Rarely, I might do the same thing with the stupidest, most corrupt politician.

E. Process Cards

You might want to type these out, get them photocopied onto card stock, and laminate them with clear plastic tape, for easy use. Sometimes I tape paper down onto cardstock, with clear tape. That works. I recommend that you develop your own process cards, out of your own understanding. These are only to get you started.

1. My version of the Hawkins scale, as described in *Power vs. Force*:
The energy that creates all form, both concrete and abstract, is rapidly moving light energy, which slows down to a crawl to become matter[20].

1000 is lightspeed, anything above this level is beyond description[21].

700+ is a place so pleasant, you may not even want to play with intent. Visit this place every so often.

---

18 Dale Carnegie noted that the first Rockefeller did this, as did the first DuPont, and many others. Claude M. Bristol notes this, as does Paula Langguth Ryan, and many others. There is something to this.

19 Revisioning is also suggested by Dr. Mansukh Patel, in his book *Mastering the Laws of Relationships*.

20 P. 123, *Sound: Native Teachings and Visionary Art*, Joseph Rael.

21 Raymond Moody's book *Life after Life* describes the tunnel of light that people go through, as part of the near-death experience. I wonder if this is simply the effect of traveling at greater than light speed, as shown in the first *Star Wars* movie? Let us imagine a person traveling into a wormhole. Light coming from our universe would be sped up. One would see our entire universe die; all of the universe's history would pass before that person in a flash= P. 161, *Parallel Universes,* Fred Alan Wolf, much like a near-death experience. Hawkins didn't say this in his book, I'm extending his ideas.

600+ Peace, Bliss. You can create instantly and effortlessly with intent, in this level.

540-550+ Joy, Serenity[22] Manifesting gets easier yet, at this level.

500±5 Love, Reverence Manifesting gets easier, here, with good intuitive guidance.

400±5 Reason, Understanding

350±5 Acceptance, Forgiveness

310±5 Willingness, Optimism

250±5 Neutrality, Trust

200±5 Courage[23]

Anything below this level takes energy from you, rather than giving energy. It is better to stay out of the lower levels, and to clear them when you find them. Also, anything below this level can only be sustained by not being in the present moment. When you go into the present moment, you automatically leave these levels.

175±5 Pride, Scorn

150±5 Anger, Hate

125±5 Desire, Craving

100±5 Fear, Anxiety

75±5 Grief, Regret

50±5 Apathy, Despair

30±5 Guilt, Blame

20 Shame, Humiliation, Death. 18-22 are disease frequencies

Note that the above are based on my experience. Alter your charts based on your experience.

3. Access Universal Intelligence dowsing sequence

- Look up at a 30-45° angle. This lowers your brainwave frequency to 10, which is the universal intelligence. This is heartspace, a good place for planting intent. Joseph Murphy would access this state, and say *"I am being made aware of the Divine Solution now. God knows the*

---

22   Be aware that these are relative. Vadim Zeland points out that Joy could actually be a limiting energy, if one sought to go higher.
23   Courage literally means having heart, "heartage", from the French word *coeur*, for heart. This is the entry into heart realm, of unity. Energies below this are based on separation, and they cost a lot to maintain, they drain energy from your system.

answer, and I and my father are one. God reveals it to me this instant."

You can also drop intent in this space. Say, in this state: *"I am totally healthy now and forever!"* Feel this to be true.

4. Make two lists- one is what the Universe takes care of for you, the other is what you want to do. The first list would be very long, longer than the second.

5. Blockage clearing intent sequence
Revision it, as Neville Goddard says, first
"Dear folks, spirit, superconscious, thank you for taking me to the original intent of my feeling/thought of feeling negative or blocked about (Insert what you want gone or different below)_____
on the most important timeline where it exists. Thank you for centering my core, and each and every area, alternate existence, aspect, layer, level, of my being on this original intent, above it. Thank you for taking it back to the light, and recrystallizing it as an intent for my highest good. Thank you for coming forward on my timeline, noting the disappearance of every intent and incident that grew out of this, in accordance with divine will, to the present moment, and then to all future and alternate timelines, so that I am filled with light, love, peace, truth, forgiveness for myself, and forgiveness of every circumstance, energy, event, person, place, and everything else which contributed to this feeling/thought. With unconditional love and forgiveness, I dissolve this intent and its outgrowths from my atoms, being, body, DNA, energy fields, heart, memory, mind, photons, and tissues. I release it, and let it go now, back to the Void!
I choose being

_____

I feel (note how you want to feel here)

_____

I am

_____

I enthusiastically allow every physical, mental, emotional and spiritual problem, and all their effects, and inappropriate behavior that grew out of this intent to quickly vanish back to the Void, until I am in the now, filled with light and truth of God/the Universe/etc. It is done and healed now. Thank you, Spirit, for helping me to recover my true magnificence. Thank you, thank you, thank you! I love you and praise God/the Universe/etc from whom all blessings flow."

If you don't believe this, or feel it is effective, commence your use of this *on that belief.*

F. Goal Cards

Focus the picture of what you seek on the screen of your subconscious mind, as often as you can, in a relaxed way, during the day, especially just after waking and before going to sleep. One way to do that is to have cards, in your pocket[24], above your bed, on your bathroom mirror, and in as many other places as possible, that others won't see. These are like portable vision boards. You can use initials, so others won't know what you're up to. What is the one thing you most seek? Choose that. Examples:

I am so happy and grateful, now that I have my health!
[perhaps with a picture, hand drawn, or from a magazine]

I am so happy and grateful, now that I can run again!

---

24   P. 85, *The Magic of Believing*, Claude M. Bristol.

Solving Problems with Dowsing **266** A book for new dowsers ISBN-10: 1482688573

It is useful to also post inspiring thoughts in your space. Here are some examples:

Your Vision is a complete kit, which comes with everything you need to realize it.

The instructions come via intuition, and loving action glues it together.

At some level, your Vision has already been realized. Find that place on the map, and start driving there.

What I seek is also seeking me.

How would I feel, if what I seek was already part of my Universe, right now?

G. An example of an intent statement:

It is time to recover my power! I have recovered it now!

Think about how we handle our power:
People have given away
their children to the school system
their choices to advertising
their happiness to the distant future
their health to the doctor
their joy to the past
their joy to the TV news
their life energy to dead food, sold in convenient coffins of plastic
or metal
their money to their banker
their peace to the media
their soul to their preacher or priest
their spirit to the television
their value to their wallet
their satisfaction and contentment to the three lies: there isn't
enough, more is better, and that's just the way it is.
Why?
So they can work long hours in jobs they hate
Using time taken from friends and family
So they can buy things they don't need
At prices they can't afford
With money they don't have
Stuffing homes that cost too much
To impress people who couldn't care less
-from a statement made by Chief Two Trees, Cherokee/Tsalagi Nation

I overlay that, with:

What are the infinite possibilities that every one of my intentions
always comes about in the most benevolent ways, for the most
benevolent outcome, better than the best I can imagine, hope
for, expect, or anticipate, in the path of healing beauty, in
wonderful ways I love to experience, that surprise and delight
me, and help me offer perfect service, as I accomplish my own
mission and purpose in life?

ISBN-10: 1482688573

I wonder what the infinite possibilities are, where everyone on the planet has already woken up to their true nature, in healing beauty, and radiance?

What would have to happen, where all the nightmares of illiusion and negativity are already forgotten in dusty history books that no-one reads?

I wonder what could occur, where we would have an economic system where people work joyfully 16-20 hours/week, to meet their needs, and have plenty of spare time to pursue their fascinations, and creative service, which was true in Stone Age times, and could be again, now?

I intend that large organizations now give back to society, out of necessity, and a desire to survive.

I intend that everyone is guided, guarded, protected, blessed, .filled with grace and serendipity on their path in life!

What would have to happen, where the energy of the entire planet has already crossed a threshold, where only the positive can be perceived easily?

I wonder what would happen, or might have already happened, where everyone is now one with perfect health, wealth, and love, in wonderful ways that surprise and delight them?

I intend that love, forgiveness, and healing are now the foundation of all human activities!

I intend that humans have already advanced so rapidly, that we start teaching dolphins how to play, better and more joyfully!

I intend that people already know that the Universe has positive intentions for them!

I intend that everything and everyone I see, hear, feel, perceive, or am otherwise aware of gets healing energy, with no need for effort on my part!

What are the infinite possibilities that everyone embodies their highest aspirations of the ideal, in wonderful ways they love to experience!

I intend that the magnificent healing beauty of the Universe now expresses, in everything in life, in a constant flow from the immanent to the manifest!

I intend that healing beauty is part of everyone's life, now, in a dynamic way!

I intend that all see the perfect beauty in everything, beyond merely the flesh, or physical, now!

I intend that everyone on the planet has already realized abundance, over scarcity, instantaneous change to the better, and beauty in the moment.

I intend that everyone is now in the right place, at the right time, in the right way, saying and doing the right things, with the right people, in the right circumstances, in the right and perfect processes, with the right and perfect results, for the highest good of all!

I intend that all darkness is now filled with light!

I intend that people are already using new, healthy technologies, that have already cleaned up the problems caused from before!

I intend that everyone already lives in an ideal, perfect community, full of people, activities, and structures that help them to grow, harmoniously!

I intend that everyone is once again in their default state, of peace, love, joy, happiness, contentment, satisfaction, beautiful expression, and all that makes life worthwhile, now!

I intend that everyone has already found their inner spiritual guidance, and uses it to achieve all their goals!

I intend that everything else I could have asked for, that serves all, has already taken place!

I intend that people have already realized that the Universe is about abundance, of everything in life, in wonderful ways.

I intend healing beauty within all, to the left, to the right, above, below, behind, and to the front, in everything!

I intend that this or something better, is here now, for the highest good of all!

I intend that all of the above intentions come together, harmoniously, to create results better than the best I can imagine, hope for, or anticipate.

So be it and so it is, now.

Thank you, thank you, thank you, thank you!

I tone the notes C, F, G, in accordance with Laurel Eliz. Keyes' book on Toning...

I am at peace, in the sacred silence of pure being.

I am. I be.

When I finish a book I enjoy, my first question is how I can find more. The book you hold in your hands consists of excerpts adapted and expanded from larger books entitled *Dowsing and Manifesting,* and *Dowsing and Healing.* This is the table of contents from that first book:

Solving Problems with Dowsing **275** A book for new dowsers ISBN-10: 1482688573

Solving Problems with Dowsing **276** A book for new dowsers ISBN-10: 1482688573

EMBODY YOUR VISION[25]

BURN BRIGHT with the power and force of your Vision
   Find a way to use everything: every chance conversation encounter
fascination gift hobby letter meeting passion question skill word
to CRYSTALLIZE YOUR VISION

BECOME the TRUTH you want to see in the world
   model it: glow with it vibrate and resonate to it play in it
   Network addictively effortlessly playfully
   through action energy feeling kindness love smiles thought

Network from the truth, the Vision, deep in your soul
   You are the Center of your Vision
         The mantle for the Flame of your Truth
You are a free, effortlessly powerful welling of intent, life, light, love, spirit,
truth, and sparkling, harmonious, joyful, healing beauty
   feel it deep within your being   know it to be true- for it is

Affirm it, project it, radiate it in concentric rings, light up your world
   Enflame yourself with its energy feeling vibration light
   and the miracle of the truth and purpose of your own life will manifest
   as you help others realize their dreams   you realize your own

Great corporations, governments, the media, all seem so powerful
   they are paper tigers   before the power of vision and networking
   and they know it

Networking to create your Vision is the healing salve, the quintessence,
   the elixir of joy Aladdin's lamp   the Holy Grail

---

25   So long as you indicate the source- that is this book, by title and author - on the page- you can use these words as you wish, in any way likely to help people.

Solving Problems with Dowsing 277 A book for new dowsers ISBN-10: 1482688573

It is freedom, the joy of creating, power to help others and self, democracy
realized, humanity working to full potential, your soul realizing itself

Happiness, joy, peace, truth, purpose in life, beauty, satisfaction, the
spiritual side of life...
    all different faces of the same thing, all flowers of the questions you ask
    and Vision crystallized through feeling and networking is the path

Things are only useful as a way to help you realize peak experiences
And all great human creations started out as a feeling in the heart of one
person who persisted at bringing it into form

Aho Mitakuye Oyasin –

For all my relations [26]

---

26 This is a Lakota way of saying we are all connected. Concept discussed also at p. 28, *Shapeshifting*, John Perkins.

Solving Problems with Dowsing **278** A book for new dowsers ISBN-10: 1482688573

What is your fondest dream?

If you were already doing it, effortlessly, playfully, lovingly, in a fun way, how would you feel?

How would you feel, if your life was better than the best you can imagine, right now?